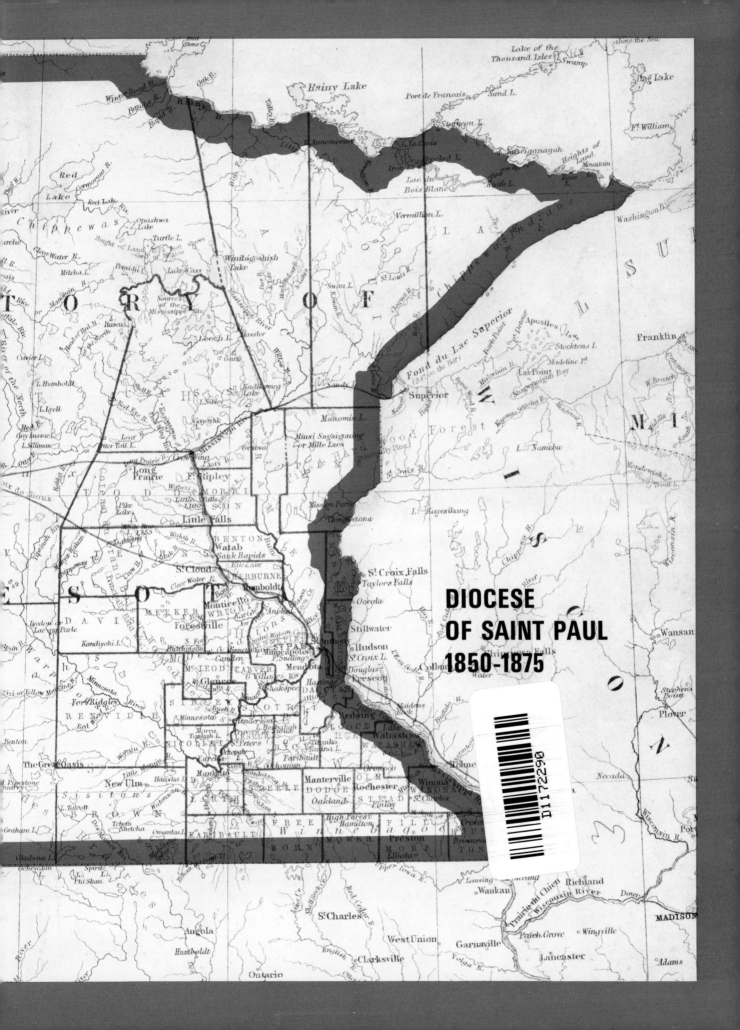

DIOCESE
OF SAINT PAUL
1850-1875

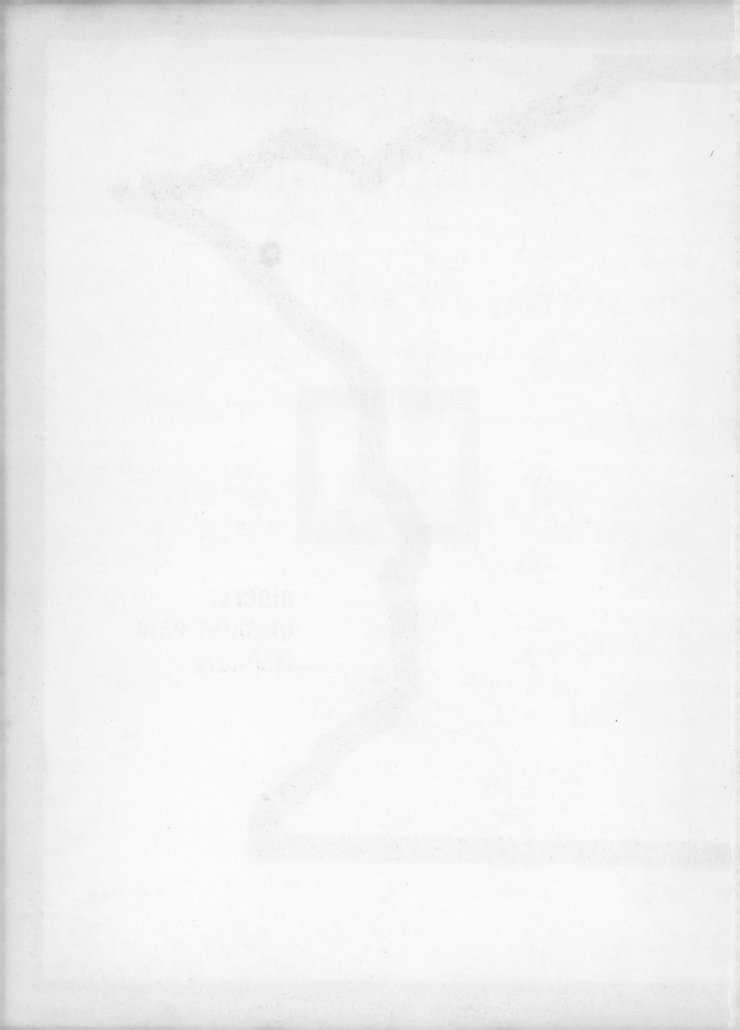

CATHOLIC HERITAGE

in

MINNESOTA
NORTH DAKOTA • SOUTH DAKOTA

*Diamond Jubilee Observance
of the Province of Saint Paul and of the
Suffragan Dioceses
of Saint Cloud, Duluth, Winona, Sioux Falls and Fargo*

Edited by

Reverend Patrick H. Ahern, M.A., Ph.D.

Published by

The Most Reverend Archbishop
and Bishops of the Province of Saint Paul

NIHIL OBSTAT
    Walter H. Peters, S.T.L., Ph.D.
    Censor Librorum

IMPRIMATUR
    ✠ LEO BINZ
    Archbishop of St. Paul
    February 10, 1964

THE COVER DESIGN shows a montage of the cathedrals of the Province of St. Paul. This device was chosen in order to emphasize that in his office and his person, the bishop of the diocese acts as the principle of unity for the people of God. The cathedral has been built and splendidly adorned in order to house the *cathedra,* the throne of the bishop, a most striking and vital symbol of his divinely instituted office of teacher, ruler and sanctifier of the faithful.

PUBLICATION COMMITTEE—The following were appointed by the Most Reverend Bishops of the province as a committee to plan this commemorative book:—Most Rev. George H. Speltz, D.D., Honorary Chairman; Rev. Patrick H. Ahern; Rev. Colman Barry, O.S.B.; Right Rev. Msgr. Bernard Drew; Rev. Jerome A. Duraczynski; Rev. Robert W. Klein; Rev. Germain B. Kunz; Rev. Marvin R. O'Connell; Rev. John T. O'Toole; Rev. Louis Pfaller, O.S.B.; Brother J. Robert, F.S.C.; Right Rev. Msgr. George W. Rolwes; Rev. A. A. A. Schmirler; Right Rev. Msgr. Leonard J. Sullivan; Rev. Gerald M. Weber; Rev. Vincent A. Yzermans.

DESIGN, LAYOUT and LITHOGRAPHY: H. M. Smyth Company, Inc., Book Publishing Division, St. Paul, Minnesota
TYPOGRAPHY: Twin City Graphic Photon, Inc., St. Paul, Minnesota

CONTENTS

Page

The Province of Saint Paul.................... 6

Minnesota History......................... 12

Archdiocese of Saint Paul................... 20

Diocese of St. Cloud 40

Diocese of Duluth 62

Diocese of Winona......................... 78

Diocese of Crookston 100

Diocese of New Ulm.......................122

The Dakotas 140

Diocese of Sioux Falls......................148

Diocese of Fargo 168

Diocese of Rapid City......................190

Diocese of Bismarck 208

THE MOST REVEREND ARCHBISHOP AND BISHOPS OF THE PROVINCE

Seated, left to right: Francis J. Schenk, D.D., Bishop of Duluth; Peter W. Bartholome, D.D., Bishop of St. Cloud; Leo Binz, D.D., Archbishop of St. Paul; William J. McCarty, C.SS.R, D.D., Bishop of Rapid City; Leo F. Dworschak, D.D., Bishop of Fargo.

Standing, left to right: Gerald F. O'Keefe, D.D., Auxiliary Bishop of St. Paul; Alphonse J. Schladweiler, D.D., Bishop of New Ulm; Laurence A. Glenn, D.D., Bishop of Crookston; Edward A. Fitzgerald, D.D., Bishop of Winona; Lambert A. Hoch, D.D., Bishop of Sioux Falls; Hilary B. Hacker, D.D., Bishop of Bismarck; Leonard P. Cowley, D.D., Auxiliary Bishop of St. Paul; George H. Speltz, D.D., Auxiliary Bishop of Winona.

THE PROVINCE OF SAINT PAUL

Pope Leo XIII

Pope Paul VI

SEVENTY-FIVE YEARS AGO, on May 4, 1888, during the pontificate of His Holiness, Pope Leo XIII, the apostolic constitution creating the Province of St. Paul was signed in Rome. To commemorate the Diamond Jubilee of this significant event, the Most Reverend Archbishop and Bishops of the province are publishing this collection of essays on the history of the Church in Minnesota and North and South Dakota as the year of jubilee is ending in 1964 during the pontificate of His Holiness, Pope Paul VI.

This commemorative volume also marks the seventy-fifth anniversary of the establishment of the suffragan dioceses of St. Cloud, Duluth, Winona, Sioux Falls and Fargo. They were created in the fall of 1889.

The Province of St. Paul, the thirteenth province established in the United States, was formed by detaching Minnesota and the Territory of Dakota from the Province of Milwaukee. The Diocese of St. Paul, erected in 1850, was raised to metropolitan rank, and the Vicariate of Northern Minnesota, established in 1875, and the Vicariate of Dakota, created in 1879, were designated suffragan churches of the Archdiocese of St. Paul.

Suffragan Dioceses

Seventeen months after the province was created five new dioceses were established in it by the Holy Father at the request of Archbishop John Ireland of St. Paul. New sees were formed in Minnesota by partitioning the Vicariate of Northern Minnesota between the dioceses of St. Cloud and Duluth and by removing from the Archdiocese of St. Paul the southern tier of counties across the state to make the Diocese of Winona. The state of South Dakota, admitted to the Union on November 2, 1889, became the territory of the newly created Diocese of Sioux Falls. North Dakota, made a state at the same time, was designated to be the territory of the Diocese of Jamestown. The see city of the latter diocese has been Fargo since 1897.

Three more suffragan sees were established in the province before the death of the first metropolitan. The Diocese of Lead was created in 1902 and assigned the western half of South Dakota. In 1930 Rapid City replaced Lead as the see city of that diocese. Bismarck was designated the see city of a new diocese that comprised the western

The six bishops consecrated by Archbishop Ireland on May 19, 1910. *Left to right:* James O'Reilly, John Lawler, Patrick Heffron, Timothy Corbett, Vincent Wehrle, O.S.B., and Joseph Busch

half of North Dakota on December 31, 1909. At the same time the northwestern corner of Minnesota was removed from the jurisdiction of the Bishop of Duluth by the creation of the Diocese of Crookston.

When the new Dioceses of Bismarck and Crookston were formed, it so happened that the sees of Lead, Fargo and Winona had been deprived of their shepherds by death or transfer. The Holy Father named five priests of the Province of St. Paul to serve as bishops in those sees and another priest of the province to assist the Archbishop of St. Paul as an auxiliary bishop. Archbishop Ireland consecrated all these newly appointed bishops at one time on May 19, 1910, in St. Mary's Chapel on the grounds of the St. Paul Seminary. Neither before nor since have so many bishops been consecrated in a single ceremony in America, and on few occasions has such an event taken place in the long history of the Church.

The final change in diocesan boundaries within the province since its formation was made on November 18, 1957. A large portion of the western part of the Archdiocese of St. Paul was then designated to be the area of the new Diocese of New Ulm.

Announcing the Gospel

A full two centuries before the canonical creation of the Province of St. Paul, the faith made its momentous if little-heralded entry into the area. In 1680, while he was a prisoner of the Sioux, the famed Franciscan missionary and explorer, Pére Louis Hennepin, baptized a dying Indian child. A generation later, in 1727, the first mass was offered in the province by one of the Jesuit chaplains accompanying an expedition of French explorers who built a stockade on the western shore of Lake Pepin, near what is now Frontenac, within the present boundaries of the Archdiocese of St. Paul. And far to the north, in the vicinity of another French outpost located near the present Canadian frontier, on the night of June 5-6, 1763, twenty-one Frenchmen were massacred by Sioux; among the victims was a young Jesuit priest named Jean Aulneau.

The flags of many nations have flown over the territory now included in the Province of St. Paul. The French, English and Spanish, not to mention innumerable Indian tribes, all held sovereignty at one time or another before the area became incorporated into the United States. The responsibility for the promotion of Catholic life has rested with a variety of ecclesiastical jurisdictions during the centuries that followed the white man's penetration. Thus, for example, parts of the present province were at various times subject to the Bishop of Santiago de Cuba and the Bishop of Quebec. It can even be argued that the

Archbishop John Ireland

first ordinary to whom this territory was subject was the Archbishop of Rouen, because he, until the middle of the seventeenth century, exercised jurisdiction over all the Catholics in New France. But the discussion of jurisdiction remained largely academic until the second and third decades of the nineteenth century when the empty land, now all part of the United States, began to fill up with settlers, many of whom were Catholics. By 1818, mass began to be offered with some regularity at the settlement of Pembina in North Dakota. Late in the 1830's the immensely fruitful apostolate of the famous Jesuit missionaries Christian Hoecken and Pierre De Smet was about to begin in South Dakota, while several hundred miles to the east, near the confluence of the Minnesota and Mississippi rivers, a log chapel was built in 1841 and dedicated to the patronage of St. Paul. During the years immediately before the Diocese of St. Paul was created in 1850, the territory west of the Missouri belonged to the Diocese of St. Louis, that east of the Mississippi to the Diocese of Milwaukee and that between the two rivers, by far the greatest portion, to the Diocese of Dubuque.

Bishop Mathias Loras of Dubuque in 1839 made the first episcopal visitation to what is now the Province of St. Paul. This proved but a prelude to the work of Dubuque priests in the area. Within a few years Fathers Lucien Galtier and Augustin Ravoux had assumed a permanent apostolate among the Indians and white settlers in the upper Mississippi Valley. Ravoux indeed carried his work as far west as South Dakota. In 1850 the vicar-general of the Diocese of Dubuque, Joseph Cretin, was named by Pope Pius IX first bishop of St. Paul. The new see included the vast stretch of land between the Wisconsin-Minnesota border on the east and the Missouri River on the west.

Growth in the Province

Thirty-eight years separate the foundation of the Diocese of St. Paul from the attainment by that see of metropolitan status. During those four decades America's relentless march westward turned forests into fields of grain and great cities sprang up on the formerly empty prairies. By 1875 the growth of the Upper Midwest dictated the detachment of the northern two-thirds of the Diocese of St. Paul, by this date ruled by Joseph Cretin's successor, Bishop Thomas Langdon Grace, O.P. The Vicariate of Northern Minnesota was placed under the charge of Bishop Rupert Seidenbusch, O.S.B., who thus became the third bishop resident in the territory. Four years later in 1879, there followed another rearrangement of jurisdiction with the creation of the Vicariate of Dakota, whose ordinary was another Benedictine missionary, Martin Marty. These two vicariates became the original suffragan churches when St. Paul was designated an archdiocese in 1888.

The sacrifices of countless men and women brought the Church in Minnesota and North and South Dakota to that point which justified this provincial organization. Though much of the story can be told in terms of statistics, the essence of it remains hidden in the faith and zeal that prompted priests, religious and laity, despite the inadequacies of sluggish human nature, to overcome all obstacles and to build the Church on sure and strong foundations. How difficult it is, a century afterward, to appreciate fully the frustration and fatigue of the missionary, the matchless endeavor of a nun teaching or nursing without any facilities, the self-denial of the pioneers who provided a fitting place for the sacrificial altar before they thought of a roof over their own heads.

The continued growth of the Province of St. Paul since 1888 stands perhaps as the greatest monument to the work of the Catholic pioneers. The statistical evidence, cold and impersonal, is nevertheless an impressive chronicle. A million and a quarter Catholics (out of a total population of four and three quarter millions) now live where 380,000 Catholics lived in the year the province was founded. Then about 350 priests were engaged in the active ministry; now more than 2,100 aid their bishops in their tasks of teaching, sanctifying and governing the faithful. In 1888 little more than a thousand sisters were scattered across the province and hardly any brothers at all; today more than 8,200 sisters and almost 500 brothers can be found devoting their lives to Christian works of incalculable benefit. There were represented in the province in 1888 eight religious congregations of men and twenty of women; today those figures stand at 27 and 74 respectively, and they include 3 Benedictine abbeys, 10 priories of the Benedictine Sisters of Pontifical Jurisdiction and provincial houses or motherhouses of Oblates of Mary

Bishop Mathias Loras

Immaculate, Canons Regular of the Holy Cross, Brothers of the Christian Schools, Sisters of St Joseph of Carondelet, Sisters of Our Lady of Charity of the Good Shepherd, School Sisters of Notre Dame, Sisters of the third Order Regular of St. Francis of the Congregation of Our Lady of Lourdes, Missionary Franciscan Sisters of the Immaculate Conception, Sisters of St. Francis of the Immaculate Heart of Mary, Sisters of St. Mary of the Presentation, and Sisters of the Presentation of the Blessed Virgin Mary.

As numbers of Catholics have grown, so have those institutions which the Church has traditionally provided for her children. In 1888 there were in the province 471 parishes and 127 missions; in 1963 there are 1,127 parishes and 307 missions, and the figure rises constantly to meet the expanding population. In the field of Catholic education, an apostolate which the Church in America has particularly fostered, the tale is much the same. In seventy-five years, the number of seminaries has grown from 2 with about 50 students, to 14 enrolling almost 1,500; where there were 2 colleges and universities with 323 students, there are now 14 with 8,294 matriculating; there were about 1,000 students in 17 Catholic high schools in 1888, while today 30,000 students are enrolled in secondary schools; and the grade school population has risen ten-fold: from 15,491 pupils in 110 schools to 151,435 in 443 schools.

All this has been accomplished under the grace of God, by people of every race and color. The descendants of the original inhabitants of this land are still here in considerable numbers: indeed the Diocese of Rapid City, South Dakota, with its more than 14,000 Indian Catholics, has the second largest aboriginal population among all the dioceses in the United States. The particular geniuses of the nations of the old world can be found in abundance, too, and Catholics of the Latin rite join in one faith, one baptism and one sacrifice with Catholics of the Byzantine, Maronite and Ukranian rites.

The Story to be Told

Some of the essays that follow sketch the history of the states in the province, and others tell the story of the people of the God, the bishops, priests, monks, brothers, sisters and faithful who have been the Church in each diocese of the three states generation after generation. The authors of the essays on the dioceses write about the spread of the Gospel, and about labors and sacrifices to erect edifices in which to worship and buildings in which to perform the spiritual and corporal works of mercy. They also mention the changes made in ecclesiastical organization to promote more effectively the spiritual formation of Catholics and the signs that indicate the health and growth of the mystical body of Christ in the Province of St. Paul.

Ecclesiastical Terminology

References to changes in the Church's organization in the province require the use of some technical language that may not be clearly understood by every reader. A few words on the terms used will make their meaning clearer. Generally the English words are similar to Latin terms used to indicate the gradation of the administrative structure of the Church.

In the United States vicariates apostolic were usually established in regions that were sparsely settled and that had not been organized into states. A bishop appointed to act as a delegate of the Pope in a vicariate has the title of vicar apostolic. When, therefore, within our St. Paul Province, the Catholic population had increased and the political organization had been completed, at least one diocese, also called a see, was eventually erected within each state.

The largest city in a diocese is usually designated the see city, the city in which the bishop is to reside. The bishop or the ordinary of a diocese, unlike the bishop of a vicariate who acts as a delegate of the Pope, has personal jurisdiction as a successor of the Apostles over the people living within the boundaries of his diocese. Vicariates and dioceses are part of a larger administrative unit called a province. The bishop of a diocese that has been designated as the provincial see, also called the metropolitan see, has the title of archbishop, and he is the metropolitan.

The area over which a metropolitan exercises jurisdiction is called an archdiocese. Dioceses and vicariates in a province are called suffragan churches or sees, and bishops in such administrative units are suffragans of the metropolitan. The rights and duties of a metropolitan in relation to his suffragans, and theirs to him, are set forth principally in Canon Law, a codification of the laws by which the ordinary affairs within the Church are governed.

There are differences in rank among the clergy, and frequently more than one word or phrase is used to identify that rank. A priest, who is a member of the lower clergy, is raised to the ranks of the higher clergy, i.e., the episcopacy, when he is consecrated a bishop. The Pope and the bishops of the world are the hierarchy of the universal Church. An archbishop and the bishops of a province are frequently referred to as the local hierarchy. Every bishop, then, is a member of the universal hierarchy. His title—pope, cardinal, archbishop, bishop, titular bishop—indicates his rank in that hierarchy. A coadjutor bishop or an auxiliary bishop appointed to aid the bishop of a diocese, for example, does not have jurisdiction over any area. Bishops who do not have jurisdiction by law over any region are called titular bishops. The title of cardinal bestowed upon an archbishop or bishop by the Holy

Apostolic Constitution of May 4, 1888, promulgating the establishment of the Province of St. Paul

Father is a mark of his special regard for the person of the prelate so honored and it raises him to the rank in the hierarchy from which the popes are selected. But the area over which he exercises jurisdiction, if he occupies a see, is not increased thereby. The title of monsignor used in referring to a priest who has been named a protonotary apostolic, domestic prelate or papal chamberlain by the Pope, usually at the request of his bishop because of the responsible position he holds or his conspicuous services to the Church, is a personal title of honor that gives him a higher position in the ranks of the lower clergy but does not change the jurisdiction that he may have previously exercised. Finally, the member of the higher or lower clergy appointed by the bishop of a diocese to the office of vicar-general is the highest official in a diocese after the bishop. At the death of the bishop of a diocese, the see and the office of vicar-general become vacant. While a see is without a bishop, a period called the interregnum, an administrator conducts the diocesan business.

—THE EDITOR

THE GOPHER STATE, land of ten thousand lakes, is in the center of the North American Continent and is numbered among the north central states of the United States. Because of its geographical position in relation to the settlements of European nations on the continent in colonial times, and because of the continental network of rivers and lakes, explorers from New France were the first to gain knowledge of water routes west of the settlements at Montreal and Quebec by which they could enter Minnesota. An expedition led by Daniel Greysolon, Sieur du Lhut (Duluth), moved into the region in 1679. It must have been a thrilling moment the next year when Duluth and his

MINNESOTA HISTORY

by Reverend Patrick H. Ahern

party, who had penetrated the area from the western shore of Lake Superior, met near Lake Mille Lacs Father Louis Hennepin, O.S.F., and his two companions, who had entered Minnesota from the south on the Mississippi River as captives of the Sioux. Having discovered the doorways to a district containing a fortune in furs, French explorers and traders, accompanied at times by priests, passed through them to exploit its resources. At strategic places near rivers and lakes in the interior and near the northern border, they erected crude forts to serve as bases for trade and for further exploration. Very few of these posts were occupied by them without interruption for very long because the unpredictable Indians frequently disputed with them the right to use the waterways and to occupy the land. The French endeavor to establish peaceful relations

with the Chippewa and Sioux Indians in Minnesota, for the purpose of trade and to make their evangelization possible, ceased in 1763 when the settlers in New France bowed to the superior forces of the British in the New World and began to live under the English flag.

British subjects controlled the fur trade in Minnesota for the next fifty years and furnished additional knowledge about its terrain to mapmakers. During this period English, Yankee and French-Canadian explorers and traders in canoes propelled by French-trained voyageurs traveled over the water paths that led to the sites of old forts and to the new posts that they erected in Minnesota, but priests did not accompany them. The British flag continued to fly over many fortified trading posts east of the Mississippi River and south of the Pigeon River after American independence was recognized by treaty in 1783. English subjects controlled the fur trade just as effectively west of the Mississippi after that region had also become the territory of the United States by purchase in 1803. It was only after the Treaty of Ghent was ratified in 1815 as the final step in the conclusion of the War of 1812 that the British subjects withdrew from their posts and American citizens began to profit from exploitation of the resources of the area.

As the British were withdrawing from the forts they had erected in the future state of Minnesota, federal officials in the War Department began seriously to take the necessary steps to obtain firsthand information about the main features of the eighty thousand square miles of land area and four thousand square miles of water area that are now within the state's boundaries. Preliminary steps for this purpose were the signing in 1815 of a treaty of peace with the Sioux Indians and the erection four years later of Fort Snelling at the junction of the Mississippi and Minnesota rivers a few miles below St. Anthony Falls. For the next thirty years chiefly military units, geographers hired by the War Department and hunters and trappers roamed about in the vast domain to fulfill their principal objectives. American fur traders established more than forty posts in the area. The posts at Mendota (called St. Peter's then) in the shadow of Fort Snelling and at Fond du Lac near Lake Superior on the St. Louis River were their chief supply and storage depots because of their strategic locations.

Father Hennepin christens the Falls of St. Anthony

Early Settlement

Fort Snelling proved to be the magnet that would draw settlers into the region. The first to be attracted by the protection it would afford were colonists at Pembina in the Red River Valley near Canada who had become discouraged by the hardships they had suffered in that isolated settlement. First a few families came early in the 1820's and then others followed, and they all squatted on the Fort Snelling military reservation until they were forcibly evicted by the commander at the fort in 1840. Moving down-river and to the east bank of the Mississippi a short distance from the fort, they settled within the triangle of land between the Mississippi and St. Croix rivers ceded by the Indians three years before. In this settlement of log huts roofed with slabs brought from a saw mill in Stillwater, a log chapel was built by Catholics and dedicated to St. Paul within the next year. This frontier village

at the head of navigation on the Mississippi was also named after the Apostle to the Gentiles, and became the chief port of entry to Minnesota.

Among the approximately seventeen hundred people who lived at St. Paul, Stillwater, St. Anthony and Mendota in the late 1840's there were a number of political leaders capable of voicing the concern they and their fellow citizens felt over the fact they had been living in unorganized territory west of the Mississippi since 1846 when Iowa was made a state and east of the Mississippi since 1848 when Wisconsin gained statehood. These men presented the arguments to Congress that moved the legislators in 1849 to establish Minnesota Territory with boundaries on the north, east and south as they are today and on the west at the Missouri and White Earth rivers. These territorial lines also became the boundaries of the Diocese of St. Paul, established the next year.

Immediately after the Territory was created

Steamboats at the St. Paul landing in 1859

the settlers, businessmen and land speculators began to press the local officials to hurry the process by which additional land would be taken from the Indians. Of course, the interest of the politicians lay in the expansion of economic opportunities in the Territory for their own financial welfare and as a means of increasing the population. It was in response to their prodding, then, that the federal government obtained in 1851 from the Sioux Indians by the Treaties of Traverse des Sioux and Mendota about twenty-four million acres in the southern half of the present state. Again in 1854 and 1855 the treaty-making fiction was employed by the federal government to acquire from the Chippewa Indians large tracts in the northeastern and north central parts of the future state. In this area were the great pine forests then coveted by lumbermen who eventually almost completely denuded them.

How quickly news spread that unlimited fertile lands and business opportunities were available in Minnesota Territory! In the settled parts of the United States and in the European nations that

Stillwater, about 1875

were the principal reservoirs from which there had been flowing a continuous stream of immigrants, people heard about Minnesota. Up the Mississippi from New Orleans, St. Louis and river towns in Illinois and Iowa, and across neighboring states the human horde and their chattels came, to exploit another agricultural and lumbering frontier. Steamboat arrivals at the wharves in St. Paul increased from 119 in 1851 to 1,025 in 1857. In the latter year over forty thousand people disembarked in St. Paul, Winona and Red Wing, and the population of the Territory was counted to be 150,000. Two-thirds of the people had come from eastern states and Canada and the rest were from the old world, mostly Germans, Irishmen, and Englishmen with a sprinkling of the earliest Scandinavians.

Prelude to Statehood

While steamboats were pushing against the current of the Father of Waters toward the territorial hub formed by St. Paul, St. Anthony and Mendota, crews under the supervision of the military establishment were toiling to fashion the roads that were the spokes going out from it. One of them went southward to points in Iowa (the Dubuque Road), another through the heart of the Big Woods to St. Peter and Mankato and on to the Big Sioux, another close to Shakopee on the way to Fort Ridgely in the upper Minnesota River Valley, another northwestward to Fort Ripley and still another in a northeasterly direction to Superior. At the same time a network of roads authorized by the territorial legislature was being constructed in the southern prairie region south and west of the Big Woods, a hardwood forest shaped roughly like a cone with its point a little below Mankato and extending toward the evergreen forests in the north. These rutted trails opened the interior to another wave of farmers whose homes were tents, log cabins or sod huts when they started to clear the land of its surface cover of hardwoods in the Minnesota and Sauk Valleys or to tear apart the thick turf of the prairie. The gradual extension of farming communities led to the development of additional agricultural service centers at Crow Wing, St. Cloud, Anoka, Monticello, New Ulm, St. Peter, Shakopee, Winona, Wabasha, Frontenac, Red Wing, Faribault and Hastings before Minnesota became the thirty-second state of the Union on May 11, 1858.

When statehood was gained the needs of the growing population for building materials, flour and manufactured goods were being met locally by enterprising businessmen who had harnessed the rivers at numerous power sites. Minneapolis and St. Anthony, located at the great falls, were rapidly emerging as the leading centers of lumber processing and flour milling, the industries that were the foundations for the prosperity of the state for many years. By 1858, too, most of the hastily constructed shanties in the towns had been replaced by substantial frame dwellings and business establishments, and many farmers could afford lumber for homes and barns because there was a market for wheat, dairy products and livestock in the growing towns that housed the bankers, manufacturers, professional men, speculators and transients.

In the early years of statehood most of the newcomers followed the well-worn paths to populated districts where fertile land was still plentiful and cheap. Even though the pace at which immigrants and investors entered the state was slowed during the Civil War and the Sioux War of 1862 and its aftermath, the population had increased to 250,000 by the end of the national conflict. During the remaining years of the decade a steady stream of ambitious and landless people came from Northern Europe and the British Isles to obtain 160 acres of land for a small fee under the provisions of the Homestead Act and to take advantage of opportunities for employment in rapidly expanding industries and in railroad construction. By the end of the decade there were about 180,000 more people in the state.

Revolution in Transportation

Railroads were essential for the extension of settlement and economic expansion in Minnesota. Rails entering from Wisconsin and Iowa as the Civil War ended had reached the Twin Cities by way of Winona and Le Roy through Owatonna and Farmington, and lines had been extended from the twin towns to Sauk Rapids, Wyoming, Cokato, Mankato and Lake Crystal in the occupied areas by 1869. Then they were extended beyond

St. Anthony and Minneapolis in the falls area, 1869

developed regions as they reached for distant points beyond the western border of the state. In 1871 trains began to run from the Twin Cities through the wilderness to Duluth and across the western prairie to Breckenridge. By the end of the 1870's the rich valley of the Red River of the North was connected by rails to the center of flour milling and to Duluth, and road beds were completed throughout the southern half of the state to form the basic rail network to which branch and feeder lines were added in subsequent years.

Railroad companies not only opened a large area for new settlement; they also conducted an aggressive campaign in Europe and America to induce settlers to occupy the land along their rights of way. Furthermore, they practically decided where settlement would take place in unoccupied areas by their choice of locations for division points, freight yards and depots and by platting towns at such sites. Brainerd, Glyndon,

Moorhead, Crookston, St. Vincent, Worthington, Jackson, Wells, Albert Lea, Willmar, Sleepy Eye and Montevideo are some of the towns located at division points or rail heads that owe their existence or their prosperity in years past to the extension of the railroads in the 1870's.

Regular transportation the year-round between communities within the state and between the commonwealth and the outside world made Minnesota more attractive to homeseekers in the post-Civil War days. Of considerable importance, too, among the factors that made it the destination of immigrants were the comparative ease with which it could be reached from Altantic ports for a low fare and the good prospects of gaining financial security in agriculture, industry, trade and the professions. The combination of so many fortuitous circumstances caused an increase in the total population to 780,773 by 1880. At that time about thirty per cent of the people in the state were natives of foreign lands.

A Growing Church

As portions of more than half of the state in the north were made accessible by the railroads, a greater number of newcomers settled there each year after the Civil War. Concern for adequate spiritual care of the approximately 15,000 Catholics among them and of the 2,200 Indians of the Chippewa nation living there on reservations moved Church officials in 1875 to place that region under the supervision of a vicar apostolic who resided at St. Cloud in the center of a large community of German Catholics. Thereafter, the Bishop of St. Paul could give full attention to the promotion of the spiritual welfare of about 100,000 Catholics then scattered throughout the more densely populated southern part of the state.

As the nineteenth century advanced and people moved into Minnesota at a faster rate, raising the population well over the million and a quarter mark in the decade of the eighties, further changes were made in ecclesiastical organization for the advance of religion. In response to a recommendation made by the bishops of the Province of Milwaukee, which then included Minnesota, the Holy See formed the Province of St. Paul in 1888, and at the same time raised the Most Reverend John Ireland of the St. Paul see to archiepiscopal rank. The new metropolitan then presented to Rome a detailed plan for new dioceses in the province. The next year the Sovereign Pontiff approved the part of his plan pertaining to Minnesota when he created the Dioceses of St. Cloud, Winona and Duluth.

The tier of counties across central Minnesota in the Diocese of St. Cloud, the counties resting on the Iowa line in the Diocese of Winona and the area sandwiched between these dioceses the width of the state in the Archdiocese of St. Paul were well populated with old stock Americans; immigrants from Germany (who were the most numerous), the Scandinavian countries, the British Isles (Ireland especially), Canada, Poland and Bohemia; and the numerous descendants of earlier immigrants from those countries.

The majority of the northern tier of counties in the Diocese of Duluth, on the other hand, were still beyond the main path of settlement. Extensive forests of white pine in the north had attracted a swarm of loggers after rail connections were established with Duluth early in the 1870's.

The port city at the head of the Great Lakes had then grown rapidly in less than two decades from 3,000 to 33,000 on the basis of lumber and wheat that was shipped to booming cities on the Lakes and in the East. But the principal industry of lumbering with its mobile front had required few permanent service centers in the interior. As the century was closing, this hinterland became the scene of the feverish activity of an army of laborers engaged in exploiting great iron ore deposits. On the mining frontier the towns of Virginia, Eveleth, Biwabik, Hibbing, Chisholm, Ely, Crosby-Ironton and Tower sprang up. These towns and other villages in the district were populated principally at first by descendants of European immigrants trained at other mining regions in the United States—Cornishmen, Scandinavians, Irish, Finns, Germans, French and Canadians, Poles, Slovenes and Italians. As the demand for laborers at the mines increased Finns, Poles, Hungarians, Rumanians, Lithuanians, Russians, Italians, Syrians and Greeks came directly from their homelands to the range towns. These men from many nations, latecomers on the Minnesota scene, started the mineral treasure on its way to the railroad and harbor towns of Duluth and Two Harbors that grew rapidly to provide for the needs of the new industry.

The phenomenal increase in the population of the eastern counties in the Diocese of Duluth, the poor transportation facilities between the see city and the western counties and the enormous area under the jurisdiction of the Duluth prelate were taken into account when the diocese was partitioned on the last day in 1909 by the creation of the Diocese of Crookston in the northwestern corner of the state. The new see city had been for three decades a center of the lumber industry that had dotted the area with small settlements like Bemidji near the eastern border of the diocese. The majority of the settlers in the region, however, were wheat growers who had flocked there after the railroads were extended through the Red River Valley in the 1870's. The rich earth of the valley produced fabulous yields of the golden crop for the small farmer as well as for the bonanza farmer who tilled thousands of acres, giving that district a reputation that drew poor people to work the soil and men with capital to invest in the productive land.

In the year that the Diocese of Crookston was

established, the foreign-born among the state's 2,075,708 residents numbered 543,595. Doorways to America were gradually closed to the subjects of foreign nations by restrictive legislation passed by Congress after the First World War. The first to be excluded from the United States were the people of eastern and southern Europe, many of whose hardy countrymen, called the new immigrants, were laboring in the mines and in the meat packing industry that had begun to flourish around the turn of the century in South St. Paul and Winona. Population growth in Minnesota after immigration from all countries was drastically curtailed in the 1920's was due principally to natural increase and to opportunities for employment in expanding industries that beckoned to alert and mobile Americans.

Hard Times and Urbanization

Minnesotans had their full quota of nightmares and headaches during the great depression of the thirties when hard times made each day gloomy and when the skies were frequently darkened by clouds of grasshoppers and of choking dust whipped by relentless hot winds from the surface of the parched fields. Even then the trend toward greater urbanization of the state's citizens continued. The movement of people to cities and towns became more pronounced during the Second World War when factories employed a multitude of men and women to produce mountains of articles needed for survival as a nation.

The twin towns on the Mississippi, where factory chimneys spewed smoke and soot, felt the crowding within their corporate limits and watched sprawling suburbs begin to take shape. These satellites of the twins were filled with people and were expanded at a phenomenal rate in the postwar decade. By 1957 about forty per cent of an estimated three and a third million residents in Minnesota lived in Minneapolis and St. Paul and their suburbs. At that time ecclesiastical authorities decided to detach the western two-thirds of the Archdiocese of St. Paul to form the Diocese of New Ulm. That was the last change made in the Church's organization in Minnesota before the seventy-fifth anniversary of the establishment of the Province of St. Paul.

The foregoing sketch of the history of Minnesota reveals the fulfillment of a vague prophecy about the future of the region written in 1778 by Jonathan Carver in these words: "There is no doubt that at some future period, mighty kingdoms will emerge from these wildernesses; and stately and solemn temples, with gilded spires reaching the skies, supplant the Indian huts, whose only decorations are the barbarous trophies of their vanquished enemies."

Church of St. Peter, Mendota, built in 1853

ARCHDIOCESE
OF SAINT PAUL

by Reverend Marvin R. O'Connell

A LEISURELY AFTERNOON drive will take you round the whole circumference of the Archdiocese of St. Paul. Begin, say, at Hugo, and proceed straight west through Anoka to Buffalo, a matter of forty minutes or so, and then swing into a sixty mile arc south and east which passes through Waconia and Montgomery and ends in the ripe, placid charm of Faribault. If you turn then to the northeast, less then an hour will bring you to Red Wing where the black bluffs, crouched along the shores of the Mississippi, invite you to remember the Sioux chief whose village once stood in their shadow. The river will stay on your right as you close the circle, traveling north and west, and it is not unlikely that as you enter the eastern suburbs of St. Paul you will see that the late afternoon sun has illumined the great green dome of the cathedral which hovers atop its hill like a guardian angel over the city below.

The color of the landscape shifts, of course, with the seasons from green to bronze to grey, tempered always by the blue of the innumerable small lakes and streams. These mementos of the primeval glacier have attracted people here for thousands of years and have served them as sources of food and avenues of trade. The produce of the country is rich and varied, and once, not so long ago, the native hunter in search of game padded through it noiselessly along trails known only to himself. He has given way now to the descendants of European farmers who brought with them from across the sea old world skills and ideals and who began in this new land the timeless gamble involved in wresting from the earth its yearly duty of corn and grain and beans. The names of the towns that dot the countryside give evidence of a nostalgia scarcely felt anymore by the bustling inhabitants, who have never seen the Derrynane, Cologne or Prague from which their ancestors came. When the roots go deep enough it is easy to forget they are there.

At the point where the Minnesota River flows into it, the Mississippi acts as though it had been struck a blow; it veers sharply north before turning in a wide loop to resume its relentless southward flow to the Gulf. Here have grown up the Twin Cities of Minneapolis and St. Paul which together form the heart of the lush countryside around them. In the ancient tradition of river towns, they owe their birth to the canoe and the steamer and the whole range of commercial activities related to inland trade. They have by now outstripped their modest beginnings, and, thanks to the boxcar and the truck, have reached far beyond the compass of the rivers to suck up into their tall elevators millions of bushels of wheat and to lead a thousand bawling cattle a day into their slaughter pens. Within this vast marketplace has sprung up a complex of mills and assembly lines which turn out cake mixes, tractors, adhesive tapes and electronic computers. In their economic foundations, then, Minneapolis and St. Paul are typical of the urban civilization that twentieth century America has produced. They provide, too, all the contrasts inherent in that civilization. They have spawned the dirt and noise unescapable in an industrial society, the gargantuan traffic snarls at the rush hours, the garish neon glitter of factory town night life, the pockets of dilapidated slums that run across their faces like ugly scars, the peculiarly desperate kind of loneliness that seems to afflict people only in the midst of a large city. But no less apparent are the quiet residential areas, with their tree-lined streets and aura of turn-of-the-century americana, the happy din of suburbs bursting with small children, the elegant new buildings crammed with the technological magic that testifies to man's conquest of nature. The Twin Cities have become an educational and cultural center of astonishing vitality, where one can learn to weave a basket or construct an atomic reactor, where one can hear the best in jazz and chamber music, where one can see major league baseball and football, paintings by Rouault and a different first-rate play every night of the week.

A million and a half people live within an hour's drive of the Cathedral of St. Paul. About one third of this total are Catholics whose lives for the most part follow a pattern similar to that of their neighbors. The urbanization of the region has affected them as profoundly as any other group and has sifted them into just about every income bracket and political allegiance. And in the absorbing interest they take in their daily work and in their children, the Catholics of east central Minnesota share in a changeless feature of human history. Just as clear, however, as their amalgamation into the culture of their times are the factors which mark the Catholics off. At the root of them is that difficult-to-define conviction, seldom consciously stated, that they are indeed the remnant of Israel, the little band whose task it is to give a unique witness to Christ. The visible form that this sense of mission has taken in the Archdiocese of St. Paul is a typically American one: the open-handed generosity which has built hundreds of churches, schools and hospitals, the enthusiastic support for good works of every description, the almost compulsive desire to make the Church understood and respected. This is not to deny that Catholics are aware of the primacy of the faith and the sacraments in their lives. They understand that precisely these things render their activity intelligible and important. They reflect upon an abiding mystery in their own inadequacy, as men and women necessarily caught up by the rhythm of contemporary events and yet, at the same time, guardians of an ancient gospel and partakers of the Divine Nature.

It has ever been so.

The Church Established

It was so when the first Catholics settled in what is now the Archdiocese of St. Paul. They were fur traders mostly, restless men who came into the wilderness as much to escape the stifling conventions of civilized society as to make their fortunes. They were French or French Canadians, and with them the first of many national geniuses was stamped upon the country. Never entirely innocent of sharp practices in their dealings with the childlike Indians, they nevertheless provided goods of inestimable value in primitive eyes and so they never lacked for customers. They did, however, lack any regular spiritual ministration, for rarely did a missionary priest penetrate to their remote trading posts.

Not until some twenty years after the first Fort Snelling had been built to guard the juncture of the Mississippi and Minnesota rivers was there a priest resident in the region. By this time a town of sorts had grown up around the American Fur Company's headquarters at Mendota, and here, in the September of 1841, Father Lucien Galtier settled into the little hut which served as a church and rectory. Galtier was a thirty-year-old Frenchman who had come to America as a mission volunteer three years before in response to the plea of Bishop Mathias Loras of Dubuque. Under that prelate's ecclesiastical jurisdiction lay all of what is now Minnesota west of the meandering Mississippi, and to this part of his vast vineyard he dispatched Father Galtier in 1840. The sensitive young man was not equal to the task, and before long he felt that he had been shuttled to the ends of the earth. He found the climate intolerable, the loneliness hardly less so, but what was to him the keenest source of unhappiness was the recalcitrance of his small and scattered flock. They were crude, hard-drinking, tough-fisted frontiersmen who responded with scant attention, it seemed to Galtier, to their priest's admonitions.

His life was further complicated by a jurisdictional problem. The settlers on the east bank of the Mississippi were technically not his subjects. Since they lived in Wisconsin Territory the Catholics among them were the responsibility of the Bishop of Detroit (and, after 1843, of the Bishop of Milwaukee). But there was no Wisconsin Territory priest within hundreds of miles, and so Father Galtier, not without complaint, had to assume the burden of their spiritual care as well as that of his own people. Altogether, he served about 650 Catholics, of whom 500 lived east of the river. For the use of these latter some kind of building had to be provided. Of the sites offered by the settlers, Galtier shrewdly chose one readily accessible to the river but standing on high enough ground to avoid the danger of

Father Lucien Galtier

spring floods, and far enough from Fort Snelling to render confiscation by an expanding military reservation unlikely. Construction, if it can be called that, began in October, 1841, and by the feast of All Saints the chapel was finished. The congregation of French, Swiss, Irish, half-breeds and Sioux, all of whom had contributed labor and materials, assisted Father Galtier in the ceremonies which dedicated the chapel to the patronage of St. Paul. (The priest observed later that its cramped and rude interior made him think of the stable at Bethlehem.) Today, toward the river from Kellogg Boulevard between Cedar and Minnesota Streets in downtown St. Paul, a simple monument marks the spot of St. Paul's Chapel, and reminds later generations how the hopes of one group of pioneers have endured. It is worth pondering that the total value of the original building was about $65.00.

Painting of Chapel of St. Paul in 1852 by R. O. Sweeny—Front built in 1841; enlarged in 1847

By 1844, Lucien Galtier, fretful and unhappy, had had enough of St. Paul and Mendota. He had received in the wilderness an exceedingly rough baptism of fire and it took a couple of years in the tranquil France of the July Monarchy to restore his spirits. Though he came back to the midwest missions, he never returned to Minnesota. His replacement, though also a Frenchman and of similar age and background, was a different type altogether. Father Augustin Ravoux possessed that combination of toughness and resilience which made for an ideal frontier priest. He began his missionary work among the Sioux, ranging miles in all directions from his permanent center near the present site of Chaska. When Galtier visited him there he found his material conditions pitiable: one broken chair, one table knife, one coffee cup, two spoons and a stove so defective that the contents of the chalice often froze when Mass was offered in the winter. Ravoux moved to Mendota after Galtier's departure, and between 1844 and 1851 he was alone in the region, serving the spiritual needs of the settlements around Fort Snelling on both sides of the river and saving as much time as he could for the Indians.

The First Bishop

In March of 1849 the Territory of Minnesota was established, and later the same year the Seventh Provincial Council of Baltimore petitioned the Holy See to set up a diocese centered in St. Paul. The Fathers of the Council judged correctly that the territorial status would bring new settlers to Minnesota who could not be served efficiently from so far away as Milwaukee and Dubuque. On July 19, 1850, the new ecclesiastical division was created with jurisdiction over 166,000 square miles, bounded by Iowa on the south, Wisconsin on the east, Canada on the north and the Missouri and White Earth rivers on the west. To head the new diocese, Pope Pius IX appointed the French-born vicar-general of the Diocese of Dubuque, Joseph Cretin.

The new bishop, who had gone home to France to be consecrated, stepped off the steamer in his see city on July 2, 1851. Father Ravoux was there to greet him, together with a goodly number of the little Catholic community. Probably

also Father Patrick James Moran was there since he had arrived in St. Paul in May. They saw a middle-aged man (he was fifty-one) of medium height, a bit on the corpulent side, with a receding hair line and strikingly dark eyes

Monsignor Augustin Ravoux in later life

behind his spectacles. Ravoux was no stranger to him, for they had come together to Dubuque with Bishop Loras in 1838. Before that Cretin had served in the Diocese of Belley where his desires to follow a missionary vocation were thwarted until finally the chance came to go to America. In Dubuque he had acted as vicar-general, rector of the cathedral, missionary to the Winnebagoes and in any other capacity (including fund raising) that his desperately shorthanded bishop selected. Thirteen years in the wilderness, to which he had come for Christ's sake, had not diminished the priestly resolutions of his youth any more than they had altered his placid manner or his rather unexceptional appearance.

Bishop Cretin had come to see as well as be

seen, and what he saw was the frontier village that had grown up in the decade since Father Galtier had dedicated St. Paul's Chapel. It was neither large nor attractive; it was simply one more raw settlement, like a thousand others, that marked a stage in America's relentless march westward. The bishop could take consolation at least in the fact that the town bore the name of the Apostle to the Gentiles rather than the nickname of one of the original settlers, whose peculiar expression had caused him (and, for awhile before 1841, the region) to be called Pig's Eye. Fewer than 1,200 people lived in St. Paul, in log shanties mostly with a more pretentious frame house here and there. Not one brick or stone building graced the town. Even so, its growth had been remarkable: four years earlier, in 1847, its white population had stood at fifty. Now the steamer from elegant St. Louis to the south stopped regularly to deliver freight and to pick up produce hauled by oxcart from the west and north. There were other signs of civilization for the bishop to reflect upon: several Protestant churches were holding services, three hotels catered to guests, the saloons were doing a thriving business and the Territory's first newspaper, the *Minnesota Pioneer,* had recently gone into operation. (Mercifully, the owner had been dissuaded from calling his publication St. Paul's Epistle, as some wag had suggested.) Bishop Cretin noted the material resources at his disposal consisted of one log cathedral, smaller churches in Mendota, St. Anthony (the nucleus of what was to become Minneapolis) and Pembina (thirty days away by oxcart to the northwest), six priests and a Catholic population of about 1,000 in a total population of 6,000 whites and 30,000 Indians.

The history of a people can never be told satisfactorily in terms of statistics, and yet it is not without importance that by 1857, when Cretin died, the Diocese of St. Paul could boast of 29 permanent churches, 35 mission stations and 20 priests who ministered to a Catholic population of 50,000. There was a hospital, too, and a theological seminary attached to the bishop's house,

St. Paul in 1860, third Cathedral marked

Bishop Joseph Cretin

where four students of theology lived and studied. Four other young men were preparing themselves for the priesthood in seminaries elsewhere, and one of these, a lad named John Ireland whom Cretin had sent to his own alma mater in France, would one day become a figure of world renown. Grammer schools and a high school had also been founded, and in 1851, a few months after Bishop Cretin's arrival, four Sisters of St. Joseph came to St. Paul from Carondelet, Missouri, and began an apostolate which has been down through the years of incalculable benefit. The sisters' first convent was a two-room shack, well ventilated by a hole in the ceiling through which passed the stove pipe. One of the four admitted that the primitive chimney arrangement did spread a chill through the ramshackle building and that it failed dismally to keep out the rain, but, she added, saying perhaps more than she knew about herself and her dauntless sisters, "through it we could count the stars."

The infant diocese grew as the Territory grew, swiftly and unpredictably. New lands were thrown open to settlers by government treaty with the Indians, and immigrants came in ever-increasing numbers to dig their plows into the rich prairie soil. Many of the Irish who had ex-

changed their famine-ridden homeland for the slums of eastern American cities turned west again, and soon Minnesota included settlements with lilting names like Derrynane and Green Isle. By 1855 there were enough Germans in St. Paul to justify a parish of their own. Joseph Cretin presided over this growth firmly but benignly and with a fine Gallic sensibility. He did most of the parochial work at the cathedral himself in order to free his handful of priests for wide-ranging missionary activity. His stout figure was a familiar sight in the town, along whose muddy streets he could often be seen carrying Holy Communion to the sick. He did not, however, neglect the countryside, and the exhausting round of visitations to his scattered parishes and mission stations used up much of his time and energy every year. If anyone protested that he drove himself too hard, he merely shrugged and remarked that every frontier clergyman, whatever his denomination, had to be a circuit rider. A chronic shortage of money, needless to say, was one of his gravest problems. The Catholic people were for the most part miserably poor; they had come to Minnesota only after having experienced failure or disaster somewhere else. Had it not been for the $40,000 he begged during his episcopate from the Society for the Propagation of the Faith, Bishop Cretin would have been unable to avert diocesan bankruptcy. Even so, ends barely met, and it was with great difficulty that the bishop scraped together enough funds to begin the construction of a modest new cathedral. He did not live to see it completed. On February 22, 1857, after several months of intense suffering, Joseph Cretin died of dropsy. It gives one pause to remember the remark he made a day or two before his death to the little group around his bed: "In my life I have asked only that the will of God be done. In the long night when I cannot sleep I pray for you."

More than two years passed before another bishop came to St. Paul. During that interval Father Augustin Ravoux acted as diocesan administrator and, of course, life went on. Far away in Washington President Buchanan served out most of his listless term against an ever-darkening background of sectional discord. John Brown raided the arsenal at Harper's Ferry, Virginia, and thoughtful men wondered if his half-mad cry was not the trumpet of Armageddon blown over a nation irreparably divided by the issue of slavery. The Know-Nothing Party, with its creed of racial and religious hatred, rose and fell like a meteor, but not before Catholics in Minneapolis were stunned to find one Sunday morning a man brandishing a pistol on the front steps of their church and threatening to shoot the first Jesuit who came in range. In 1858, Stephen Douglas defeated Abraham Lincoln in the Illinois senatorial election, and that same year, amid great jubilation, Minnesota was admitted to the Union.

Bishop Thomas Langdon Grace

Despite the new dignity of statehood, the episcopal vacancy in St. Paul, to which neither the telegraph nor the railroad had yet come, did not attract very many candidates. The first appointee was so upset that he undertook the long and expensive journey to Rome where he succeded in persuading the Pope to select some "worthier" person. Not so successful was the Dominican pastor of SS. Peter and Paul Church in Memphis, Tennessee. When he returned the documents of appointment to Rome with a polite refusal, he was promptly informed that the Holy Father had decided to send him to Minnesota anyway. And so, with some understandable reluctance, Thomas Langdon Grace, of the Order of Preachers, became second Bishop of St. Paul. Born in Charleston and raised in Cincinnati, Grace, now in his middle forties, had established a fine reputation as an educator and administrator. When he left Memphis to assume his hazardous new duties in the north, the local press extolled his public virtues and hailed him as a "gentleman," not a small tribute for a Catholic priest to have received in ante bellum Tennessee. He was installed in the unfinished cathedral (at the corner of Sixth and St. Peter Streets) on July 29, 1859, about six weeks before Minnesota's first gubernatorial election.

Bishop Grace had scarcely finished his first visitation to his sprawling diocese (during which he had been particularly charmed by a sixteen-mile sleigh ride through a sharply cold, bright November night) when the United States exploded into Civil war. Governor Alexander Ramsey took

Bishop Thomas Langdon Grace, O.P.

steps immediately to form the First Minnesota Regiment which was destined for bloody immortality at the battle of Gettysburg. Altogether, more than 20,000 Minnesotans fought on the northern side during the four-year struggle. The agony of this war that divided friends and brothers had a special poignancy for the Bishop of St. Paul who had been born within sight of Fort Sumter. Though his loyalty to the Union was never doubted, Bishop Grace's position made it hard for him to see without sorrow the victory of either side. Something of the same emotion moved him (and many others) when, in the summer of 1862, the Sioux in Minnesota rose in a hopeless bid to drive the white men out. From the Lower Agency near Redwood Falls, 1,500 braves swept across the Minnesota River, slaughtering more than 400 whites and sparing only the women and children whom they wanted to take captive. With the repulse of the Indians at the German settlement of New Ulm, the uprising collapsed and judicial vengeance followed. Thirty-nine unfortunate Sioux were hanged, though many more than that were condemned to death. When President Lincoln commuted the sentences of all not proved guilty of murder or rape, he brought down upon himself the angry resentment of most white Minnesotans. Such is the bitterness engendered by war.

The guns fell silent in 1865 and Johnny came marching home to a nation suddenly plunged into a period of unprecedented economic expansion. Minnesota had its share of the boom. By 1870 its population had reached nearly half a million and it doubled again in the next ten years. Wheat and timber created huge fortunes for a few and provided jobs and income for countless others. The railroads revolutionized transportation and commerce and as they poked their iron fingers out in all directions across the countryside the frontier image of the state began to fade.

 1. Bishop Grace
 2. Augustin Ravoux
 3. John Ireland
 4. Augustine Wirth, O.S.B.
 5. Valentine Sommereisen
 6. Magnus Mayr
 7. Francis Toplak
 8. Patrick K. Ryan
 9. Thomas Cahill
10. Maurice E. Murphy
11. Felix Tissot
12. Alois Plut
13. John Schenk
14. William Riordan
15. Theodore Venn
16. James Trobeck
17. John McDermott
18. Gregory Koering
19. Francis Pierz
20. William Lette
21. Retreat Master
22. Thomas Kennedy
23. Patrick Glennon
24. Joseph Herman
25. Eustice Barszez
26. Charles Koeberl
27. Prosper Mauer
28. Francis Sturenberg
29. George Keller
30. Pius Bayer
31. Bernard Baumann
32. Claude Genis
33. John Mullins
34. John Zuzek
35. Anatole Oster
36. Alexander Berghold
37. Thomas O'Gorman
38. D. A. Reville, O.P.
39. Joseph Buh
40. George Schmirer
41. James McGlone
42. Arthur Hurley
43. Ignatius Schaller
44. Louis Caillet
45. Joseph Goiffon
46. James McGolrick
47. Claude Robert
48. H. Povolny
49. Anthony Lechner

Clergy of the Diocese of St. Paul on retreat, 1871

By the early seventies Minneapolis and St. Paul could choose between two rail lines to Chicago, and they were linked as well to the Great Lakes by way of Duluth and to the Red River wheat lands in Dakota. In 1884 the first cargo of Minnesota iron ore was shipped across Lake Superior to markets in the east. This frenzied agricultural and industrial development brought cruelties and social dislocation in its wake. Unrest among urban workers and farmers became increasingly a sign of the times, and organizations sprang up to carry their protests against exploitation to the voters.

Life among the Catholics in the Diocese of St. Paul reflected the exhilirating and painful growth of America in the years after the Civil War. They did their part in converting the wilderness into a prosperous, civilized community, and when calamity struck, like the financial panic of 1873 or the locust plagues between 1873 and 1876, they took their share of the lumps. For Bishop Grace, it was a matter of trying to keep up with an exploding population. Although the Scandanavians who poured into Minnesota were mostly Lutherans, many of the Germans and practically all the Irish, Polish and Bohemian immigrants were Catholics who needed priests, churches and schools. They also needed amalgamation into the broad American cultural pattern, and this, given language barriers and old world suspicions, was not an easy thing to achieve. The desperate personnel shortage was partially alleviated by Grace's policy of inviting into the diocese the religious orders which for the most part still flourish a hundred years later. In 1875 some of the weight was lifted from the bishop's shoulders by the formation of the Vicariate of Northern Minnesota, and four years later a similar ecclesiastical jurisdiction was established for Dakota. Even so, by the time he retired in 1884, the Catholic population of his diocese, which now included only southern Minnesota, totaled 130,000. It should never be forgotten that the solid, unspectacular accomplishments of the Grace episcopate laid the foundations for the dramatic progress the diocese was to make under his successor. After his retirement the old bishop lived quietly, looking every day a little more like a character out of Dickens, until he died, by curious coincidence, on the fortieth anniversary of Cretin's death, February 22, 1897.

Bishop John Ireland

"A man was sent from God whose name was John." Those who knew and loved him best never blushed when they applied the gospel text to John Ireland, Thomas Grace's successor as Bishop of St. Paul. For them no praise of Ireland appeared extravagant. He won the almost unanimous adulation of the people among whom he worked. They admired his absolute fearlessness, his energy, his daring and imaginative approach to the problems of the day. There was a massive virility in everything he did. He fought Demon Rum and religious bigotry and free silver, all with a zest that astonished lesser men. He was never overawed by his episcopal colleagues from the great eastern centers of population for whom there was probably only a hazy geographical distinction between St. Paul and Dodge City. He plunged ahead where others hesitated, not always successfully and not always to the benefit of his personal career, but in matters as disparate as the defense of organized labor and the promotion of the Catholic University of America his willingness to take action (and to take a chance) won the day. Even his failures were on a grandiose scale, like the famous Faribault-Stillwater school plan which, had it been adopted, would have altered profoundly the course of education in the United States. Ireland was a shrewd and practical man, an idealist but no dreamer. When he had become counsellor to popes and presidents, he never lost the common touch. Without breaking his stride, he could move easily from the parlors of the rich to a meeting of exploited workingmen and not for a moment compromise himself or his principles. He could arouse the enthusiasm of a group of intellectuals and he could backslap his way through a GAR encampment. In an age when formal oratory was the indispensable art of the public man (and before the invention of electric public address systems), Ireland spoke easily and effectively to any sized audience from almost any kind of platform. A whole generation of St. Paul priests paid him the highest personal tribute of all: they imitated him —in rhetorical style, in habits of dress, in posture, even in a throaty voice placement. He was, as one of his most ardent admirers put it in a now famous bit of redundancy, "an international figure, both here and abroad."

Archbishop Ireland in later years

It is difficult after the passage of so many years to appreciate the deep affection and almost awesome regard that his contemporaries felt for Archbishop Ireland. He was more than a spiritual father to them, more than a great leader. In the adulation they gave him was expressed something of their own hopes, for he epitomized in his person all that the immigrant Catholics most admired: knowledge, courage and, above all, acceptance. Himself an immigrant, he was as American as the flag he so often extolled in the florid rhetoric fashionable at the turn of the century. He walked with his fine head erect among a rootless and harrassed people and assured them that America was their country, that they should be proud of it and of themselves, that they needed to fear no hostile Ascendancy any more. And so they glowed with pride when Theodore Roosevelt, no less, described Ireland as one of the great citizens in the land, because the triumph was theirs as well as his.

John Ireland was consecrated coadjutor to the Bishop of St. Paul in 1875, when he was thirty-seven years old. He had already served as an army chaplain in the Civil War, as rector of the St. Paul Cathedral and as his bishop's delegate at the First Vatican Council (1869-70). Bishop Grace observed in these as in all young Ireland's undertakings a remarkable combination of energy and sound judgment, and when it appeared that Rome would appoint Ireland to a vicariate in Nebraska, Grace intervened successfully to have him named coadjutor in St. Paul instead. There existed between the two men, so different in age and temperament, a genial and mutually respectful relationship which made it possible for Ireland gradually to assume a greater portion of the more onerous duties of diocesan administration. In 1884, a week after the celebration of his silver jubilee as a bishop, Thomas Grace resigned the affairs of Catholic St. Paul into Ireland's younger, stronger hands.

The First Metropolitan

Four years later Bishop Ireland became Archbishop Ireland when St. Paul was established as a metropolitan see with the Vicariates of Northern Minnesota and Dakota as suffragan churches. A year after that (1889) another re-alignment was effected with the creation of the five new suffragan dioceses of St. Cloud, Duluth, Winona, Sioux Falls and Jamestown. Within this new framework, the Archdiocese of St. Paul included in its territory twenty-six counties running across south central Minnesota from Wisconsin to South Dakota, a form it was to maintain for nearly seventy years.

For about half this period, through those years of the "Gilded Age," John Ireland was probably the most influential ecclesiastic in America. Hardly an area of national life did not feel the impress of his personality and his boundless energy. In a time of prevailing optimism, when the young United States was feeling the first exhiliration of world importance, his vivid nationalism struck a respondent chord among his countrymen of all faiths. He adopted the general position that America, with its youthful dedication to the principles of democratic government and free enterprise, was the best and perhaps the only hope the Church had in an increasingly hostile world. On every possible occasion he pointed out the similarity of ideals he discerned between the American Republic and the Catholic Church. Patriotism, he maintained, ranked as a virtue only after religion itself. As competition in business affairs made for a healthy economy, so competition among religious sects was a challenge and an opportunity for Catholic accomplishment, not just a shameful instance of heretical malice. The conversion of America to Catholicism, he never tired of insisting, would not interfere with the basic rightness of American political and economic institutions. So when he plunged furiously into the advocacy of total abstinence it was with the plea that the drunkard is a bad citizen as well as a bad communicant. When he defended the public school system, the applause welled up on every side.

That quality which is a man's greatest strength, when viewed from a different angle, is sometimes found to be also his most serious weakness. So it was with Ireland. The forthright way he worked to implement his convictions, while it endeared him to many, appeared to others as thoughtless and rash. Thus Archbishop Ireland's open and unabashed support of the Republican Party, though it gave him opportunity to accomplish good things for his Church and country, naturally annoyed the Democrats. His advocacy of the rights of organized labor dismayed the prominent industrialists who were his close friends and upon whom, more than once, he had to call for financial assistance. He championed speedy amalgamation of the immigrants into the American culture, surely an admirable and necessary program; but in so doing he paid too little attention to the sensibilities of foreign-language groups and involved himself as a result in one painful controversy after another. He gained the particular enmity of a bloc of German-speaking bishops who, because they were talented and dedicated men themselves, were able to cause him no end of trouble. His lack of sympathy for the Society of Jesus was returned in kind; he thought the Jesuits calculating, they thought him bumptious. During the uncertain days of the Catholic University of America's infancy, when it seemed that the institution might suffocate in the fog of hesitations and factional intrigues, Ireland's iron will no doubt saved the project, but he paid dearly for his victory by alienating permanently two powerful prelates, the Archbishop of New York and the Bishop of Rochester, who felt that he had ridden roughshod over them. And indeed from their point of view he had. Meanwhile, the wary men in the Vatican, whose task it was to weigh and sift, watched Archbishop Ireland closely. They applauded his selfless service to the Church and made direct use of his talents on more than one occasion. In every crucial test they supported him. But there was little real sympathy between him and them. Perhaps his youthful exuberance did not quite ring true in the ancient city that had outlived all of history's enthusiasts; perhaps, accustomed as they were to dealing with European governments composed of gangs of apostate Catholics intent on the destruction of the Church, they mistrusted his voluble patriotism. More likely, Archbishop Ireland, as has been so often said, was a man far ahead of his time, and the Church of Christ must be governed here and now, with tomorrow's troubles to be awaited in turn. However that may be, they refused to bestow upon him the seal of their ultimate approval. The cardinal's hat was never given him.

Those who disliked Archbishop Ireland often maintained that his preoccupation with affairs on the national and international levels distracted him from his real business, the governing of the Archdiocese of St. Paul. Significantly, this charge was not made by his own people who appeared perfectly satisfied with Ireland's priestly endeavors in their behalf, and the record of his administration seems to confirm their favorable judgment. As a matter of fact, except for extraordinary matters like the part he played in the negotiations prior to the Spanish-American War and, later on, in the politico-ecclesiastical crisis in the Philippines, there is discernible a striking single-mindedness in Ireland's activities. This is not surprising. Minnesota, after all, was a microcosm of America of the "Gilded Age," and the problems which confronted American Catholics in their joint national identity could be seen, more modest in their scale, in Archbishop Ireland's own back yard. Like the rest of the country west of the Alleghenies, Minnesota before the First World War suffered the sharp growing pains of rapid expansion. The state's population soared to more than two million by 1910, and its industrial and agricultural production was valued at that date in the hundreds of millions of dollars. The swift and the strong fared well enough, but there were many for whom the race was a painful, bewildering experience and for whom the nineties were anything but gay.

The Catholics in the Archdiocese of St. Paul possessed an ancient answer to the tumults and uncertainties of their age. The faith and the sacraments would provide not only the supernatural avenues of individual salvation but also a genuinely civilizing force in contemporary society. Under the leadership of Archbishop Ireland, who recognized the goals in his archdiocese as not essentially different from those of the whole Church in America, they turned their hands to a multitude of good works. They built, first of all, at a furious pace, and, if the truth be told, without always the highest aesthetic standards. But their primary anxiety was to keep up as best they could with an exploding population, to make their religion a permanent, concrete part of their environment, and in this they were singularly successful, if one judges simply by the evidence which survives, in usable form, two generations later. Their churches and schools, and the parish life they expressed, came to make a real difference in the lives people led all across the state. There were times when the financial demands involved in this building program al-

James J. Hill
(Etching by Alfonso Muller — Ury, 1898)

most crushed the Catholic people; in the wake of the Panic of 1893, for example, the archbishop avoided disaster only by begging money from his eastern friends. But they did not let bad moments hobble them for long, and in 1907 they laid the cornerstone of the magnificent Cathedral of St. Paul, the culmination of their building activity, the permanent reminder of their work and sacrifice.

Brick and mortar, however, occupied only part of their interest. They took a leading part in the local total abstinence movement, a favorite cause of Archbishop Ireland. They supported a Catholic Colonization Bureau which sponsored immigration of Catholics into the archdiocese and provided the newcomers with a realistic opportunity to create for themselves a dignified, economically independent life. They realized that once this was accomplished the greatest barrier to the immigrants' Americanization would have been removed. (It is worthy of note that Archbishop Ireland, who carried on a running battle with certain German-speaking bishops, had little difficulty winning the love of his own German people.) Education was a further key to the full American life, and so the Catholics of the Archdiocese, again at the cost of stupendous sacrifice,

crowned their grammar and secondary schools with facilities for higher education for their young people, the College of St. Thomas for men and the College of St. Catherine for women. Pondering their zeal for the good of their church and their community, James J. Hill, the railroad magnate and financier, though not himself a Catholic, built and endowed the St. Paul Seminary, which received its first class in 1894. This great and open-hearted man could have done nothing more important for the Catholics of the Archdiocese and, at the same time, he paid them a tribute they richly deserved.

When Archbishop Ireland died, at eighty, in September, 1918, he could look back upon an amazing record of achievement. He was full of honors, too, though the cardinal's hat had eluded him and had been given instead to more careful men. It proved to be a quite fitting moment for the old warrior to die, because the world he had known and had helped to shape was about to give way to something new. Science and technology were poised to change radically the everyday life of ordinary people, while the First World War, which ended a few weeks after his death, would shortly come to be viewed as a significant historical watershed. But one phase of civilization cannot be born without the labor of the one that went before, and in that world that has now vanished John Ireland was a great man. This is not said lightly, nor is it a judgment based upon a computation of building projects, speeches or diplomatic adventures. To be sure, Ireland was a great builder, in an era when the Church needed first of all a roof over her head, and he was a spellbinding orator and a skillful diplomat. One does not despise any of these accomplishments, however, by recognizing that true greatness is a spiritual phenomenon which lasts because neither rust nor robbers can disturb it. Even the most splendid of Ireland's material monuments, the Cathedral of St. Paul, is but a sacrament, an outward sign of the man's unseen vitality, and long after that building has been replaced by another the spirit of John Ireland will continue to pervade the Archdiocese of St. Paul. With almost every facet of life among Catholics who never heard Ireland's voice or experienced the magic of his handshake, from concerns as different as education and race relations and organized charity, he is still the ideal of the Christian Church whose task it is to make the love of Christ mean something in a sluggish and sinful world. A fine sentiment was expressed in the words from the first book of Machabees engraved upon John Ireland's tomb: "He was renowned even to the utmost part of the earth, and he gathered them that were perishing." Nevertheless, the greatest monument to him still stands in the hearts of his people.

The Dowling Decade

The unenviable assignment of succeeding Archbishop Ireland fell to one Austin Dowling, Bishop of Des Moines. Dowling was fifty-one years old when he came to St. Paul in 1919. He had been born in New York City, raised in Newport, Rhode Island, and ordained for the Diocese of Providence where he earned his elevation to the episcopacy in 1913 by outstanding work as teacher, editor and parish priest. Of a slight physical build and delicate health, painfully reserved, the bookish scholar rather than the man of action, Dowling was in most respects the antithesis of

Archbishop Austin Dowling

his predecessor from whose shadow he never managed quite to emerge. He was, however, very much his own man, and he did not hesitate to strike out in his own direction, despite the nostalgic grumblings of his priests and people. He inherited a diocese with a Catholic population of about a quarter of a million, hundreds of churches and schools, and the usual financial and administrative headaches which are the lot of any archbishop. Most of his time, of course, was consumed in the normal episcopal round of teaching, sanctifying and governing. Though everybody made it clear that his worst handicap was that he was not Archbishop Ireland, Dowling did not let this unalterable condition impede his activity. He had a mission of his own.

To make relevant the unchanging gospel in an ever-changing society: this, as ever, was the problem. Archbishop Dowling recognized better than most that the age of the immigrant Catholic had passed, that now, in the twenties of the twentieth century, the process of maturation of the Church in America had to take precedence. For America, after experiencing some of the horrors of the 1914-18 war, had itself suddenly grown up. Women's suffrage, prohibition, the jazz age, the generation that felt itself "lost," each of these things in its own way reflected the coming into majority of a nation which no longer could burn up its energy in an undeveloped western frontier. Secular science was bringing people to new frontiers with electricity and the internal combustion engine, and Catholics could not afford to lag behind. In Archbishop Dowling's judgment this necessarily involved Catholics in a strong movement to improve their own education. What had sufficed before would not suffice now. Only an elite of highly trained Catholic scientists, educators, professional men and priests at the head of a generally well-informed populace could meet the needs of the day. Only if they became increasingly proficient in the sacred sciences could Catholics hope for a successful apostolate; otherwise, the world, distracted by the analysis of its own wonders, would not listen. Dowling never ceased harping on this theme: American Catholicism, he said, must be as adult in its aims and interests as the society it wanted to save.

Few today would dispute this view, but it came as a hard saying to many Catholics forty years ago. This was partly attributable to Archbishop Dowling's extraordinary candor; he spoke bluntly and directly and sometimes with a verbal edge which understandably irritated his listeners. In his own archdiocese the reaction was often one of injured pride, because it was so easy to forget that St. Paul's world-wide fame rested upon the personality and achievements of Archbishop Ireland, not upon some inherent virtue which rendered the region immune from progress. Nevertheless, opposition and his own inadequacies notwithstanding, Dowling threw himself into the gigantic job of upgrading Catholic education. His national influence in this area was quiet and unobtrusive but nonetheless of permanent value. He served for years as episcopal chairman of the National Catholic Welfare Conference's education department at a time when that organization was in its crucial, formative stage. Perhaps his most spectacular accomplishment came with the successful conclusion of the series of litigations known as the Oregon School Case, which, in 1925, was settled in such a way as to guarantee by legal precedent the integrity of the Catholic school system.

Archbishop Dowling staked his hopes at home upon the success of the Archbishop Ireland Educational Fund. The results at best were mixed. The establishment of a minor seminary, the construction of consolidated Catholic high schools to serve the rural areas of the archdiocese, the endowment of a Bureau of Education, the foundation of a teachers' college, the subsidization of existing institutions, particularly the two colleges: all of these goals, Dowling explained in 1919, were worthy of the memory of Archbishop Ireland and his contemporaries who had left behind them a fine educational legacy but also an unfinished educational system. The next year a formal campaign to raise $5,000,000 was begun. It was accompanied by a massive attempt to inform the Catholic public, through the pulpit and the press, of the archdiocese's educational needs. An uncertain economic climate, however, blunted enthusiasm for the project, and, though final figures were never released, it is doubtful that much more than sixty per cent of the proposed total was ever collected. Even so, the Ireland Fund did bring into being a centralized superintendant's office and a Normal School, and, in 1923, the new minor seminary, Nazareth Hall, the Fund's showpiece

ZINTSMASTER

Archbishop John Gregory Murray

and Archbishop Dowling's greatest single contribution to the Church in St. Paul, opened its doors to the first young students for the priesthood. Although the Ireland Fund failed to achieve many of its original objectives, Dowling did not hesitate to maintain its overall success. Despite some disappointments, he always said, the Fund proved what Catholics of quite ordinary means could do if they banded together in the name of a high ideal.

A heart ailment gradually incapacitated Austin Dowling after 1927 and he died at the end of November, 1930. For fourteen months the throne in the cathedral remained vacant, until, on January 27, 1932, John Gregory Murray, since 1925 Bishop of Portland (Maine), was installed as third Archbishop of St. Paul. He was a small, plump man with a shy smile and a surprisingly quick step and a New England twang in his voice which twenty-five years in Minnesota did nothing to lessen. He was born in Waterbury, Connecticut, in 1877, and after completing his theological studies at the University of Louvain he was ordained for the Diocese of Hartford in 1900. His early priestly duties ran through an improbable spectrum: he was chaplain of the Hartford city jail, a professor of Greek, chancellor of the diocese and finally, from 1920 until his promotion to Portland, auxiliary bishop of Hartford and pastor of a large parish.

Thus Archbishop Murray brought with him to his new responsibilities a wide experience. He also brought an indefinable sympathy for people which was to make him one of the most beloved men in the recent history of the Upper

Eucharistic Congress Emblem and Altar

Midwest. The times were hard. First came the grim days of the Great Depression when the desperation of a large segment of the population was attested to by soup kitchens or, more graphically still, by the thousands of able-bodied men who every day milled aimlessly about Minneapolis' Gateway District because no one would hire them. The economic picture had scarcely begun to brighten when the Second World War suddenly thrust itself into every American home, to shatter the lives of millions, some of them irreparably. And in 1945, when the killing stopped, one mushroom-shaped war cloud refused to roll away, and its shadow fell across the paths of civilized men everywhere so that fear and uncertainty tended to become a habit of life. Minnesotans, and Catholics in Minnesota, were not spared the troubles of the time, and that is why, perhaps, they learned to have a special regard for good John Murray.

He was never too busy or to preoccupied to do a kindness. His personal comfort or convenience meant nothing to him. He gave his money away as fast as it came into his hands. The administrative burden of a large and sprawling archdiocese, the perpetual financial difficulties, the endless round of official functions, none of this distorted Archbishop Murray's conviction, rooted in the ancient tradition of the Church, that the bishop's first duty is to let the people experience in his person direct contact with a man of God. This awesome sense of vocation was his, and the sick, the aged and the poor were therefore more aware of his presence than anyone else. Small children, whose instincts about adult intentions are very sharp, always recognized his gentle concern. He was an inveterate trolley car rider, and a kind of mythology has grown up in connection with the friendships he made with people of all ages, professions and persuasions whom he met hanging onto a strap in the long yellow cars of the Twin City Rapid Transit Company. Indeed, his conversational feats, on these and other occasions, are already legendary. There was, in short, about Archbishop Murray a meticulous sense of duty: literally nothing could be too much trouble for him, even in his later years when he was old and very ill, if he considered it part of the obligations of the Archbishop of St. Paul. His death struggle with cancer was long and

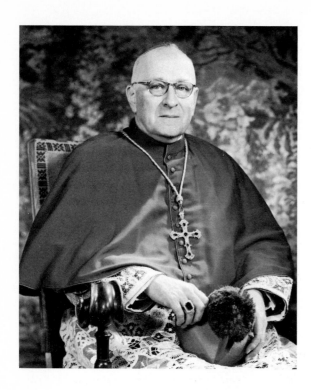

Archbishop William O. Brady

cruel, but not till the very end did he modify his busy routine and not once did anyone hear from him a word of complaint or self-pity. When he died, in October of 1956, people of all faiths and no faith joined to mourn their common loss.

Almost eight years have passed since then. In that short space momentous things have happened in the Archdiocese of St. Paul and in the Catholic world at large. Pope John has come and gone, and so has Archbishop William O. Brady. A great Ecumenical Council has been summoned, the effects of which will be felt as long as the Christian Church prevails on this planet. A martyr to the Council was Archbishop Brady who died in Rome in the autumn of 1961 while working with his usual vigor on one of the conciliar preparatory commissions. Born in Fall River, Massachusetts, in 1899, William Otterwell Brady was ordained a priest of the Archdiocese of St. Paul in 1923, served successively as professor of moral theology and then rector of the St. Paul Seminary and, from 1939 until the summer of 1956, was Bishop of Sioux Falls. He was a man of singular charm and eloquence, and his wide administrative experi-

ence combined with an intimate knowledge of the archdiocese's needs promised great things for the future. But less time was given him than any of his predecessors, and though he initiated many important projects he was not to see the completion of them. A brief five years his episcopate lasted, time enough, however, for his particular genius, in the tradition of Ireland, Dowling and Murray, to have left its bold impression.

Today that noble line is represented by Leo Binz, by the grace of God and the Apostolic See, fifth Archbishop of St. Paul. A priest of the diocese of Rockford, Illinois, Archbishop Binz, before his arrival in St. Paul in 1962, had served as a pastor in his home diocese, as a member of the staff of the Apostolic Delegation in Washington, as Bishop of Winona and as Archbishop of Dubuque. One cannot help but recall that Mathias Loras, another ordinary of the see of Dubuque, came up the Mississippi exactly 125 years ago and that under his direction the faith took its first root in what is now the Archdiocese of St. Paul. It takes a great deal of effort to remember that all this country then was wilderness, with the savage and simple beauty of empty land. Today it teems with people and machines and the whole complicated apparatus of modern life. Archbishop Binz, unlike Bishop Loras, found here a thriving Catholic life. He found that his predecessors had provided a vigorous parochial tradition and an educational system at all levels unsurpassed anywhere. Instead of two or three priests to help him, he can count upon hundreds, headed by two auxiliary bishops, Leonard P. Cowley and Gerald O'Keefe. The handful of Catholics whom Bishop Loras met in 1839 has grown to half a million, some of them men of great eminence, like Ignatius A. O'Shaughnessy, whose benefactions to the Church and society will never be forgotten, and others of lesser fame but of equal zeal and good will. And yet, despite all this growth or rather because of it, the immensity of Archbishop Binz' burden is if anything greater than that of Bishop Loras. For those of us who, with Archbishop Binz, pick up the task where our ancestors left it, it is worth pondering that, though a century and a quarter is not a long time in the history of the Church, it has proved to be long enough to make a good beginning.

36

Provincial House of Sisters of St. Joseph of Carondelet
and College of St. Catherine, St. Paul

Provincial House of Sisters of Our Lady of
Charity of the Good Shepherd, St. Paul

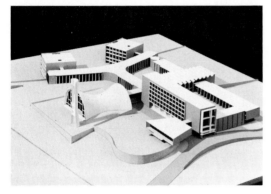

Model of St. Paul's Priory, Maplewood

Oblate Provincial House, St. Paul

RELIGIOUS IN THE ARCHDIOCESE OF ST. PAUL

Benedictine Fathers (St. John's Abbey)
Brothers of the Christian Schools
Conventual Franciscan Fathers
Crosier Fathers
Dominican Fathers
Franciscan Fathers
Jesuit Fathers
Maryknoll Fathers and Brothers
Marist Fathers
Missionaries of the Sacred Heart
Oblate Fathers of Mary Immaculate
(Central Province)
Paulist Fathers
Priests of the Congregation of Holy Cross
Redemptorist Fathers
St. Columbans Foreign Mission Society
Society of the Precious Blood
Third Order Regular of St. Francis

Benedictine Sisters of Pontifical Juris-
diction (St. Paul's Priory)
Benedictine Sisters of Pontifical Juris-
diction (St. Benedict's Priory; St.
Scholastica's Priory; St. Gertrude's
Priory)

Congregation of Our Lady of the Retreat
in the Cenacle
Daughters of the Divine Redeemer
Daughters of the Heart of Mary
Discalced Carmelites
Dominican Sisters of the Sick Poor
Dominican Sisters of the Third Order of
St. Dominic
Felician Sisters
Franciscan Poor Clare Nuns
Franciscan Sisters of the Immaculate
Conception
Little Sisters of the Poor
Missionary Sisters of St. Peter Claver
Oblate Sisters of Providence
Poor Handmaids of Jesus Christ
School Sisters of Notre Dame
School Sisters of St. Francis
Servants of the Holy Heart of Mary
Servants of Mary
Sisters of Charity of Our Lady, Mother
of Mercy
Sisters of Charity of the Blessed Virgin
Mary
Sisters of Christian Charity
Sisters of the Congregation of St. Agnes

Sisters of Divine Providence of Kentucky
Sisters of Mercy
Sisters of the Most Precious Blood
Sisters of Our Lady of Charity of the
Good Shepherd
Sisters of St. Casimir
Sisters of St. Dominic of the Congrega-
tion of St. Rose of Lima
Sisters of St. Francis (Waltbreitbach)
Sisters of St. Francis of the Congrega-
tion of Our Lady of Lourdes
Sisters of St. Francis of the Holy Family
Sisters of St. Joseph (Crookston)
Sisters of St. Joseph of Carondelet
Sisters of the Holy Humility of Mary
Sisters of the Presentation (Aberdeen)
Sisters of the Presentation (Dubuque)
Sisters of the Third Order of St. Francis
of Assisi
Sisters of the Third Order Regular of
St. Francis of the Congregation of Our
Lady of Lourdes
Sisters, Servants of the Immaculate
Heart of Mary
Ursuline Nuns
Visitation Nuns

37

OUR LADY OF VICTORY

This statue is an exact replica of an image of the Mother of God in the Church of Our Lady of Victory in Paris. It was brought to St. Paul from France by Bishop Joseph Cretin in 1851.

One day in 1853 Bishop Cretin led John Ireland and Thomas O'Gorman to the image that had been placed in the second cathedral and said: "My dear boys, let us kneel and say a prayer. I put you under the protection of God and of His blessed Mother; you are the beginning of my diocesan seminary, the first seminarians of St. Paul."

The statue is now located in the vestibule of St. Mary's Chapel at the St. Paul Seminary.

SEVENTY-FIVE YEARS AGO, in 1889, the Sacred Congregation for the Propagation of the Faith issued the apostolic constitutions which established the Diocese of St. Cloud and four other dioceses in the Province of St. Paul. It is not entirely without significance that this development of major importance to the future growth of the Church in the United States coincided with the centenary of the establishment of the American hierarchy in the person of John Carroll, first bishop of Baltimore.

The Diocese of St. Cloud was formed from part of the Vicariate Apostolic of Northern Minnesota with Otto Zardetti as its first bishop. It was assigned sixteen counties in central Minnesota for

The Kensington Runestone

The prologue of the story of the Church of St. Cloud may well be a curious oblong stone with strange markings unearthed in 1898. Much disputed by both historian and archeologist, it is nevertheless worthy of mention. The Kensington Runestone, as it is called, may well be the oldest native historical document on the continent, perhaps in the entire western hemisphere. It was accidently discovered by a Swedish farmer on his land three miles northeast of Kensington in Douglas County.

The stone is approximately 30 by 16 by 6 inches in size, and weighs over two hundred pounds.

DIOCESE OF SAINT CLOUD

by Reverend William P. Furlan

its jurisdiction: Stearns, Sherburne, Benton, Morrison, Mille Lacs, Kanabec, Isanti, Pope, Stevens, Traverse, Grant, Douglas, Wilkin, Otter Tail, Todd and Wadena. It covers an area of 12,251 square miles and its present total population is 330,021 of which 128,898 are Catholics.

Though the Church of St. Cloud—viewing it only as a diocese—goes back in history a mere seventy-five years, its roots probe much deeper. As a minute part of the living organism that is the Church Universal of Jesus Christ, it justifiably shares her glorious history, her venerable traditions and her sublime mission. Even as a transplant from the ancient vine that was seeded and nurtured in the civilization and culture of the old world, the Catholic Church in the United States holds a place and enjoys a prestige that no one can take from her. America was baptized by Catholic zeal and piety.

Inscribed on it in 206 runes, 3 Latin capitals and 12 numerals is a message that has been translated as follows:

> Eight Goths (Swedes) and twenty-two Norwegians upon a journey of discovery from Vinland westward. We had a camp by two skerries (rocks in the water) one day's journey from this stone. We were out fishing one day. When we returned home we found ten men red with blood and dead. A V M (Ave Maria or Ave Virgo Maria) save us from evil.
>
> We have ten men by the sea to look after our vessel, fourteen days' journey from this island. Year 1362.

If this stone is a genuine document and not a cleverly perpetrated fraud, it offers strong evidence that the light of the Catholic faith first shone on what was to be the Diocese of St. Cloud more than five hundred years before the arrival of its first bishop. It antedates the discovery of

America by more than a century. And the simple invocation of the Virgin Mary by these unknown Vikings may well have been the very first prayer addressed to her in this diocese whose mother church is under her patronage.

Explorers and Missionaries

Three centuries of silence separate this alleged expedition of Vikings into Minnesota and the beginning of recorded history. Then was initiated a period of exploration, exploitation and evangelization under the aegis of the French flag. Explorers and traders, soldiers and priests came westward from the forts and settlements of New France over the waterway of the Great Lakes to find entry into this rich and unexplored country. Each came obsessed with a mission. The land of the Sioux and Chippewa became a checkerboard for their activities.

Daniel Greysolon, Sieur du Lhut, was the first French explorer, and probably the first white man, to have traveled with a party within the boundaries of the diocese. In 1679 he reached the western end of Lake Superior and from there veered south into the region around Mille Lacs and beyond. In the following year he rescued the Franciscan, Father Louis Hennepin, and his two companions, Antoine Auguelle and Michel Accault, who had been taken captive by the Sioux. Although Hennepin could not offer mass during his detention at the Sioux encampment on Mille Lacs because he had no wine and his vestments had been stolen by his captors, he did preach to the savages and he baptized at least one dying child whom he christened Antoinette. So a twist of fate deprived him of the honor of offering the first mass in Minnesota and perhaps the first mass in what is now the Diocese of St. Cloud.

After the departure of Hennepin from Mille Lacs in 1680, there is no evidence of another priest being in the region until more than a century and a half later. By that time New France had passed under English rule and France's possessions west of the Mississippi had been ceded to Spain. In 1803 the trans-Mississippi area became a part of the United States. When the new period of missionary activity commenced, which was to have such a deep and

KENSINGTON RUNESTONE

lasting affect on the growth and development of the Church in the Northwest, its source was no longer the Church of Quebec but Dubuque. Its first bishop, Mathias Loras, was quick to see that the prospects for the Church in Minnesota were good after making a pastoral visit into the area in the summer of 1839.

The zealous labors of Father Lucien Galtier and Father Augustin Ravoux who came to Minnesota at Loras' bidding laid the foundation for the Diocese of St. Paul established by Rome on July 19, 1850. Ravoux made extensive missionary journeys throughout the territory and in September, 1842, one of them took him as far west as Brown's Valley on Lake Traverse, now the most westerly parish of the diocese. This was famous "Traverse des Sioux" at the juncture between Lake Traverse and Big Stone Lake where the savages carried their canoes and baggage overland during their periodic migrations. Later when the white man arrived it became equally important to him on his journeys westward. Ravoux's memoirs indicate that he remained here almost a month. He had hoped to find an encampment of several hundred Sioux families but his arrival was ill-timed. All but a few had departed on a massive buffalo hunt to obtain their winter's supply of meat. He rejoined Galtier at Mendota the following month. He returned again in 1845, this time baptizing

41

twelve half-breeds and blessing two marriages.

In July of 1851 the first bishop of St. Paul, Joseph Cretin, appointed Cannon François de Vivaldi as missionary to the Winnebagoes at Long Prairie. The Winnebagoes formerly lived on the Turkey River in Iowa but had been resettled in the Minnesota Territory by government order to act as a buffer tribe between the mutually hostile Chippewa and Sioux. De Vivaldi was the second son of a noble Italian family and a canon of the cathedral of Ventimiglia. He had the misfortune of becoming embroiled in a local revolution and was living in exile in France when he met Cretin who was seeking recruits for his new diocese. He offered his services to the frontier prelate and returned to America with him. For a time his work at Long Prairie was completely satisfactory to Cretin. The young priest was energetic and zealous and obviously devoted to his Indian wards. But his work among them was relatively brief. Throwing caution to the winds and refusing to accept the prudent counsel of his bishop, de Vivaldi amassed debts far beyond his means to pay, incurred the displeasure of the government agents and caused havoc at the mission both among his charges and his co-workers. One act of rebellion led to another until finally he abandoned his mission and left the diocese.

"Father of the Diocese of St. Cloud"

The bitter disappointment and heartache that de Vivaldi caused Bishop Cretin was in some measure compensated by the zealous and able missionary labors of another priest working in his diocese, Father Francis Xavier Pierz (Pirc). This Slovene priest born in the Austrian province of Carniolia (Krain) was no novice in the mission field. Before coming to Minnesota in 1852, he had spent almost twenty years among the Ottawa Indians of Michigan. At the age of sixty-seven years he began in Minnesota what was actually a new career and for more than two decades labored tirelessly among both Indians and whites, establishing missions and founding parishes in what is now the Diocese of St. Cloud. In recognition of his notable contribution to the future growth of the Church in this region, he is revered as the "Father of the

Diocese." The honor is well-deserved for, as Archbishop Ireland declared on the occasion of the twenty-fifth anniversary of the erection of the Diocese of St. Cloud, Father Pierz was "first in time, as first in zeal and in the out-put of energy."

Bishop Cretin gave him complete charge of the Indian missions of the upper Mississippi with the exception of Long Prairie which was still under the supervision of Canon Vivaldi. He established his headquarters at Crow Wing, a flourishing trading post about ten miles south of present-day Brainerd. The military authority at nearby Fort Ripley granted him permission to select any piece of land on the reservation, not exceeding twenty acres, on which to build his church and residence. With Crow Wing as his base of operations, he labored through the entire territory among Indians, half-breeds and whites. He was a familiar figure as he trudged from one Indian village to another and from one white settlement to another. Though primarily remembered for his work in behalf of the red man, his contribution to the colonization of Minnesota must not be overlooked.

Pierz was a realist. He was quick to recognize that the days of the Indians were numbered. He realized that before long government policy would restrict them to reservations. Looking ahead to that eventuality, he decided to use

Father Francis X. Pierz

42

Cemetery cross at old Crow Wing

whatever influence he had to persuade Catholics looking for new oportunities to take over the lands vacated by the Indians. So he began a single-handed campaign by means of letters and advertisements in the leading German newspapers in the East and in Europe urging Catholic immigration to Minnesota.

Pierz Promotes Settlement

"I do wish, however," he wrote in his brochure *Eine kurze Beschreibung des Minnesota-Territoriums,* "that the choicest pieces of land in this delightful Territory would become the property of thrifty Catholics who would make an earthly paradise of this Minnestoa which heaven has so richly blessed, and who would bear out the opinion that Germans prove to be the best farmers and the best Christians in America. I am sure that you will likewise do credit to your faith here in Minnesota; but to prove yourselves good Catholics do not bring with you any freethinkers, red republicans, atheists or agitators."

The colonization of Minnesota began in earnest after the federal government concluded treaties with the Sioux in 1851 that opened vast lands west of the Mississippi to homeseekers. The settlers came from the East—New York, New England, Ohio, Indiana and Illinois—and from the countries of northern Europe. Though Pierz had appealed to his own countrymen, he was disappointed in their response. Some came and these settled for the most part in the low-lying hills north and west of St. Cloud. Here they built St. Stephen, the oldest Slovenian settlement in America. Germans came by the score. By 1855 more than fifty families had settled on the rich, fertile farm lands of the Sauk River valley. Catholic as they were, these pioneers christened the towns they founded with distinctively Catholic names: St. Joseph, St. Augusta, St. Martin, St. Nicholas.

This influx of Catholic settlers created a new problem for the missionary. He was still the sole pastor of both Indians and whites in the immense territory placed under his jurisdiction by Cretin. In his appeals to the Germans to settle in Minnesota, he assured them that provision would be made to care for their spiritual needs. He visited them as often as he could but these visits were few and far between. In the fall of 1853 he called at Belle Prairie, a small settlement of French Canadians near Crow Wing. Here he said mass in the home of Antoine Bisson. On October 17, 1854, he said mass for the first time in the little log church just completed in Sauk Rapids, a stopping place on the stage road between St. Paul and Fort Ripley. The following year he offered mass at St. Joseph where a group of German families had settled. The first mass in Jacob's Prairie was said in the home of Michael Fuchs. Exactly when and where the first mass was offered in St. Cloud is a matter of dispute. Xavier Braun, one of the earliest pioneers in the area, maintained that it was said in the open under a huge tree which stood on the property now occupied by the Children's Home. Another tradition holds that the first mass was said in the home of James Keough, the first Catholic settler in St. Cloud. Pierz is also known to have offered mass in the homes of Joseph Edelbrock and John Schwarz.

However, these infrequent pastoral visitations were not acceptable either to Father Pierz or to the settlers. As a solution, Pierz turned both to his bishop and to the German mission aid societies for priests to help him. He indicated his preference for a religious order to come into the territory and take over the parishes already established as well as those to be organized in the immediate future.

Bishop Cretin obtained a sympathetic hearing for this problem from Abbot Boniface Wimmer at St. Vincent's Abbey in Pennsylvania. The Abbot and his capitulars responded early in 1856 by sending a contingent of monks "to the place where the need is the greatest."

Arrival of Benedictines

The Benedictines, oldest religious order in the western Church and apostles of civilization from time immemorial, arrived on the Minnesota scene on May 2, 1856. This date marks the beginning of an apostolate that not only preserved from extinction the work begun so well by Father Pierz but endowed the Church in the entire Northwest with vigor and strength. The monks laid the foundation upon which in later years the Church of St. Cloud was to rise. They also contributed immeasurably to the growth and development of the Church in several other dioceses of the area. Not even the most optimistic observer of the contemporary scene in 1856 would have ventured to predict the phenomenal success of this monastic foundation in frontier Minnesota in the century ahead. Nor could anyone in that far-off day have dreamed that the influence of St. John's Abbey would grow and develop to reach far beyond the diocese in which it was situated.

The vanguard consisted of five monks: the prior of St. Vincent's, Demetrius di Marogna; two clerics soon to be ordained, Cornelius Wittmann and Bruno Riess; and two lay brothers, Benno Muckenthaler and Patrick Greil. Bishop Cretin's joy was boundless when the weary travelers from Pennsylvania presented themselves at the episcopal residence. They remained in St. Paul as his guests for two weeks. The time was well spent: Father Demetrius assisting in the pastoral ministry; the two clerics preparing themselves for their ordinations which took place May 18; and the two lay brothers doing manual work for the bishop and the Sisters of St. Joseph of Carondelet. Cretin himself escorted them to Sauk Rapids where he installed them in Father Pierz's little log chapel on May 21. The veteran missionary himself had already returned to Crow Wing and his beloved Indians.

St. Cloud, about 1858, first Catholic church in foreground

St. John's Abbey in 1886

Only a note signed by him indicated that he eagerly awaited their arrival and warmly welcomed them as co-workers.

Relieved of his responsibility for the spiritual care of the German Catholics of St. Cloud and Stearns County, Father Pierz intensified his activity in the northern part of the territory. From Crow Wing his missionary journeys radiated in all directions: Mille Lacs, Red Lake, Millerville, Rush Lake, Perham, Elizabeth, etc. Occasionally he returned to the vicinity of St. Cloud, for records show that he offered mass at Duelm, St. Stephen, North Prairie, Rice, Clear Lake and Foley after the Benedictines arrived.

It is remarkable how much was actually accomplished by the old missionary. He conducted a singlehanded apostolate among Indians and whites in an area now embraced by three dioceses. For one brief period in 1858 he experienced the joy of an assistant when Father Lawrence Lautishar, a fellow Slovene, joined him at Crow Wing. Pierz seized the opportunity to open a mission at Red Lake and took him there in early August. Four months later word came to him at Crow Wing that Lautishar was

dead. Inexperienced with the severity of Minnesota winters, he had set out on a sick call and frozen to death in a blizzard on the icebound lake.

During the winter of 1863-64 Pierz received permission to go to Europe to make a personal appeal for priests in the German and Slovene dioceses of Austria. One priest, Father Joseph Buh, and fifteen students offered to return to America with him. They included James Trobec (later a bishop of St. Cloud), Ignatius Tomazin, John Zuzek, Alois Plut, John Tomazevic and Jacob Erlah, all Slovenes; also Katzer (future archbishop of Milwaukee), Stern, Berghold, Pauletic and Spath, who were Germans. Of course, Pierz did not personally reap the benefits of all these men whom he had recruited. Only Buh, Tomazin and Zuzek actually joined him on the Indian missions. The rest were assigned elsewhere. His own missionary days came to an end in the fall of 1871 when he retired to the small community of Rich Prairie (now Pierz) to spend the last years of his active ministry as a simple parish priest. On September 6, 1873, he returned to his native land, advanced in years (eighty-eight) and broken in health. He died January 22, 1880.

Benedictines Lay Foundations of Diocese

Many and serious problems confronted the Benedictines upon their arrival in Minnesota. The area of their labor was vast: six hundred square miles actually under their jurisdiction, and for sick calls two thousand four hundred square miles. Although they had come to care for souls, they also had the duty of reconciling the active life on the frontier with their monastic life. Moreover, as Benedictines, they were the heirs of thirteen centuries of educational tradition which they were determined to transplant to the wilderness.

Their efforts were crowned with remarkable success despite the usual complement of trials and errors and failures. The rudimentary missions that they had taken over from Pierz became under their administration strong and flourishing parishes. To the original six—St. Cloud, St. Augusta, Sauk Rapids, St. Joseph, Jacob's Prairie and Richmond—they added new ones as their numbers increased and the need arose: Luxemburg, New Munich, Avon, Duelm, St. Martin, Spring Hill, Meire Grove, North Prairie, St. Nicholas, Albany and St. Wendel. Still later they organized parishes at Belle River, St. Stephen, Sauk Centre, Melrose and Foley.

The Benedictines laid the foundations of the future Diocese of St. Cloud. It would be safe to hazard the opinion that their contribution to the stability of ecclesiastical life in this diocese can find no parallel in the early beginnings of any other diocese in the United States. Without their labors and sacrifices the future of the Church in this territory would have been uncertain.

No less important than their pastoral ministry to the rapidly increasing number of Catholic settlements, predominantly German in nationality, during these booming years of expansion in Minnesota were the efforts of the monks to implement the Benedictine tradition of education as an essential part of their apostolate. From humble and inauspicious beginnings in St. Cloud arose a great institution of learning, St. John's University, which for more than a hundred years has been molding the minds and hearts of its students according to the principles of Christian thought and action.

The Benedictine nuns joined the monks only a

Bishop Rupert Seidenbusch, O.S.B.

year later. They came in the summer of 1857 from St. Mary's in Elk County, Pennsylvania, but had originally emigrated to the United States from Eichstadt in Germany under the leadership of Mother Benedicta Riepp. Their arrival in St. Cloud seemed premature to many, including such responsible persons as Abbot Wimmer, Father Ravoux, and even Prior Demetrius. But the fears that the foundation was courting disaster and failure proved unwarranted. The little band of four nuns and two candidates, soon to be augmented by Mother Benedicta Riepp and a companion, was equal to the task. Although the beginnings were difficult and the nuns suffered much from poverty, they built a firm foundation. Even before they were able to move into a house they could call their own, they opened a school in the boardinghouse where they lodged. The people took them to their hearts as the following excerpt from a letter of Father Demetrius attests: ". . .The Sisters are honored, respected and loved; they edify the people by their modest behavior. The Americans are amazed and wonder how it is possible to live such a mortified life. They admire the Sisters and cannot help respecting them." In 1863 the community moved to St. Joseph and today it holds the distinction of being the largest Benedictine convent in the world. So successful was the courageous undertaking of Mother Benedicta a century ago that six daughter foundations trace their origin to it and, like nearby St. John's, St. Benedict's Convent exerts an influence that goes far beyond the diocese.

Within the confines of the diocese was also born another religious family whose activities are world-wide in scope, the Missionary Franciscan Sisters of the Immaculate Conception. It was founded at Belle Prairie in 1873 by Mother Mary Ignatius Hayes, a remarkable woman who was converted from Anglicanism. A convent was built and completed in 1875, and the first novices made their profession of vows in 1878. In 1888 the convent was destroyed by fire and was not rebuilt immediately. The sisters stationed at Belle Prairie working among French-Canadian settlers were directed by Mother Hayes to go to the community's foundation in Georgia.

This tragic setback of the struggling congregation proved to be a blessing in disguise for the diocese inasmuch as it led to the birth of a new congregation of religious women. When the Belle Prairie nuns received orders to proceed to Georgia, some of them under the leadership of Mother Mary Beauchamp expressed the desire to remain in Minnesota. The idea appealed to Bishop Zardetti and they made a new foundation at Little Falls. They were canonically erected as a diocesan congregation March 1, 1891, to be known as the Franciscan Sisters of the Immaculate Conception.

Meanwhile, the community founded at Belle Prairie continued to grow. Foundations were established in Europe, Canada, Australia and Africa, as well as elsewhere in the United States. Not until 1911 did the Missionary Franciscan Sisters of the Immaculate Conception return to "the cradle of the institute" at Belle Prairie when the foundation was reestablished by permission of Bishop Trobec.

By 1875 ecclesiastical life in the territory that had been under the care of the Benedictines almost exclusively since 1856 had developed to such an extent that the time seemed opportune for dividing the Diocese of St. Paul and establishing a new see in northern Minnesota. As early as 1871 Bishop Grace had advocated the division of his diocese for the good of souls.

Bishop Seidenbusch and diocesan priests

47

"Grasshopper chapel" near Cold Spring

Vicariate of Northern Minnesota

On February 12, 1875, the Holy See erected the Vicariate Apostolic of Northern Minnesota and named Abbot Rupert Seidenbusch, first abbot of St. John's, as titular bishop of Halia and vicar apostolic of the new territory with residence in St. Cloud. The new vicariate included all the area formerly a part of the Diocese of St. Paul north of the southern boundary of Chisago, Isanti, Sherburne, Stearns, Pope, Stevens and Traverse counties in Minnesota, and of Richland, Ransom, La Moure, Logan and Burleigh counties in North Dakota. It extended from the Wisconsin border on the east to the Missouri and White Earth rivers on the west, and from the already mentioned southern boundary to Canada on the north. While it was not a full-fledged diocese, its canonical effects were the same. The choice of a Benedictine as the first ordinary was anticipated and met with general approval. There was no question that the monks richly deserved the recognition that the appointment brought them.

Rupert Seidenbusch was born in Bavaria, in Munich, on October 13, 1830, and came to America in 1850 to join the Benedictine community at Latrobe, Pennsylvania. He was ordained in 1853, and in 1866 was elected the first abbot of St. John's Abbey at Collegeville. On May 30, 1875, he was consecrated the Vicar Apostolic of Northern Minnesota in St. Mary's Church, St. Cloud. In the absence of Bishop Grace from his see, Bishop Michael Heiss of La Crosse was the consecrator, assisted by Bishops Joseph Dwenger, C.PP.S., of Fort Wayne and Louis Fink, O. S. B., of Kansas. Bishop John Hennessy of Dubuque, an old friend of the new bishop, delivered the sermon.

After his consecration, Bishop Seidenbusch turned his attention to the needs and problems of the vicariate. He made St. Mary's Church his episcopal church and also lived in the rectory until the following year when the Joseph Broker house near the corner of Sixth Avenue and Third Street North became his residence. He requested the Benedictines to turn over to him this church for a cathedral but was refused by Abbot Alexius Edelbrock, who had succeeded him as abbot, and by the monks. He then built Holy Angels Church, which was the procathedral until 1937 when the Holy See designated St. Mary's Church as the cathedral.

The first order of business for the new bishop was a pastoral visitation of the parishes and missions of his vast jurisdiction. Within this territory there were 29 priests—8 diocesan and 21 religious; 42 churches and 40 missions; 1 religious order of men, the Benedictines; 3 religious orders of women, Benedictines at St. Joseph, Franciscans at Belle Prairie, and Sisters of Charity at Fort Totten, Dakota Territory. The Catholic population was approximately 18,500.

In the course of Bishop Seidenbusch's first tour, he conferred Confirmation in places where the sacrament had never been administered. Among the places he visited were Duluth, Brainerd, White Earth, Moorhead and Pembina, as well as Fort Totten, Jamestown and Wahpeton in the Dakota Territory. In Fargo he selected the site for a new church, and at St. Augusta he blessed a new church.

On October 24 of that same year (1875) he conferred the abbatial blessing on his successor, Abbot Edelbrock, at St. Mary's Church, St. Cloud.

After long and serious discussions with the abbot, he persuaded the Benedictines to assume the care of the Indian mission at White Earth. Father Tomazin was in charge of the mission but Seidenbusch felt it was necessary to remove him because of his difficulties with the Indian agent and his own erratic behavior. Father Aloysius Hermanutz, O.S.B., arrived at the White Earth mission on November 4, 1878. Ten years later, on November 11, 1888, the Benedictines established the Red Lake mission.

A serious problem to Bishop Seidenbusch through all the years of his regime was the lack of diocesan priests to assist him in the fast-growing vicariate. He made every effort to find them in Europe as well as in America. That his efforts met with at least partial success is evident in the fact that during his fourteen years as vicar apostolic he increased the number of his diocesan clergy from eight to thirty-seven. They worked principally outside Stearns County which was almost exclusively Benedictine territory. As priests came to the diocese, new parishes were established at Red Lake Falls, Crookston, Rush City, Fergus Falls, Browerville, Wadena, Brainerd, Long Prairie, Little Falls and elsewhere. In the Dakota Territory there were resident priests only at Pembina, Bismarck and Grand Forks. In Stearns County the Benedictines founded new parishes at Cold Spring, Holdingford, Farming and Freeport. They also helped Bishop Seidenbusch by sending priests to Millerville, Alexandria and Osakis in Douglas County and to Moorhead in the west.

The grave problems and the strenuous duties connected with the work of his vicariate exacted their toll from Bishop Seidenbusch. In the spring of 1885 the fifty-five-year-old prelate suffered a serious heart attack from which he was not expected to recover. Even after the mortal danger had passed, he never resumed the duties of his office but had to agree to a slow convalescence. Abbot Edelbrock was appointed administrator of the vicariate during this period. Seidenbusch resided at St. Cloud only for a brief time in 1886-1887, and afterwards left again for treatment in Europe. He resigned as vicar apostolic on October 30, 1888. Archbishop John Ireland was appointed administrator of the vacant vicariate by the Holy See. Bishop Seidenbusch spent the remaining years of his life in retirement, alternating between residence at St. John's Abbey in the summers and rest homes in the south in the winters. He died at Richmond, Virginia, on June 3, 1895.

The resignation of Bishop Seidenbusch became the occasion for the reorganization of the Church in Minnesota and Dakota Territory. This move had been anticipated for some time but the rumor was that it would be delayed until the ailing vicar apostolic resigned. When St. Paul was raised to Metropolitan rank on May 4, 1888, it seemed almost certain that new dioceses would also be created as suffragan sees. Temporarily the Vicariates Apostolic of Dakota and Northern Minnesota fulfilled this function. The long-awaited event came in the fall of 1889, when five new dioceses were erected. The Diocese of St. Cloud was created on September 22. On October 3, Father Otto Zardetti, vicar-general of the Vicariate Apostolic of Dakota, was named the first bishop of St. Cloud.

Bishop Otto Zardetti

Otto Zardetti was a native of Rorshach, Switzerland, where he was born January 24, 1847. As a deacon he accompanied his bishop to Rome where he witnessed the opening of the First Vatican Council and attended two of its sessions. It was during this Roman sojourn that he met Father Martin Marty, O.S.B., who was to have such a profound influence on his life in the years to come. He was ordained August 21, 1870. After extensive travels in Europe and America, he accepted the offer of Archbishop Heiss of Milwaukee to teach dogmatic theology at the pro-

Bishop Otto Zardetti

vincial seminary. In 1886 Bishop Marty, the Benedictine whom Zardetti had met in Rome and who was now the Vicar Apostolic of Dakota, invited him to be his theologian at the First Provincial Council of Milwaukee. Soon after this council Marty asked him to be his vicar-general. Zardetti was in Rome when he received the news of his appointment to the see of St. Cloud. He was consecrated at the Abbey of Einsiedeln in Switzerland on October 20, 1889, by Archbishop William Gross of Oregon City. He arrived in St. Cloud on November 21 where he received an enthusiastic welcome from both civil officials and his Catholic flock. On Sunday, November 24, he was formally installed as the first bishop of St. Cloud by Archbishop Ireland.

The problems that faced Zardetti as he began the administration of his diocese were the problems shared in common by most of the bishops in the early days of the Church in this country: lack of financial means, fewness of priests and extensive territories. In addition St. Cloud had its own peculiar problem. Since the Benedictines had done the pioneer work of the Church in this area when there were few diocesan priests to be had, they were in charge of most of the flourishing parishes. This was an irritant to Bishop Zardetti from the inception of his regime and was solved only in part when he and Abbot Bernard Locnikar reached an agreement in 1892. Zardetti was anxious to have some of the parishes then under Benedictine administration handed over to the diocesan clergy even though he did not have the priests to staff them. He took a long-range view of the situation and had in mind the future welfare of the diocese. The monks, on the other hand, were reluctant to part with these parishes because they felt that they had a title to them in view of their past labors.

Bishop Zardetti stated his case forcefully in the report that he left for his succesor: "On coming here I found the diocese existing by name and *de jure,* but otherwise yet the confusion of a vicariate existed. The diocese was nearly in the power of the Benedictines. There were but 15 secular priests in the poorest missions.... From the beginning I strove to build up a diocesan clergy, to educate young men and to provide the secular clergy with missions so that I could hope to attract a new generation of priests and destroy the prevalent impression

that the St. Cloud diocese was but a dominance *(sic)* of the Benedictines. . . ."

Through negotiation with Abbot Locnikar, he obtained the following missions—Holdingford, St. Anna, St. Stephen, Belle River, Perham, St. Nicholas, Lake Henry, Spring Hill, Kraintown, Kimball Prairie and Alexandria—but, as he observed, they were "poor, most of them only stations," so that his priests "justly complained" when assigned to them. He tried to get at least six of the flourishing Benedictine parishes in Stearns County but the abbot refused to accede to his request. Instead Abbot Bernard appealed to Rome and obtained from Propaganda a rescript granting to the Benedictines in perpetuity the following parishes, all of them in Stearns County and in the immediate vicinity of the abbey: Richmond, Cold Spring, St. Martin, Farming, Meire Grove, New Munich, Freeport, Albany, St. Joseph and St. Mary's Church in St. Cloud. By the same rescript the Benedictines turned over to Zardetti the following: Luxemburg, Melrose, Millerville, St. Augusta, Rich Prairie (Pierz) and Rush Lake. The bishop seemed satisfied with the arrangement. He considered the abbot "fair and just" and observed that "the condition of the diocese is now satisfactorily and permanently settled. The secular clergy can no more complain. They have now a good number of good missions. Small and new ones will grow and multiply. All counties except Stearns are now free from the religious. . ."

Bishop Zardetti wielded his episcopal authority with a strong hand. It was fortunate for the diocese that its first incumbent should have established the authority of the bishop so firmly. He acted decisively in all his undertakings and both clergy and laity soon discovered that they had a strong man at the helm.

Only a year after he came to St. Cloud, he inaugurated a monthly clergy bulletin. "The Diocese of St. Cloud," as it was called, was to contain, as the bishop announced in the first issue, January, 1891, "all official documents, circulars, ordinances, which from this date will exclusively be promulgated in this paper." He himself seems to have done most of the writing for this bulletin, and it provides an interesting and informative account of the early years of the diocese.

Zardetti was an eloquent preacher and a prolific writer. From the beginning of his episcopate he made it a practice to preach once a month at Sunday mass in his procathedral. He also preached frequently at Sunday vespers at which he pontificated. His sermons were delivered sometimes in English and sometimes in German and frequently in both languages at the same service. It is obvious that his ability as a preacher was recognized far and wide from the many invitations he received to preach at religious celebrations throughout the country. His penchant for writing is evident from the long list of historical and theological monographs he published. A list of these appeared in the March, 1892, number of his bulletin and this list included works written the year after his ordination twenty-two years before. Undoubtedly his finest literary work was the pastoral letter he addressed to his flock in Minnesota from Einsiedeln Abbey on the day of his consecration. It was a lengthy and learned treatise on the office and dignity of a bishop that perhaps has seldom been equalled by another bishop writing to his priests and people with the same purpose in mind.

Shortly after his arrival in St. Cloud he took it upon himself to clarify the obscure background of the patron saint of his see city. From the days of the vicariate Roman documents, presuming that St. Claude (Claudius) was the patron of the city, used that name in the official correspondence. However, Bishop Zardetti, with his meticulous passion for detail, was not satisfied that this was historically accurate. He consulted with John L. Wilson, "Father of the City of St. Cloud," and ascertained that the city took its name from the suburban city of St. Cloud near Paris. He presented this data to the Holy See with the petition that St. Cloud (Clodoaldus), a monk who founded a monastery in the French city that now bears his name, be declared the patron of the see city and the diocese. As a result, the Holy See decreed that St. Cloud was the patron saint of the diocese, that his cult should be canonically established there and that September 7 is the patronal feast day.

Bishop Zardetti's administration as the first ordinary of the see of St. Cloud came to an end early in 1894. On January 15 he received a cablegram from his friend, Cardinal Ledochowski, informing him that he had been promoted to the see of Bucharest in Roumania as arch-

bishop. This personal communication was followed by the official appointment dated March 5. He was also directed to request Archbishop Ireland to act as temporary administrator of the diocese until the Holy See appointed his successor. He left St. Cloud shortly after Pentecost. In his farewell sermon, he said in part: "Others have laid the foundations. Others will build up and finish the work. I only laid the water table. I feel some comfort in the idea that I will be recorded as St. Cloud's first bishop and remain a citizen of their (sic) country." He was installed at Bucharest on December 8, 1894, but his reign there was short-lived. By June of 1895 he had resigned and had retired to Rome where he died May 10, 1902.

Bishop Zardetti built firm foundations for the Church of St. Cloud. Though he was not always understood by those around him and at times seemed to act in an arbitrary fashion, there is no doubt that he had the best interests of the diocese at heart. His episcopate was a fruitful one. At his departure the diocese had about 40 diocesan priests, 52 parishes with a resident pastor, 39 parochial and district schools with 4,680 pupils, and a Catholic population of approximately 40,000. He established 6 new parishes and was instrumental in organizing the Franciscan Sisters of the Immaculate Conception as a diocesan congregation at Little Falls (1891). The estimation of him expressed by Archbishop Ireland at his installation proved to be prophetic, "I feel that in presenting to you your new Bishop I present to you a Bishop who would do justice to any see in America."

Bishop Martin Marty, O.S.B.

The Benedictine Martin Marty, who succeeded Zardetti as the second bishop of St. Cloud, is a study in contrast to his predecessor. He did not possess Zardetti's aristocratic demeanor nor was he interested in outward display and pomp. At heart he always remained a missionary even after he was elevated to the episcopal dignity. He was a man of action with the soul of a contemplative.

He was born in Schwyz, Switzerland, on January 12, 1834. He entered the famed Einsiedeln Abbey where he was ordained to the priest-

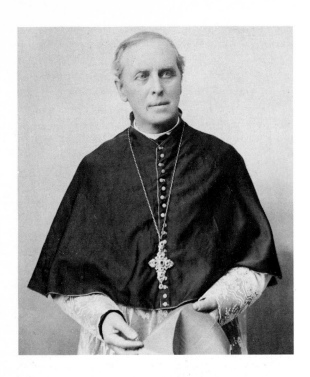

Bishop Martin Marty, O.S.B.

hood on September 14, 1856. When Einsiedeln received urgent requests from America for priests to minister to the many Catholic immigrants of German and French origin settling in Indiana, Father Marty was among the first to volunteer. He came to St. Meinrad in 1860 and was a prime mover in the development of this Swiss Benedictine foundation in America. In 1865 he was appointed the prior, and in 1870 Pope Pius IX named him its first abbot.

He welcomed the opportunity extended to his monks to staff a mission among the Sioux in the Territory of Dakota, and decided to answer the call personally. Leaving the abbey in charge of his prior, he and a companion set out for the mission in 1876, arriving at Fort Yates on July 31 just in time to save the Indian agent from death at the hands of the warring Sioux. Marty commenced his work among them during troublesome times. From the start he exerted a remarkable influence upon them. Despite their disillusionment with the empty promises of the federal agents and the frequent brutality of the military, Indians continued to respect the Catholic priest. It is interesting to note that Marty was one of the few white men who was trusted by Sitting Bull and though he was unable to

persuade the old warrior chief to return to the reservation and give up the fight against the military, he was respectfully received by him.

In 1879 the Dakota Territory was cut off from the Vicariate Apostolic of Northern Minnesota and established as the Vicariate Apostolic of Dakota. Abbot Marty was appointed the vicar apostolic and consecrated titular bishop of Tiberias on February 1, 1880. Bishop Marty immediately launched an intensive program to build up the Church in this vast territory. The conversion of the Sioux and their adaptation to a settled mode of life was his ultimate goal. He recruited priests and brought in nuns to staff the missions and schools he opened for the benefit of the Indians throughout his jurisdiction. He organized societies for the red man to give him an opportunity to use his native talent for oratory and these became study clubs in which the savages learned the fundamentals of the Catholic faith from their own leaders. He inaugurated Catholic congresses for the Indians to keep them from participating in the pagan gatherings convened by medicine men. These congresses were a happy blend of traditional Sioux rites and Catholic ceremonial. The climax was always a Pontifical High Mass celebrated by Bishop Marty. His deep love and fatherly concern for his Indian children were evident in his practice of allowing each one of them to shake his hand during this annual powwow. Never once did he give any intimation of the personal sacrifice it involved. Exhausted from his rough ride over the prairies and suffering from a chronic headache, he stood in line for hours to accord this courtesy to them. They in turn sensed his devotion to them and honored him by naming him "Lean Chief."

When the Diocese of Sioux Falls was established in 1889, Bishop Marty was appointed its first bishop. Six years later he was moved to the see of St. Cloud and was installed by Archbishop Ireland on March 12, 1895. He came to the diocese prematurely aged and in failing health. By special permission of the Holy See, he retained the Sioux Indians under his jurisdiction. During the summer of 1896, he returned to the scene of his former labors to preside over the Indian congress at Holy Rosary Mission. He was only a shadow of his former self, weak and emaciated. A priest had to support him as he celebrated mass for the

Indians and preached to them for the last time. It was his leave-taking and the Sioux sensed this as he praised them for their piety, commended them for their progress and urged them to remain faithful to their Chief of Chiefs, Jesus Christ. As he prepared to leave, they crowded around him and saluted him with the phrase "Sinasapa Itanca Tamahetscha" (Black Robe Lean Chief).

Bishop Marty's tenure in St. Cloud was of short duration. He administrated the affairs of the diocese less than two years. He established eight new parishes—St. Peter's at Browerville, Assumption at Eden Valley, Mora, Browns Valley, St. Adalbert's at Little Falls, Mayhew Lake, Flensburg and Moran. He laid the cornerstones for new churches in Wadena, Foley and Princeton.

He planned for the construction of an addition to the cathedral parish school and laid the cornerstone for the new parochial school in Little Falls. With difficulty he set out on his confirmation tour in the summer of 1896. On September 15, he administered this sacrament for the last time at St. Wendelin's Church, Luxemburg, where he was fatally stricken. He died September 19, 1896.

Although Bishop Marty's episcopate in St. Cloud was so brief that the historian might be tempted to pass over it as of no significance, this would be a mistake. He came to St. Cloud with a reputation for quiet and efficient work. The diocese profited immeasurably from his tenure. He exemplified for his priests and people the beautiful image of the Good Shepherd who has

Sunday dinner

Harvesting time in early Stearns County

Clearing the land

the salvation of souls as his primary concern. He shunned public acclaim and vain display. While he demanded much of his clergy, he did not spare himself and faithfully discharged his duties as a bishop to the very end. Archbishop Ireland, who gave the eulogy at his funeral, summed up his life as a total dedication to the demands of his conscience. "He loved his God supremely," Ireland said. "He sought by all his acts to do God's will. When his conscience told him to stop, all of the powers of earth would not move him. His whole purpose in life was to hearken to his conscience and to obey, for he knew that the voice of conscience was the voice of God, and in this absolute obedience to conscience consists his lifework."

Bishop James Trobec

On July 28, 1897, James Trobec, then pastor of St. Agnes' Church in St. Paul, was notified of his appointment as the third bishop of St. Cloud. He was consecrated September 21, and installed in his see seven days later. Bishop Trobec was no stranger to the diocese over which he was to rule for seventeen years. He was intimately associated with the "Father of the Diocese" with whom he had thrown in his lot in 1864 when Father Pierz visited the seminary of Ljubljana to find recruits for his missions in America. He was born in Log, Carniola, and was enrolled in the diocesan seminary when he volunteered to join his renowned countryman in Minnesota. He completed his studies at St. Vincent's Abbey, Pennsylvania, and was ordained by Bishop Thomas Grace on September 4, 1865. Prior to his appointment to St. Cloud, he achieved notable success in his priestly work at Faribault, Wabasha and St. Paul.

His years as spiritual leader of the Diocese of St. Cloud were fruitful in every respect. Catholic life reached maturity under his wise and patient guidance. The diocese experienced its greatest growth during this period. Thirty-three new churches were built; twelve churches were remodeled or enlarged; sixteen new schools were erected and one rebuilt. He established eighteen new parishes, and the number of parishes with resident priests increased from fifty-five to ninety-four. Hospitals were erected at Breckenridge

Bishop James Trobec

and Perham, bringing the number to four in the diocese. Many parishes built new rectories and convents. Between 1897 and 1914, the Catholic population showed an astounding growth of more than sixty per cent.

Especially worthy of note is the cordial relationship he established between the diocese and the religious communities working in it. His intimate friendship with Abbot Peter Engel, whose administration of the Benedictine community at Collegeville almost coincided with the years Trobec headed the diocese and the period of his retirement, gave him a rare insight into the nature of the life of religious and a balanced appreciation of their status and function in diocesan life.

Three new communities established themselves in the diocese during his episcopate. The Crosier Fathers, formally known as Canons Regular of the Order of the Holy Cross, laid the foundation for their successful American venture at Butler, a hamlet in the northern reaches of the diocese in the spring of 1910. Two priests, Father William Van Dinter and Father Henry Yzermans, and a lay brother, Henry Van der Aa, were joined in this enterprise by sixty-eight Dutch immigrants. Bishop Trobec received them kindly and granted the priests full faculties of the diocese. In a report to the Master General, they described Trobec as "kindness personified" and remarked on his gracious gesture of stuffing some good cigars into Van Dinter's suitcase, "truly the mark of a good man," as they observed. Trobec insisted that they observe canonical procedure in making their foundation by deeding the property on which the church was to stand to the diocese through the parish corporation. Otherwise they were given complete leeway and had permission to locate anywhere in Otter Tail or Mille Lacs counties. That same fall they decided to accept a parish at Onamia while also keeping one at Butler. It was at Onamia that they built their monastery and opened a seminary for the training of both diocesan and religious priests.

In 1911 the Missionary Franciscan Sisters of the Immaculate Conception, originally founded at Belle Prairie in 1873, returned to the scene of their congregation's birth. By a fortunate turn of events, they were able to secure the original property in Belle Prairie and the second foundation was made by Mother Mary Columba Doucette, a native of Belle Prairie who was then superior general of the institute. While the convent and school were under construction, the nuns lived in the basement and sacristy of the Holy Family Church. Bishop Trobec blessed their new building on December 8, 1911.

In 1913, another Franciscan community, the Sisters of St. Francis of the Immaculate Heart of Mary, came to the diocese to supervise the domestic department of St. John's University. They remained at this post until only recently when an acute need for more nuns to staff the congregation's missions elsewhere made it necessary to give up this work.

Bishop Trobec strongly advocated Catholic education in the diocese and made a notable contribution in this field. During his administration sixteen new schools were opened and secondary education on a diocesan level took a step forward when the Cathedral High School in St. Cloud was established in 1902. Before his resignation, he had the pleasure of laying the cornerstone for a new and more commodious Catholic high school in the see city on June 10, 1914. The college of St. Benedict, a liberal arts school for women, opened its doors in 1913. Undoubtedly the bishop had played a decisive role in its inauguration, if only by his wise counsel and warm encouragement.

Bishop Trobec's insistence on Catholic education for the youth of the diocese stemmed from his conviction that it was their sole guarantee in a pluralistic society for growing up and growing strong in the faith of their fathers. He gave expression to his policy in this matter when he wrote:

Arrival of immigrants

The principles which the parish school maintains are the same as those which are obtained in Christian schools of every age and under all conditions. Those principles spring from the relationship of man to God, principles as unchangeable as Christianity itself. Moral training or the education of the will is one of the fundamental aims of the Christian school, for it is generally admitted that moral character is even more important than mere knowledge in the struggle of life. All educators agree on this point as also in the fact that a child to be thoroughly educated, must be taught religion. In public schools, which are frequented by pupils of different creeds, religion cannot be taught, it is simply impossible, hence the necessity of private schools for those who wish to receive a Christian education.

On June 7, 1914, Bishop Trobec announced that, because of his advancing age and failing health, his resignation as the Bishop of St. Cloud had been accepted by the Holy See. He was asked to continue as administrator until his successor was named. At the farewell reception tendered him by his flock, he gratefully accepted an automobile given him by his priests and a modest purse from the laity. The remark he made upon accepting these gifts was characteristic of the man, his simple manner of life and his detachment from material goods: "It has never been my ambition to be the owner of an automobile but now I must yield to the wishes of my priests and accept it."

Bishop Trobec retired to the peace and solitude of St. Stephen-in-the-Woods to spend his last days. Though he occasionally assisted in St. Cloud and other dioceses by administering Confirmation and Holy Orders at the request of the respective ordinaries, he rarely left his retreat in the hills. He took special delight in performing the simple duties of a parish priest, especially in hearing confessions and preaching. He died suddenly while working at his desk on December 14, 1921. In deference to a wish he often expressed, he was laid to rest in the parish cemetery.

Bishop Joseph F. Busch

The formative years of the Diocese of St. Cloud came to a close with the resignation of Bishop Trobec. Bishop Joseph F. Busch, then ordinary of the Diocese of Lead in South Dakota, was named to succeed him on January 19, 1915, and

installed by Archbishop Ireland on the feast of St. Joseph. During the thirty-eight years that he occupied the See of St. Cloud, he expedited the transition of the diocese from pioneer days to full maturity. He came well qualified to perform this task.

Bishop Busch had been elevated to the episcopal dignity on May 19, 1910, at the historic ceremony in St. Paul at which six successors of the Apostles were consecrated to fill posts in the same ecclesiastical province. At Lead he revealed himself to be a man of courage and conviction.

Bishop Joseph Busch

He became a fearless champion of the miners by assuming the leadership in their struggle to obtain just and equitable living and working conditions. In this he was attempting to implement the social teachings of Pope Leo XIII.

When he came to St. Cloud, he recognized that the diocese had been built on firm foundations by his predecessors and was well organized. But he was not content to rest on their achievements. He realized his own obligations as a bishop to advance the kingdom of God. It was soon apparent to his clergy and people that their new spiritual shepherd was a man of vision and action. The diocese began to throb with activity, spiritual as well as physical.

New parishes were established at Waite Park, Sauk Rapids, Little Falls (Our Lady of Lourdes), St. Cloud (St. Augustine and St. Anthony), Dent, Greenwald and Brennyville. Others, like Tintah,

Millerville and Dumont, opened parochial schools. Still others expanded or replaced existing facilities to keep pace with growth. In 1922 the Crosier Fathers opened a preparatory seminary at Onamia that has served the diocese well. The following year, 1923, the contemplative Order of Poor Clares established a cloistered monastery in Sauk Rapids to become the "power house of prayer" for the diocese. A strictly cloistered community following a rigid rule of life, it has met with notable success. In 1953 a daughter foundation was begun in Richfield. In 1937 St. Mary's Church in St. Cloud was designated by the Holy See as the cathedral church replacing Holy Angels Procathedral which had been destroyed by fire in 1933. For eighty-five years the parish had been under the care of the Benedictines and its transfer into diocesan hands was the culmination of prolonged and spirited negotiations between Bishop Busch and Abbot Alcuin Deutsch of St. John's Abbey. A diocesan newspaper, *The St. Cloud Register*, which was printed at Denver as a part of the Register System of Newspapers, was inaugurated in 1938. In the twenty-five years of its existence it has grown in circulation and in influence and at the present time goes into every home and institution of the diocese. It is now affiliated with the *Our Sunday Visitor* chain of diocesan papers.

Indicative of Bishop Busch's social consciousness were several notable undertakings. In 1917 the St. Cloud Institute was erected in the see city as a Catholic cultural and social center. In 1923

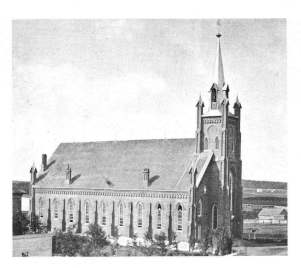

Second St. Mary's Church, St. Cloud

he built the St. Cloud Orphanage (now known as the Children's Home) which pioneered the cottage-plan of housing homeless children. The present St. Cloud Hospital, generally acclaimed as one of the finest medical centers in the Northwest, was begun in 1925 and completed in 1928. A new Cathedral High School to accommodate the steadily growing enrollment opened its doors in 1938. He also used his personal inheritance to build a new episcopal residence that served as his home until his death and has since been converted to use as the Chancery.

Less tangible but equally real were his contributions in the spiritual realm. He directed the establishment of the Confraternity of Christian Doctrine in every parish as an effective means for developing an educated Catholic laity. He was equally insistent that the Confraternity of the Blessed Sacrament and the Confraternity of the Holy Ghost become vital forces in the parishes for the promotion of divine worship and social action. He organized the Society for the Propagation of the Faith and its Auxiliary on a diocesan basis. He founded the Ladies Guild as his personal instrument for dispensing charity to the poor and needy. He encouraged the laity to join the Third Order of St. Francis, of which he himself was a member, as a means for personal sanctity.

As one lists the many and diversified interests of Bishop Busch, one cannot help but express awe and admiration for the balanced program he proposed to his flock. It was an effective program, for Catholic life in the diocese flowered during his episcopate. Proud as they were of their material accomplishments in parishes and on a diocesan scale, priests and people were even more gratified by their growing awareness of the implications of the doctrine of the mystical body of Christ. This was the theme that Bishop Busch expounded constantly in his sermons, his pastoral letters and his conferences to priests and religious. He developed this theme even more explicitly in a slender volume he published in 1930 entitled *The Art of Living with God*. This book set forth a profound subject in simple terms.

The year 1939 witnessed the joyful celebration of two important events of historic significance: the fiftieth anniversary of the establishment of the diocese and the fiftieth anniversary of the ordination of Bishop Busch. This double Golden

Jubilee was appropriately commemorated by the priests, religious and laity of the diocese. From Rome came an autograph letter of the Sovereign Pontiff, Pius XII, to congratulate the jubilarian "on the years-long, prudent discharge of your sacred office."

Bishop Peter W. Bartholome

A new period of diocesan history opened on December 6, 1941, when it was announced that the Holy See had appointed a coadjutor bishop *cum jure successionis* (with the right of succession) to assist Bishop Busch in carrying out the duties of his office in his declining years. The new bishop was Peter W. Bartholome, a priest of the Diocese of Winona and the pastor of St. John's Church in Rochester. He was consecrated titular bishop of Lete on March 3, 1942, and was formally welcomed to the diocese on April 7. When the news of this appointment reached St. Cloud, Bishop Busch issued this statement: "The coming of a Coadjutor Bishop to share the cares and burdens of the Ordinary will enable the former to avail himself of the experience of the past and to formulate wise and zealous plans for the future good of religion and the salvation of souls."

Bishop Bartholome worked closely with Bishop Busch as his coadjutor for more than a decade. During these years the Church of St. Cloud continued to grow and develop both in numbers and in spiritual strength. As Bishop Busch had indicated, the coadjutor bishop did avail himself of the "experience of the past" to formulate "wise and zealous plans for the future." By interviews and by personal observation, he carefully surveyed the needs of the diocese, noting particularly where new parishes or new schools were needed. In St. Cloud, which had experienced a major population growth, three new parishes were erected: St. Paul's in 1946, St. Peter's in 1948, and Holy Spirit in 1952. He also established St. Francis Xavier parish in suburban Sartell to accommodate the many Catholic families who had joined the exodus from the city to enjoy life in a rural atmosphere. In the outlying reaches of the diocese he laid the groundwork for new parishes. He encouraged the old and established parishes to replace outmoded and obsolete buildings with modern struc-

tures. New hospitals were built at Alexandria, Parkers Prairie and Sauk Centre, and the existing hospital at Breckenridge was replaced with a completely modern facility. New schools, both elementary and catechetical, were constructed in many parishes. While this surge of activity took place in the closing years of Bishop Busch's episcopate, there is no doubt that the impetus came from Bishop Bartholome.

When he came to St. Cloud as coadjutor bishop, he sensed the vast potential of this diocese which has been described as the most Catholic in the nation and he regarded it as a duty to harness these untapped resources for the work of the Church and the welfare of souls. Methodically he developed a policy that would in time supply the needs he had discerned and patiently awaited the opportune time to introduce each project. His constructive thinking about the basic problems of society is evident in his programs. If Bishop Bartholome could be said to have an overall philosophy that permeates his thought and action, it must be described as a strong and unwavering faith in the common sense of the human individual which will, given the opportunity, seek to defend and preserve the simple things of life. Nowhere has he manifested this philosophy more explicitly than in the two areas that have been his primary concerns as priest and bishop: the stewardship of the land and the sanctity of family life. In both areas he has attained national prominence and has often been invited to address secular as well as Catholic gatherings of people interested in the same objectives. For many years he headed the Family Life Bureau of the National Catholic Welfare Conference and for a number of terms held the office of president of the National Catholic Rural Life Conference. While he held these national posts, he exerted his influence to achieve on a national level what he was accomplishing in his own diocese.

In 1948 he inaugurated a course of marriage preparation for engaged couples and issued a directive that all young couples in the diocese contemplating marriage enroll in it. What was begun on a modest scale the first year has become an annual workshop and approximately 6,000 couples have attended these classes since their inception. It is interesting to note that not one of these has required the marriage counselling service which is also provided in the diocese.

He has vigorously promoted the family size farm in his own diocese, which is predominantly rural, as well as elsewhere where mechanization and moneyed interests threaten to undermine the basic economy of the nation. "The family-sized farm," he said on one occasion, "has to be larger than in former years because equipment for the farm and education for the farmer's family cost more than they used to. But the land is personal and the Creator intended it to provide a living. Soil conservation—preserving the land as you found it—is a matter of conscience."

Bishop Bartholome's interests, however, are not one-sided. Though rural living and family life have been among his primary concerns, he has what might be called a catholic view of life. The importance of Catholic education both for the welfare of the youth of the diocese and for the future of the Church has been emphasized from the day he arrived in St. Cloud. The numerous schools that have sprung up throughout the diocese are a tangible evidence of his conviction in this matter. Perhaps the crowning achievement of his years as the coadjutor bishop was the establishment of a diocesan seminary for the training of young men for the priesthood. For years the diocesan clergy had received their education either at St. John's University or at some other seminary in the country. Bishop Bartholome conceived the plan of establishing a seminary in which the administration would be in diocesan hands and the academic program remain under the School of Divinity at St. John's. The agreement between the diocese and the abbey embodying these provisions was signed in April, 1949. St. John's diocesan Seminary opened its doors in September, 1950.

On July 28, 1949, Bishop Busch celebrated the completion of sixty years in the priesthood. His health declined visibly in the years that followed and his coadjutor bishop was obliged to assume more and more of the responsibility of conducting the affairs of the diocese. During 1952, which the diocese commemorated as a "Century of Living with Christ" to mark the coming of Father Pierz to central Minnesota in 1852, Bishop Busch presided at the principal events of the year-long observance but Bishop Bartholome acted as the official host to the visiting prelates and other dignitaries. Bishop Busch died May 31, 1953. He had ruled the diocese for thirty-eight years and at the time of his death

was the dean of the American hierarchy.

By virtue of his original appointment to the see of St. Cloud "with the right of succession," Bishop Bartholome automatically became the fifth ordinary. The transition was hardly noticeable for he did not introduce any drastic changes in the over-all pattern of diocesan life. The policy he followed was the same one that he had developed as coadjutor bishop. He had had the wisdom and vision at that time to formulate a long-range program that would provide for the needs of the Church in the diocese for many years to come. This program was initiated while Bishop Busch was still living and it has continued to unfold year after year. The postwar years witnessed a remarkable growth in population throughout the diocese. While he noted this with satisfaction, it presented new problems by taxing facilities already overcrowded. This was especially so in the schools. But he met the situation with characteristic optimism and unbounded confidence in Divine Providence. He inspired the priests and people to share his own confidence. He was firmly convinced that if his priests and people worked together, there was almost no limit to what they could accomplish. A tour of the diocese and a look at its churches and schools, its hospitals and homes for the aged, its convents and monasteries, would amply bear this out.

Epilogue

Seventy-five years have gone by since Pope Leo XIII established the Church of St. Cloud. Its first shepherd, Bishop Zardetti, who came to a frontier town in 1889 to assume charge of a diocese woefully lacking priests and material resources upon which to build for the future, would be astounded to see it today. The "mustard seed" of the Gospel planted so long ago has taken deep root in good ground and become a mighty tree. The hand of Providence is everywhere evident in the history of the Diocese of St. Cloud but nowhere more so than in the illustrious succession of bishops who have ruled over this portion of Christ's vineyard. Each in his own right has well deserved the title of shepherd for each has admirably heeded the counsel of the Apostle Peter, "becoming from the heart a pattern to the flock" (I Peter 5:3).

St. John's Abbey and St. John's University, Collegeville

Motherhouse of Franciscan Sisters of the Immaculate Conception, Little Falls

Crosier Monastery, Onamia

St. Benedict's Priory, St. Joseph

RELIGIOUS IN THE DIOCESE OF ST. CLOUD _____

Benedictine Fathers
Crosier Fathers
Society of the Precious Blood
Third Order Regular of St. Francis

_____

Benedictine Sisters of Pontifical Jurisdiction (St. Benedict's Priory)
Benedictine Sistert of Pontifical Jurisdiction (St. Gertrude's Priory)
Franciscan Sisters of the Immaculate Conception

Franciscan Poor Clare Nuns
Franciscan Sisters of the Poor
Misioneras Guadalupanas de Cristo Rey
Missionary Franciscan Sisters of the Immaculate Conception
School Sisters of Notre Dame

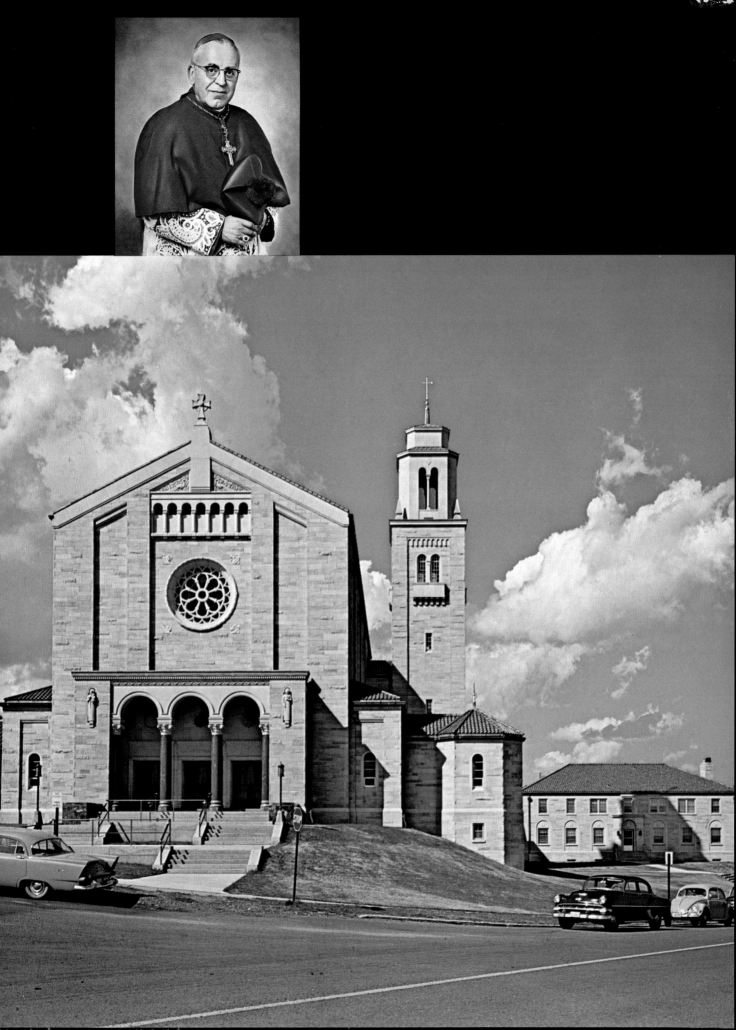

DIOCESE OF DULUTH

By Reverend Robert W. Klein

IN AN APOSTOLIC letter dated October 3, 1889, Pope Leo XIII communicated his decision that 39,439 square miles of the territory then known as the Vicariate Apostolic of Northern Minnesota was to be established as a separate and autonomous diocese, with its see located in Duluth. Eight weeks later, on November 29, Father James McGolrick of Minneapolis was chosen to be the first bishop of the newly created Diocese of Duluth.

Bishop McGolrick was consecrated by Archbishop John Ireland on December 27, together with the bishops of two other newly formed dioceses, the Most Rev. Joseph B. Cotter of Winona and the Most Rev. John Shanley of Jamestown, North Dakota.

When Bishop McGolrick arrived in Duluth, on January 9, 1890, to take possession of his new diocese, he was greeted by an ovation which was termed "unequalled in the history of the Northwest." In the minds of everyone present on that memorable winter evening was the realization that the Church in northern Minnesota was on the threshold of a new and significant era in her history.

Not that Catholicism was something new in the territory encompassed by the infant diocese. In 1641 Father Isaac Jogues preached at the Sault Ste. Marie, and asked permission to cross the big sea water and visit the Indians at its western end. His superior felt the Jesuits were already overworked in the Lake Huron region, and advised Father Jogues to "pray Heaven to hasten their conversion."

It was for others to fulfill Jogues' wish to spread the light of the Gospel in the west. Perhaps the very Indians who had listened to him in 1641 did this according to their own humble station and ability. But, starting in 1658, more sophisticated travelers entered the scene.

Frenchmen Probe the Area

First came Medard Chouart, Sieur des Grosseilliers, and his brother-in-law, Pierre Esprit Radisson. Merchants rather than missionaries, they came to trade. From a warehouse-like fort they built at Chequmegon Bay, they traveled the South Shore of the lake among the Hurons and Chippewa, moved inland through the Sioux territory to a river "as mighty as the St. Lawrence," crossed from Bayfield peninsula to Two Harbors to contact the Cree Indians and passed down the North Shore through what is now Duluth, the first white men to see the mouth of the St. Louis River. In the fall of 1660 they returned to Montreal rich in furs and adventure stories, the latter of which Radisson wrote up in 1669 in his famous travelogue.

While these Marco Polos were busy gathering data for books—and furs—Father René Ménard, a veteran missioner, set up a small station among the not too friendly Indians at Keweenaw Bay, which he renamed the Baye de Ste. Thérèse. His "small hermitage," as he called it, must have been quite wretched. He said that the evergreen branches did not really shield him from the ravages of the winter of 1660, but they did "correct my imagination and persuade me that I am sheltered."

The following spring Father Ménard attempted to visit some Hurons who had been driven into the neighborhood by the Sioux. Because he was already worn out with decades of work in New France, his friends urged him not to take the trip. "I must go," the Jesuit replied, "even if it costs me my life. Are we to serve God only when there is nothing to suffer and no risk left?" This time the risk proved too great and Father Ménard never returned. But his short stay had borne a little fruit. He had carried the Gospel further into the northwest than any previous missionary. When his replacement, Father Claude Allouez, passed through St. Theresa's Bay in 1665, he found some remnants of Father Ménard's labors: "two Christian Indian women who had always kept the faith and who shone like two stars in the darkness of that infidelity."

With Father Claude Allouez, called "a second Xavier" by his companions and "the founder of Christianity in the west" by historians, the Gospel was at last preached at the western end of Lake Superior. From his mission of the Holy Spirit at La Pointe on Madeline Island, he ranged up and down both shores of the lake. While his zeal drove him on in search of souls and fired his tongue for preaching, his ever curious eyes roved the rocky shores noting the location of "copper rocks," and his keen mind memorized the region so well that his map of Lake Superior became the best to be had. His visitations along the North Shore extended from the Nipigon River westward to the mouth of the St. Louis River, and inland toward another river he tells us is called the "Messipi." It was probably at Fond du Lac that the Chippewa, who had a village there from 1665 to 1669, presented him

with a gift of wild rice, a resource that to this day remains one of the choice offerings of the region.

How many souls did Father Allouez harvest? Some accounts say that he baptized over 10,000 Indians. His records for the Lake Superior mission list only four or five hundred; they also reveal that he was quite discouraged. He asked permission to work among the Indians to the south where he thought (and correctly) that he would have more success. Accordingly, in 1669, Father Allouez moved to the Green Bay area, and Fathers Claude Dablon and Jacques Marquette came to Lake Superior.

Father Marquette worked among the Indians near La Pointe for a year. After the Sioux drove the Hurons and Algonquins east along the South Shore, Father Marquette founded the mission of Point St. Ignace, in Michigan.

The activites of Father Allouez in mapping and describing Lake Superior, and of Father Marquette in helping to discover and explore the upper Mississippi in 1673, underline a very important aspect of what these missionaries attempted to accomplish. Trained in the finest universities of Europe, they were men deeply interested in

Chippewa gathering wild rice

the territory they worked and the people they encountered. They not only preached and converted; they studied and described. A modern historian has written of their activities:

> In the *Jesuit Relations,* the folklore, the religion, the mythology, the manners and morals, even the speech and detailed daily living of those vanished [Indians], what they did and what they were, are set down minutely, keenly, zestfully by men than whom no men in the 17th and 18th centuries were more shrewdly trained in the subtle arts of rhetoric, diplomacy, observation, psychology, and humanity.

Read, for example, Father Dablon's classic description of the vast lake that stood in the center of his "parish":

This lake has almost the form of a bent bow more than 180 leagues long. The south side serves as the string, and the arrow seems to be a great tongue of land projecting more than 80 leagues into the width of the lake. The north side is frightful by reason of a succession of rocks which form a prodigious mountain chain which finally loses itself in the end of this lake.

We should also remember that the work of the missionaries was part of a French master plan to open the new continent and win it for King Louis XIV. The interesting and colorful ceremony that took place at the Sault in 1671 was only one of many such pageants intended to flaunt the claims of Spain and England and to awe the Indians. On June 4, Simon François Daumont,

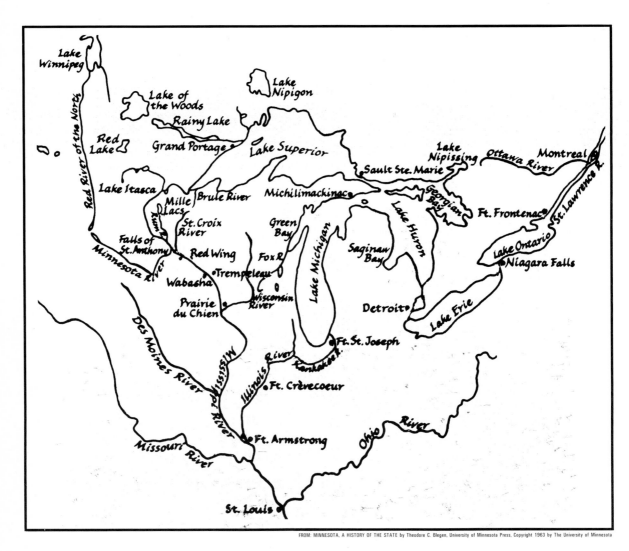

The water routes from Montreal west.

Sieur de Saint Lusson, took formal possession of the entire western domain in the names of God and the King of France. Fathers Dablon and Marquette were present, and watched the cross and standard of the King rise together over the rapids.

Then Father Allouez preached. He pointed to the cross and explained to the Indians how Christ redeemed all men—Indians and white men, noble men and humble men. Then he pointed to the king's banner and hailed his monarch as "the Captain of the greatest captains" and assured the savages that they had "not his equal in the world."

Duluth Arrives

A fusion of somewhat similar idealisms and ambitions is to be found in the man for whom Duluth is named. Daniel Greysolon, Sieur du Lhut, was born at Saint-Germain-en-Laye, France. His father was of the petty nobility under the Bourbon Kings, his mother of the wealthy Patron family at Lyons. Duluth lived most of his boyhood at Lyons. After spending a few years in military service, where he found advancement too slow, he came to New France in 1672, settling in Montreal. He made his first Holy Communion here two years later. When family affairs called him home that year, he also took time out to enter the Royal Guard and help France with her war on Holland. At the bloody battle of Senef in August, 1674, he met Father Louis Hennepin, a Franciscan, who was chaplain of his troops. He was back in Montreal before winter, out of the army and trying to settle down to a routine life.

But opportunity was insistent. Duluth dreamed the common dream of finding a water route to the Indies. At the same time France dreamed of settling the war between the Chippewa and Sioux which, from 1661, had all but stopped the fur trade. Was there a man courageous and diplomatic who could negotiate a settlement, draw trade away from the British posts at Hudson Bay and insure a French monopoly? Add some more circumstances. Legend has it that Duluth was disappointed in love. His intended, it is said, was of an upper class and refused the hand of a mere merchant. The sense of adventure is heightened by the fact that a royal decree forbade all Frenchmen to enter Sioux territory.

The authoritories feared that their presence would only aggravate the intense tribal rivalries, take higher tolls among the already depleted French forces and help the British fur trade.

In 1678, with neither license for trade nor commission to explore—only a gentleman's agreement with Governor Frontenac of Quebec—Duluth sold the house he had purchased only a year before and set out with twelve companions. He wintered at the Sault and held preliminary conferences with the Chippewa. The ice out, he paddled up the lake, landing at the present site of the Duluth Ship Canal about June 28, 1679. After making some initial contacts with the Sioux at Mille Lacs he held his historic meeting with the tribes either at Fond du Lac or Minnesota Point.

Representatives of the Monsious, Crees, Assiniboines and Chippewa gathered here with their own common enemy, the Sioux, on September 15, 1679. Duluth skillfully wove ties of peace and amity and spent the ensuing winter at Grand Portage drawing them together by fostering intertribal marriages and hunting parties, all of which were accompanied by merry feasts. In the following spring, after convincing the Indians that the British and Dutch were lying when they accused the French of spreading a contagious disease among the Indians, Duluth was able to send a delegation from the tribes to Montreal. He had to offer himself as a "hostage" until the delegates returned.

Now he was able to look for his water route. He had heard reports of "a great lake where water is not good to drink" twenty-days journey away, and his informants had brought him salt. Eagerly setting out in June, his party paddled up the Brule, portaged into the St. Croix and moved on down to the Mississippi.

It was here that something made him change his plans. There were rumors out that the Sioux had captured some "white spirits." Two days later, Duluth traced down his old friend, Father Louis Hennepin, who had been captured with two companions during their exploration of the upper Mississippi.

Using all the diplomatic skill at his disposal—including undisguised threats and the equivocation that Hennepin was his brother—Duluth succeeded in saving the lives of the priest and his companions. His boldness also preserved the dignity of France and set a precedent that would protect Frenchmen in similar scrapes in the future. Because he felt he had to escort his friend to safety, Duluth gave up all hope of finding the "Great Salt Sea" that summer.

Then a further complication developed. While spending the winter at Mackinac Island, Duluth learned that one of the informers of Louis XIV, Jacques Duchesnau, had charged him with conspiring with Governor Frontenac, illegally trading with the Indians and treasonably trading with the British. Later the famous explorer La Salle made similar charges. Duluth was placed under "arrest" in Quebec, where he dined each night at Governor Frontenac's table. In 1682 he went to France and was able to clear his name. He returned to Montreal where he served his country as guide and interpreter until his retirement in 1707.

Historians agree that Daniel Greysolon was unique among explorers. Though his bravery was well known—he once told Governor Frontenac, "I fear not death, only cowardice and dishonor" —his personal writings betray modesty rather than boastfulness. While he sought personal glory

Holy Rosary Church at Grand Portage built of logs in 1865, covered with siding in 1940

as the discoverer of a water route to the west and used his great influence among the Indians to advance the cause of France, he was more concerned for their welfare than his own profit. For example, of the French and English practice of giving brandy or rum to the Indians, Duluth once wrote: "I have seen that the trade in *eau de vie* produced great disorders . . . and I maintain that morally speaking, it is impossible to export brandy to the woods and distant missions without danger of its producing misery."

Duluth may have cut a dashing figure as a soldier and explorer, but we should not forget that for forty years he suffered from gout, attacks of which lasted as long as three months. He prayed to Catherine Tekakwitha, the famous Mohawk virgin, to help him in his sufferings. His last will and testament revealed his devotion to the Church as well as his personal poverty. He left legacies to the three religious orders working in North America, the Recollects (Franciscans), Sulpicians and Jesuits. When he died on February 25, 1710, his desire to be buried in the Recollect cemetery was granted. In notifying King Louis XIV of Duluth's death, the Governer General of New France said simply, "he was an honest man."

In the years following the death of the great-hearted Duluth, few if any missionaries visited the western end of Lake Superior. Those who came west, Father Charles Mesaiger in 1731 and Father Jean Aulneau four years later, passed through Grand Portage and along the water routes to the north where they preached the Gospel at International Falls.

Political troubles in the old world, military conflicts with Great Britain in the new were upsetting France's master plan for control of the Great Lakes. The missionaries were frustrated, not only by superstition and hostility among the savages, but also by the more civilized idolatries of their fellow countrymen, that is, greed and corruption. The end was in sight when Quebec fell to General James Wolfe in 1759. The Jesuits evacuated the Sault, Mackinac Straits and Green Bay. Three years later, at the Treaty of Paris, the lion of England closed the continent to France. It was as if a glacier crept down from Hudson Bay, locking off the inland sea from Christianity and the civilization, pure and undefiled, that came with it.

Activity of Missionaries

But the fires of faith that had been ignited and spread in the northwest by the missionaries were not entirely snuffed out. In 1830 a spark blew west again in the person of the remarkable Pierre Cotte, a retired half-breed voyageur and lay missionary.

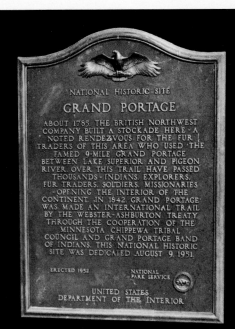

NATIONAL HISTORIC SITE

GRAND PORTAGE

ABOUT 1785, THE BRITISH NORTHWEST
COMPANY BUILT A STOCKADE HERE - A
NOTED RENDEZVOUS FOR THE FUR
TRADERS OF THIS AREA WHO USED THE
FAMED 9-MILE GRAND PORTAGE
BETWEEN LAKE SUPERIOR AND PIGEON
RIVER. OVER THIS TRAIL HAVE PASSED
THOUSANDS - INDIANS, EXPLORERS,
FUR TRADERS, SOLDIERS, MISSIONARIES
- OPENING THE INTERIOR OF THE
CONTINENT. IN 1842, GRAND PORTAGE
WAS MADE AN INTERNATIONAL TRAIL
BY THE WEBSTER-ASHBURTON TREATY.
THROUGH THE COOPERATION OF THE
MINNESOTA CHIPPEWA TRIBAL
COUNCIL AND GRAND PORTAGE BAND
OF INDIANS, THIS NATIONAL HISTORIC
SITE WAS DEDICATED AUGUST 9, 1951.

ERECTED 1952   NATIONAL
                      PARK SERVICE

UNITED STATES
DEPARTMENT OF THE INTERIOR

Restored stockade at Grand Portage

We find Cotte in that year at his home among the shacks of Fond du Lac, a busy trading post since the 1820's, "zealously" conducting services for the Indians. He told our informant, the famous Presbyterian missionary, Edmund Ely, that he expected "a Catholic from the Sault to open a school." The teacher apparently never came. Four years later Cotte and his wife were still on the job, armed now with a copy of Father Baraga's Indian Prayer Book, which had been published in Detroit in 1832. Reverend Ely, who opened his own Indian Mission School at Fond du Lac in 1834, recorded the following ecumenical confrontation which occurred on October 17 of that year:

> This morning Mr. Cottee [sic] read Catholic prayers, but I was ignorant of it. Why he did not invite me to be present I do not know. This evening I informed Mr. C. that I intended to sing with those of my scholars who had come in. He invited me into his home. When we entered the room was filled. He said we would first say prayers. Accordingly the Catholic service was read, in which the Indians and children joined. They spent half an hour, or more, in singing Catholic hymns, and then told me there was an opportunity for my children to sing. We accordingly sang several hymns, one or two of which his congregation knew . . . I then asked him if I should join in prayer. To this he made no answer. I called on all to join me, and we knelt down. I concluded in Indian, in which one voice joined me.

Cotte was, of course, preparing his congregation for the day when a priest would come (and, no doubt, "holding the fort" in true post-Reformation style). The priest finally did come in 1835. With the arrival of Father Frederick Baraga another brilliant and, this time, permanent phase of Catholicism in America began.

Born in Carniola, part of what we today call Yugoslavia, Father Baraga had been working among the Indians in Michigan for a year when his prayer book was published. The trip from the Sault to La Pointe in July of 1835 on a "trading vessel" took eighteen days. Father Baraga wrote his patrons in Austria that although July is "the hottest month, yet some mornings it was so cold on the water that I was obliged to put on my coat over my cassock and envelop myself in my cloak, not to take cold."

After baptizing eighty-six Indians at La Pointe and getting the construction of a church underway there in August, Father Baraga came to Fond du Lac. A joyful throng of Indians greeted him like a long-awaited friend. Cotte had prepared many of them so well that Father Baraga could baptize them without adding any instructions. Twenty-one Indians were christened on September 6.

Back at La Pointe, Father Baraga noted that "a considerable number of pagans have already been received into the bosom of the Church, namely, one hundred and forty-eight." Since snow flakes were already falling, he sent off another letter to the Leopoldine Mission Society in Vienna commenting on the need for warm clothing.

Father Baraga evangelized western Lake Superior and the Indian and French villages that ringed it. Sometimes he sailed up and down aboard the trading ship *John Jacob Astor.* At other times he joined Chippewa flotillas. In 1846

Father Baraga monument near Cross River where the missionary erected a wooden cross

Duluth in about 1870

he made the famous crossing of Lake Superior during a storm that is commemorated by the little shrine of "Baraga's Traverse" at the mouth of the Cross River.

Father Baraga also sailed the ocean many times to beg funds and to enlist priests. Upon his return from the voyage of 1837, a letter from the Indian Chief at Grand Portage informed him that a missionary would be welcome there. Father Francis Pierz, a fellow countryman of Father Baraga who had come to Detroit two years earlier, was placed in charge of the new mission.

And who was on hand to meet him? The American Fur Company had opened a fishery at Grand Portage about 1835, and Pierre Cotte, the manager, was on hand ever since instructing a "new congregation." Father Pierz not only found many of the Indians ready for baptism, but also a temporary chapel which the catechumens had put up. Father Pierz began a mission school, and stayed at Grand Portage until October of 1838. Called away by the needs of missions elsewhere,

he was able to visit Grand Portage only occasionally. In 1842 he put up a chapel and opened a school for forty-five children at the mouth of the Pigeon River. Five years later he visited the great carrying place again. After 1846 Grand Portage was attended by the Jesuits from Fort William. Father Dominic du Ranquet in 1851 built the chapel which serves as the sacristy of the present church. Four years later he founded the mission at Grand Marais.

Other names also belong on the list of those who re-established the Lake Superior missions. Father Otto Skolla, a Franciscan who had come to Detroit from the Austrian Province of Dalmatia in 1842, served at Grand Portage in the 1840's and at Fond du Lac and in the Sandy Lake region in the 1850's. Father Lawrence Lautishar came from Carniola to Red Lake in 1857 after three years on the Michigan missions. He froze to death while on a sick call in December a year later.

Regional developments at mid-century seemed to assure the permanent settlement of the head

69

of the lakes. In 1853, the year Father Baraga was named Vicar Apostolic of Upper Michigan, engineers began the dredging of the Sault. Two years later the million dollar project was completed and the way opened for direct shipping of lumber, furs and farm produce down the lakes, and manufactured goods up. In that same year Congress ratified the treaty of La Pointe which settled certain grievances held by the ten tribes of the region and opened the North Shore for permanent white settlement. When the Diocese of Sault Ste. Marie was created in 1856, with Frederic Baraga as the first ordinary, fourteen towns in various stages of development stretched from Fond du Lac to Beaver Bay. Duluth, the settlement on Minnesota Point, received its name and became the seat of St. Louis County.

White Settlement at Duluth

The early years were not secure years. When Father John Cebul, whom Bishop Baraga brought to Michigan from Carniola in 1859, came to Duluth from his station at La Pointe in 1860, he found only eight persons living there. The financial panic of 1857 and the smallpox a year later all but wiped out the settlement.

But as the nation turned from civil conflict to a continuation of its conquest of the continent, men once again moved to the head of the lakes. Now it was rumored that gold glittered in the quartz around Lake Vermillion. In 1866 the prominent entrepreneur, Jay Cooke, came to town talking about a railroad and stimulating development. By 1870 there were 3,100 merchants, shippers, bankers and workers and their families living in Duluth. Hundreds more labored in the area cutting lumber, laying track and transporting grain. Commercial and tourist boats regularly plied through the Sault and stopped at the growing port. The city had two newspapers, a YMCA, and in that year organized its public school system. The first passenger train arrived on August 1, and four days later the business leaders created a Chamber of Commerce. Perhaps we can place the establishment of Catholicism at Duluth in this same year. In 1870, Father John Cebul erected the first church in the city.

Father Cebul was a remarkable man, even as missionaries go. An accomplished musician

who could sing well and play several instruments, he also composed or adapted many songs for the Chippewa. He could speak several other Indian dialects and was fluent in five Slavonik idioms and in German, French and English. He could also do well in Latin, Greek and Arabic. Jay Cooke did not respond to his request for property for the proposed Church, but Luther Mendenhall, one of the founders of the Chamber of Commerce, arranged for the donation of land through the Western Land Association. The first Catholic church went up where Sacred Heart Church now stands. Completed in February, 1871, when Father George Keller became pastor, it was a small frame building. Eventually, its gleaming white paint was visible against the green hillside for many miles out into the lake.

And by the time the ice was out of the bay, the church had an organist. Mrs. W. P. Farrell lived over in Superior, but every Sunday an Indian rowed her and her melodeon across the bay, and the two (helped, no doubt, by Mr. Farrell) somehow got the thing up the hill to the church on time.

But not all relations between Superior and Duluth were so cordial. The St. Louis River and Bay emptied into Lake Superior at the Wisconsin end of Minnesota Point. Superior's harbor, accordingly, enjoyed an advantage and offered more promise. Duluthians decided to change the course of history by digging a canal through their end of Minnesota Point, thus altering the flow of the river and bay into the lake, and at least approximating the advantage Superior enjoyed from its natural canal.

A great and dramatic fuss arose over all this, but before the Superiorites could close down the Duluthian's project by a court order, shovels and picks wielded by the citizenry throughout the weekend of April 28 and 29 opened a linking trench. This done, the force of the river did the rest, and as dawn rose from over the Sault on Monday, April 30, 1871, George W. Sherwood guided his yacht through the fifty-foot-wide channel.

Unfortunately, Duluth's hopes sailed smack into the Panic of 1873. Jay Cooke and Company failed in September, the population dropped from 5,000 to 1,300, and by 1877 the "Zenith City of the Unsalted Seas" (so named in 1868) was pronounced dead. Father Cebul had left the area to rest in Europe, his eyesight weakened by the smoke in the many Indian huts he had visited. Father Keller had also gone, and his successor, Father Jean Baptiste Marie Genin, O.M.I., was in France. Father Joseph Francis Buh, who had come to Minnesota in 1864, helped out in Duluth, along with Fathers Joseph Staub and Charles Verwyst. The three divided their time between the head of the lakes, the numerous missions Buh had founded near Belle Prairie, where he built the first concrete church in Minnesota in 1877, the stations from Duluth to Pine City and those on the South Shore between Superior and Bad River, Wisconsin.

When Father Buh in 1878 took over St. Joseph's Church near Perham, where he was to remain until 1885, Duluth was showing the first signs of recovery. Grain shipments from the Red River Valley were flowing stronger than ever due to the increased activity following the migrations from the cities in 1873. In the forests from Grand Rapids to Virginia, axes flashed and saws screeched as dozens of crews of cruisers, choppers, swampers and barkers fought timber, mosquitoes, liquor and smallpox to hack out an existence and a new frontier. By 1879 George Stuntz, builder in 1852 of the first house on Minnesota Point, proved to the satisfaction of eastern

Monsignor Joseph Buh

financial interests that the real "gold" near lake Vermillion was iron ore. Six years later Charlemagne Tower's two million dollar railroad connected these sites with Two Harbors, and Minnesota's first ore shipment, 62,000 tons of high grade hematite, was off to the Sault and the furnaces beyond. A year later, 1885, the population of Duluth had soared to an all-time high of 33,000, and the year after that, when the port handled 1.9 million tons of commercial shipments, the Chamber of Commerce said that the panic was over.

Growth of the Church

But the panic was just beginning for the church builders because the growth of the area, gradual as it was, was only just starting.

From the south farmers and merchants were now pushing up the St. Croix and Mississippi valleys and the fertile highlands between them. Poles, Irishmen, Frenchmen, Germans, Scandinavians and Finns mingled with the "old Americans" in settling rural communities and railroad centers, and in developing neighborhoods in Duluth. The Poles built a log church at Gnesen in 1876, the year after Abbot Rupert Seidenbusch of St. John's Abbey became Vicar Apostolic of Northern Minnesota. Ten years earlier the first Catholics had arrived in the Pine City region. Between the opening of Immaculate Conception parish there in 1880 and the appointment of Father Buh as pastor of Tower-Ely-Two Harbors in 1888, parishes were established at Cloquet (1881), Brainerd and Aitkin (1885) and Carleton (1886). In Duluth, St. Mary Star of the Sea for the Poles (1883), St. Jean Baptiste for the French and St. Clement for the Irish and Germans (1885) joined the original Sacred Heart parish.

Abbot Seidenbusch promoted Catholic education. In 1880 he asked three Benedictine Sisters from St. Joseph, Minnesota, to establish a school in Sacred Heart parish. Their first attempt in 1881 began in a carriage shop converted into a convent and school. Due to financial difficulties it failed. Four years later the sisters moved with 150 pupils into a vacant public school. In 1886 St. Thomas School was opened across the street from Sacred Heart Church, and St. Mary Star of the Sea parish began its parochial school. A year later the "faculty house" at St. Clement was ready for occupation. Because pastor-professors did not arrive to teach in the proposed "Business Academy for Young Men," but a typhoid epidemic did, the Benedictine Sisters turned the sturdy building into the first St. Mary's Hospital.

That was 1888. Duluth and Superior were now a single port under federal title, and members of the Chamber of Commerce in Duluth not only felt the panic was over; they believed that the future was rosy. There were more than 20,000 Catholic whites living in Duluth and the villages in the area and about 2,000 Catholic Indians scattered over a large area.

The Diocese is Established

In 1871 Father Cebul, after his first train ride from St. Paul to Duluth, had written a friend in Austria that "the times are changing and we change with them." In 1889 the Holy See responded to the developments at the head of the lakes by erecting the Diocese of Duluth. One might wonder how Father Cebul would have described the changes that took place in the two decades after his departure that led up to this event; or how he would have reacted to the dynamic and furious growth that followed the opening of the iron mining industry in the 1890's. When he died at Spring Garden, Michigan, in 1898, Bishop James McGolrick, who was now

Bishop James McGolerick

First mass at Warba in 1912

caught up in the turmoil of the new period, looked back on the pioneer days with gratitude and wrote: "Father Cebul was as simple as a child, a man without ambitions." That is, like all the pioneering priests and laymen we have met, he had the sole ambition of doing God's work on earth.

Bishop McGolrick, when he entered his new diocese, could be grateful for the work of his pioneering predecessors, but he must have realized only too clearly that theirs was but the work of laying foundations.

To assist him in the gargantuan task of building on those foundations he had fifteen diocesan priests and five religious priests, who exercised their ministry in 32 churches and 10 stations. The new diocese had 5 schools, with total enrollment of 800 pupils.

The first years of the new diocese show a record of methodical progress, slow and deliberate at first, and not devoid of heartbreaking set-backs. In the midst of a business recession in 1892, the cathedral church and rectory were destroyed by fire.

In spite of this and similar handicaps, the Church in the Diocese of Duluth was making gains. The first decade of Bishop McGolrick's adminstration had seen the establishment of seven new parishes.

Bishop McGolrick was instrumental in another major step forward when he encouraged Mother Scholastica Kerst, O.S.B., to establish the Duluth Benedictine community in 1892.

The new Benedictine community founded by

Mother Scholastica found ready acceptance in the young diocese. Within ten years of their arrival, the sisters had built hospitals in Duluth, Grand Rapids, Brainerd, Bemidji and Crookston. In 1908, they established a school of nursing in the see city.

The year 1909 saw the construction of two more institutions staffed by the sisters, St. James' Orphanage and the College of St. Scholastica. In addition, Benedictine Sisters administered two homes for the aged and staffed the diocese's six new schools.

On December 31, 1909, the diocese was divided, and its western portion became the Diocese of Crookston. On May 19 of that year, Father Timothy Corbett, rector of Duluth's Sacred Heart Cathedral, was consecrated bishop of the new diocese.

When Bishop McGolrick died, on January 23, 1918, the Diocese of Duluth was no longer the struggling infant it had been thirty years before. Its Catholic population had increased nearly threefold. There were now 51 priests serving the faithful in 43 parishes, 48 missions and 35 stations. A significant start had been made, but it was only a start.

Second Bishop of Duluth

The vacant chair of Bishop McGolrick was filled by Bishop John T. McNicholas, O.P. During his seven-year reign was begun the task of erecting the superstructure of the spiritual edifice whose foundations had been laid by Bishop McGolrick and the pioneer missionaries.

The population of the area, which had surged upward during the years of discovery and development on the iron ranges, remained surprisingly stable during these same seven years. This "breathing-space" permitted the diocese to augment the number of its clergy, whose numbers had failed to increase in due proportion to the booming population.

The years between 1918 and 1925 witnessed an expansion of the diocese's educational facilities. Bishop McNicholas added four new schools to the diocesan system. To staff them, he brought into the diocese the Dominican and Franciscan Sisters in 1923, and the Sisters of the Holy Name of Jesus and Mary in 1924.

In 1921, the Dominican tertiaries from England came to Duluth, under the leadership of Mother Mary Ellerker. Their novitiate, Corpus Christi House, became a center for working girls, and later, a girls' home. The tertiaries also were engaged in catechetical work among the Italians who had moved into the city. The little group entered the Order of Mt. Carmel in 1928 and, as

Bishop John T. McNicholas, O.P.

Carmelites, has continued in its apostolate of charity until the present.

Bishop McNicholas established 12 new parishes during his episcopate. He founded a central mission house, from which a group of priests attended 40 missions.

He also set up the Council of Catholic Women in the diocese and chartered the Holy Name Society in thirty-eight parishes. On July 7, 1925, he was appointed Archbishop of Cincinnati, a post which he held until his death in April, 1950.

Bishop Welch's Administration

Bishop McNicholas' successor Thomas Anthony Welch, was born November 2, 1884, in Faribault. He was the son of Mr. and Mrs. Thomas Joseph Welch. He attended elementary and secondary schools in Marshall. Later he was enrolled in St. Thomas College, St. Paul, from which he was graduated in 1903.

From St. Thomas, he went to the St. Paul Seminary in St. Paul. He was ordained a priest by Archbishop John Ireland of St. Paul on June 11, 1909, in St. Mary's Chapel on the seminary campus.

Shortly after his ordination he was appointed secretary to Archbishop Ireland, a post which he held until July, 1911. At that time, Father Welch was named chancellor of the St. Paul archdiocese. Archbishop Ireland, who died in September, 1918, was succeeded by Archbishop Austin Dowling. Under Archbishop Dowling, Father Welch continued in the same post.

In February, 1924, he was elevated to the rank of Domestic Prelate by Pope Pius XI. In Decem-

Bishop Thomas A. Welch

ber of the same year, Monsignor Welch was appointed vicar-general of the Archdiocese of St. Paul. One year later, on December 17, 1925, Pope Pius XI appointed him Bishop of Duluth.

His consecration to the episcopacy took place in the St. Paul Cathedral on February 3, 1926. Archbishop Dowling was the consecrating bishop. Co-consecrators were Bishop James O'Reilly of Fargo, North Dakota, and Bishop Joseph Busch of St. Cloud. The sermon on that occasion was preached by Archbishop McNicholas.

On the following day, February 4, he was formally installed as bishop of the Duluth diocese in Sacred Heart Cathedral.

As spiritual leader of the diocese, Bishop Welch saw the Catholic population of the area grow from 61,000 to nearly 100,000. The years of his administration witnessed the erection of 47 new churches in cities and towns throughout the diocese.

In the thirty-three years of Bishop Welch's administration, the number of parishes with resident priests grew from 55 to 86. The number of parochial schools increased by almost 50 per cent.

Bishop Welch successfully steered the diocese through the trying years of the depression. He also succeeded in reorganizing and stabilizing many diocesan offices and institutions.

He encouraged the growth of the Council of Catholic Women in parishes throughout the diocese, and played a major role in the establishment of the Council of Catholic Women on a diocesan basis. At his urging, the Confraternity of Christian Doctrine was set up in each parish, and he lent his wholehearted support to the inauguration of religious vacation schools. A program of religious retreats for lay people was among the many projects that benefited by his encouragement.

The Bureau of Catholic Charities (now Catholic Social Service) was expanded by Bishop Welch. Auxiliary Bishop Laurence A. Glenn (consecrated in September, 1956) was the bureau's first full-time director.

Bishop Welch also inaugurated the Newman Club and the Serra Club.

The Duluth Register, the official newspaper of the diocese, was established in 1937, under the direction of Bishop Welch.

The work of the Benedictine Sisters of Duluth won his support and encouragement. The facilities of the Villa Scholastica were greatly expanded with his cooperation and guidance. This expansion included the construction of Our Lady Queen of Peace Chapel and of Stanbrook Hall, a girls' high school. It was largely at his promptings that the College of St. Scholistica was raised to the status of a complete four-year college for young women.

The years of his reign saw the construction of two new hospitals staffed by the sisters—Miners' Hospital in Crosby and the Hibbing General Hospital. During the same years, St. Joseph's Hospital in Brainerd was considerably enlarged by the construction of a new wing. St. Mary's Hospital in Duluth underwent two major expansions during Bishop Welch's episcopate.

Two building projects which gave Bishop Welch particular satisfaction were the completion of a new diocesan chancery (in 1954) and of the new Church of Our Lady of the Rosary (in 1957). The title of cathedral was transferred to Our Lady of the Rosary in November, 1957.

Bishop Welch died September 9, 1959, after an illness of several weeks. Bishop Laurence A. Glenn, in his funeral sermon over the deceased prelate, noted three major contributions made by Bishop Welch to the life and growth of the diocese. These were careful preparation of priests for the diocese, the improvement in religious teaching and the substitution of permanent for temporary structures. "These more than other factors," observed Bishop Glenn, "mark the transition from the status of a missionary to a well-organized diocese, and because of them he merits the undying gratitude of the faithful."

The Present Bishop

On February 3, 1960, the Holy See announced the appointment of the Most Rev. Francis J. Schenk, then Bishop of Crookston, as the fourth Bishop of Duluth.

Francis Joseph Schenk was born April 1, 1901, in Superior, Wisconsin, the son of Mr. and Mrs. Nicholas Schenk. Shortly after his birth, the Schenk family moved to Gaylord, Minnesota, where the future bishop attended the elementary public school.

Later he attended St. Thomas Academy and St. Thomas College in St. Paul, before entering the St. Paul Seminary in the fall of 1920. He was ordained a priest of the Archdiocese of St. Paul by Archbishop Austin Dowling on June 13, 1926.

After his ordination, young Father Schenk attended the Catholic University of America in Washington, D. C., where he received his doctorate in canon law in 1928.

Upon his return to St. Paul, he was named vice-chancellor of the archdiocese and secretary to Archbishop Dowling. He remained in these posts under Archbishop Dowling's successor, the late Archbishop John Gregory Murray, until 1934, when he was named professor of canon law and moral theology at the St. Paul Seminary.

Father Schenk was appointed rector of the St. Paul Cathedral in 1942 and at the same time was elevated to the position of vicar-general of the archdiocese.

His appointment as Bishop of Crookston came on March 10, 1945. He was consecrated on May 24 of that year by Archbishop Murray. Co-consecrators were Bishop (later Cardinal) Aloisius J. Muench of Fargo and the late Bishop Thomas A. Welch of Duluth.

His installation as Bishop of Duluth took place on Easter Tuesday, April 19, 1960.

It has been three centuries since ambassadors of the Catholic Church first set foot in northern Minnesota. And the Diocese of Duluth has been in existence for a scant third of that time. For most of its three generations the diocese has been governed by three bishops, each of whom has contributed to the growth of the Church in this area.

The diocese welcomed its fourth Bishop as it headed into the last quarter of its first century. The task allotted by history to Bishop Schenk is one which will differ considerably from that of his predecessors. The years of laying foundations, of expansions, of "setting up shop" are over. After seventy-five years of existence, the Diocese of Duluth has reached adulthood.

The future will contain, to be sure, more building, more expansion, even more beginnings. The economic future of the area bears promise of new developments in mining, shipping, commerce and manufacture. Under Bishop Schenk's hand, the diocese has already begun to respond to the changing climate of the 1960's.

During his four years in Duluth, Bishop Schenk has already brought to fulfillment three major projects: the remodeling of the former West Duluth YMCA into a diocesan youth center (named for his predecessor, Bishop Welch); the construction of the new St. Ann's Home for the aging; and the opening of the new Duluth Cathedral High School, a modern co-institutional school with a potential enrollment of 1,500 students.

But by and large, the years ahead will witness a progression in depth more than a growth in expanse. Led by the bishop, who shares the human warmth and pastoral concern of the late Pope John XXIII, the diocese will become more intent on the task of deepening and intensifying its own spirit, its own sense of mission. The task will be one of education, development, formation.

It may be that, before its first century of life is complete, the Diocese of Duluth will reap in rich abundance the full fruits of the seeds of Catholicism planted in the pine forests of northern Minnesota 300 years ago.

St. Scholastica's Priory

RELIGIOUS IN THE DIOCESE OF DULUTH _____

Benedictine Fathers (St. John's Abbey)
Congregation of the Missionaries of the
   Holy Family
Conventual Franciscan Fathers
Crosier Fathers
Oblate Fathers (Central Province)

Pious Society of the Missionaries of
   St. Charles

——————————

Benedictine Sisters of Pontifical Jurisdiction (St. Scholastica's Priory)
Carmelite Sisters of Corpus Christi

Dominican Sisters of the Third Order of
   St. Dominic
Sisters of the Holy Names of Jesus and
   Mary
Sisters of St. Joseph of the Third Order
   of St. Francis

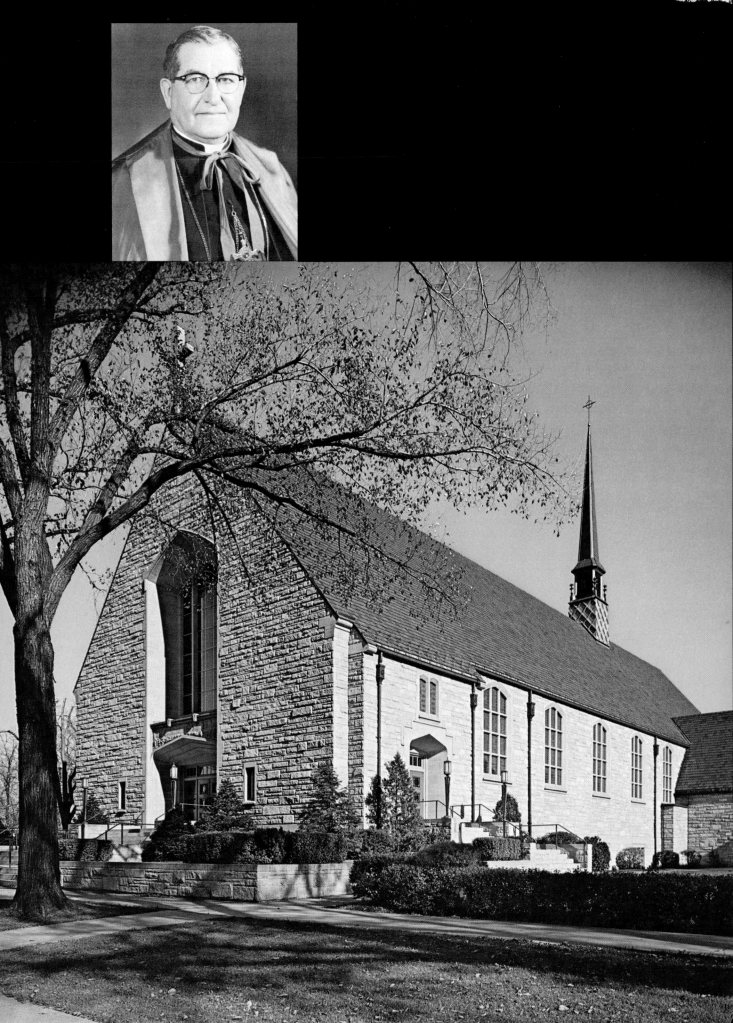

DIOCESE OF WINONA

by Brother J. Robert, F.S.C.

NATURE PROVIDES the means for its own conquest. The rivers have been the routes by which the interior of our country has opened itself to explorers, trappers and settlers. It has been chiefly by the rivers that the wilderness has been penetrated. Quite naturally, then, it has been on our rivers and along their shores that the first missionaries to the Midwest raised the cross of Christ. Today the cathedral churches of five of Minnesota's six dioceses are located on rivers. Three of them are on the great Mississippi. The sixth is found upon the shores of one of the Great Lakes, well known to trappers and missionaries who followed the St. Lawrence River into the northern wilderness.

It was out of the heart of French power on the St. Lawrence that came the first missionaries to the upper Mississippi Valley. The first of these, and believed to be the first white man to have come to this area, was the Belgian Recollect, Father Louis Hennepin. Along with two companions he was captured by a band of Sioux while ascending the Mississippi in April, 1680, and taken to the Indian village on the shore of Mille Lacs Lake. His movements with his captors brought him into the region of Lake Pepin, and thus he became the first priest associated in any way with the territory of the present Diocese of Winona. Six years later Nicholas Perrot, following orders to establish a trading post among the Sioux on the upper Mississippi, built Fort Antoine on the eastern shore of Lake Pepin. In his company was Father Joseph Marest, S.J., who, considering that he was with Perrot for at least three years (1686-1689), undoubtedly said mass in this region.

France's rivalry with Great Britain in North America lay behind the erection in September,

1727, of Fort Beauharnois at Point au Sable on the west side of Lake Pepin. Named after the governor of New France, intended as a trading post in a rich fur area, it was also to be a center for missionary activity. Thus within its walls was erected the Chapel of St. Michael the Archangel, and here, on November 4, 1727, was offered the first mass in Minnesota of which there is historical record. The commission by Governor Beauharnois to erect the fort had specified that two missionaries should accompany the expedition; these were Fathers Michael Guignas and Nicholas de Gonner, both Jesuits. Both of them returned to Canada in 1728 but Father Guignas came west again in the summer of 1731 to continue his missionary activities. In view of the fact that the site of Fort Beauharnois lies just beyond the northern boundary of the Diocese of Winona, there is excellent reason for considering the northeastern section of the diocese as the first scene of extended missionary activity within its present limits.

Time, diplomacy and the fortunes of war brought the upper Mississippi Valley into the possession of the United States. In 1819 our country began the erection of Fort Snelling at the confluence of the Minnesota and Mississippi rivers to guard its northwestern frontier. The presence of a government fort at the junction of the two most important rivers in Minnesota led to the establishment there in 1820 of St. Peter (renamed Mendota in 1837), a center of commercial life and an important point in the fur trade. Located across the Minnesota River from Fort Snelling it became the first center on the upper Mississippi with enough Catholics to attract the attention of the bishop within whose jurisdiction it lay, Mathias Loras of Dubuque, and to merit a visit from him in June, 1839. When making his departure, he promised to send a permanent priest to the settlement. This turned out to be Father Lucien Galtier, who arrived in April, 1840. From Mendota he served several posts and missions including Wabasha in the present Diocese of Winona. During his years on the upper Mississippi he was assisted by Father Augustin Ravoux, who also replaced him when he left for Keokuk, Iowa, in May, 1844.

The first mass celebrated in Wabasha by Father Galtier, most probably in 1840, was the first of record in the Diocese of Winona. The record, however, is not too clear. One of his remarks on the distance from Mendota to Wabasha suggests that he probably visited Wabasha only on his trips to and from Dubuque. Wabasha was known at that time as Rocque's Landing, because a French trader, Augustine Rocque, had erected there a trading post along the banks of the Mississippi. It was at either Rocque's home or his post that Father Galtier said his masses for the settlers, most of whom were French.

Father Ravoux, who visited Wabasha probably for the first time in 1843 on a trip to Prairie du Chien, carried on Father Galtier's work. Having labored among the Sioux in the valley of the Minnesota, he was accustomed to traveling great distances to care for souls. So, though his flock was scattered among many places, he managed, beginning in 1845, to visit Wabasha twice a year, at Easter and in the fall, until 1851.

Thus Wabasha became the first area within the Diocese of Winona in which mass was celebrated and the sacraments administered with some measure of regularity. It was the Mississippi which had brought Fathers Hennepin, Marest, Guignas and de Gonner, and it was the same river which brought Fathers Galtier and Ravoux. Along its banks the Diocese of Winona had its first beginning. It is fitting that the cathedral church of the diocese should look out today from those same shores across the waters by which Christ first came to the area over a century ago.

The first settlers in Wabasha, appreciating their first priests and first masses, set an example of great zeal and sacrifice in obtaining their first church. It was also the first church in the diocese. As their first priests came to them by the river, so did even their first church. It was a log chapel and was erected at the northern end of the village. Father Ravoux was largely responsible for it.

These facts have been rather clearly established. The only question seems to be one of date.

Father Ravoux, while working among the Sioux on the Minnesota River, had erected a combination chapel and rectory in 1843 in Little Prairie, not far from Chaska. In 1845 he secured money from Bishop Loras to move it to Shakopee that he might be closer to the Indians whom he wished to convert. He never managed to settle there. In the following year, 1846, hearing that the Indians were talking of burning it, he requested Bishop Loras for permission to move it to St. Paul to replace the smaller building which Father Galtier

Site of first chapel in diocese, Wabasha

had erected there in 1841. Because the east bank of the Mississippi was then under the jurisdiction of Bishop John Martin Henni of Milwaukee, Bishop Loras suggested that the structure be taken instead to Wabasha. Accordingly Father Ravoux and four Wabasha pioneers dismantled the cabin and in November, 1846, floated its logs by way of the Minnesota and Mississippi rivers to Wabasha where they were reassembled into Wabasha's first church, ready for use in the spring of 1847. Other accounts give the year of removal as 1850, 1851, or 1852, and Bishop Cretin rather than Bishop Loras is responsible for the choice of Wabasha. A point which lends support to the earlier date is that in 1847 Father Ravoux was obliged to build an addition to the original St. Paul Chapel which, because of the growth of St. Paul, had become much too small. Yet even should the latest year ultimately be established as the correct date, Wabasha's little church would remain the first in the diocese.

Wabasha's log church soon ceased to be adequate, for in the 1850's Wabasha enjoyed a rapid growth. Wabasha's growth was part of the growth that was taking place in the territory as a whole.

On March 3, 1849, Congress set up the Territory of Minnesota. Previously the desire for public land had brought thousands of settlers into Iowa. Thousands more were moving toward Minnesota. Many of these were native-born Americans, but many too were immigrants—Irish fleeing the famine at home; Germans dissatisfied with political developments in the Fatherland; Swedes who had heard of the glories of Minnesota; Norwegians brought to America by colonizers; and Canadians who came for many reasons. A generous estimate of the population in 1849, one used at the time in seeking territorial status, is four thousand. By 1852 the figure had jumped to twenty thousand; by 1855 it was estimated at forty thousand and in 1856 at one hundred thousand. A census taken in 1857 on the eve of statehood gave 150,092. The decennial census of 1860 listed 172,023.

In so many ways the growth of the Church in Minnesota in the 1850's paralleled the growth of the Territory. The creation of the Territory was followed in May of the same year by the Seventh Provincial Council of Baltimore. Upon the urging of Bishop John Hughes of New York, the Council petitioned Pope Pius IX for the appointment of a bishop for the new Territory. The Holy See acquiesced, and on July 19, 1850, erected the Diocese of St. Paul to be coterminous with the Territory of Minnesota. On July 23, 1850, it named Reverend Joseph Cretin, then vicar-general of the Diocese of Dubuque, to be the first bishop. He arrived in St. Paul on July 2, 1851.

He learned that there were about two thousand Catholics in his diocese. He was also to discover that the increase in the number of Catholics was far too rapid for the meager facilities of the diocese and that meeting the need for both institutions and priests would challenge him during the years of his administration. They coincided with the boom of the fifties. In 1855 he wrote to his sister that more than twenty thousand Catholics had come into the diocese and "next year it will be doubled." Since the majority of these arrivals in Minnesota settled in the southeastern part of the territory and since so many of them were Catholics, it was in the 1850's that several of the parishes that were to be later included within the Diocese of Winona were established.

Mankato and Vicinity

"The mecca attracting most immigrants (in the 1850's) was the Minnesota River Valley. The fertile lands bordering the stream were rapidly engulfed by farms or towns—Shakopee, Le Sueur, Mankato—all little hamlets with a few log cabins." It was in Mankato that the second church in the diocese was established. This site is at the big bend of the Minnesota River close to where it is joined by the Blue Earth. To this site came the first settlers in the spring of 1852, and there they founded the town. Others came almost upon their heels and among these early arrivals were the first Catholics. In the following year another half-dozen Catholics came, including Clements Kron who opened the first hotel in Mankato.

In 1854 there arrived a group of German Catholics from St. Charles, Missouri. They had heard of the wonderful opportunities for settlers in Minnesota and had sent one of their own, Anton Ilg, to look over the territory and to find a suitable spot in which they might locate. Ilg had gone to Bishop Cretin for advice, but not wishing to exercise undue influence, the bishop mentioned Mankato, St. Cloud and Atchison, Kansas, as possible sites. Ilg visited St. Cloud but, not liking it, returned to St. Paul. There he gathered some acquaintances made on the boat coming up the river from St. Louis and with them pushed south to Mankato. They found only five block (log) houses, but the land looked good so his companions decided to remain while Ilg went to Atchison. He soon returned to St. Charles where his report decided five families and two single men to migrate to Mankato.

They found no conveniences to brighten their spirits at the end of their journey. The settlement then had five houses, a hotel, the "Mankato House" and a shop. Yet only two months later, December 30, 1854, fourteen Catholic men met at Kron's hotel to plan a church. They chose the site occupied today by the church of Saints Peter and Paul. It was a city block in size. P. R. Johnson, one of the founders of Mankato, donated half the land. Michael Hund, one of the St. Charles group, put up two hundred dollars to buy the other half on condition that he be paid back later.

It was also Michael Hund who on January 1, 1855, presented a log house on his claim for use as a church until the one planned should be built. This little structure, 16 feet by 24 feet, was the first Catholic church in Mankato, the first in Blue Earth County, and the second in the present

First Catholic church in Mankato, 1855, left background; second church, 1856, rear section of stone building

Diocese of Winona. It was to this little church that Bishop Cretin came on June 23, 1855. There he heard confessions and on the following morning, Sunday, June 24, celebrated the first public mass in Blue Earth County. That afternoon he baptized eleven children. He slept overnight in the blockhouse church and, after an early mass on Monday morning, he departed.

During his visit he contributed twenty dollars toward the new church. This provided inspiration, for on July 2, 1855, a subscription list for the church was begun. Construction started twenty days later. But time was scarce for struggling new settlers, and money was not more plentiful; so the building of the church was a slow process. It was not used until the closing services of the first parish mission on September 29, 1856, and it was not until 1857 that the doors, windows, floors and plastering were completed.

In the meantime the Catholic population of Mankato continued to grow. Though lacking a church, they did at times enjoy having mass and the sacraments. In 1855, the Winnebago Indians had been moved from Long Prairie to a new reservation in Blue Earth County. With them was Father Francis de Vivaldi, who had come to America with Bishop Cretin when the latter returned from France in 1851. The Agency was located twelve miles from Mankato. From the Agency Father de Vivaldi occasionally came to say mass in the log chapel. Even after Mankato received a pastor, his duties elsewhere were so heavy at first that he could say mass in Mankato on only one Sunday of each month. On the other Sundays, many parishioners drove or walked to the Winnebago Agency as they had done before their pastor arrived.

During his visit in June, 1855, Bishop Cretin had promised the Mankato Catholics a resident priest. He turned out to be Father Valentine Sommereisen, who arrived on March 16, 1856, only eight days after he had been ordained by Bishop Cretin. He thus became not only the first resident pastor in Mankato, but also the first resident pastor in the Diocese of Winona. A straightforward man, he was likewise a man of great endurance. This was necessary since in addition to caring for the Catholics in Mankato, he cared also for those in thirty-six other places in fourteen different counties. Many of these stations were at sites now within the diocese, so it is not uncommon to read in parish histories that Father Sommereisen said the first mass offered within their boundaries. In Mankato he lived and said mass in the blockhouse church. In June, 1856, it was moved to the church property where the new stone church was being built. On this occasion a kitchen was added to the log chapel, and even after it ceased to be used as a church he continued to live in it.

Mankato enjoyed a steady growth. In 1860 its population was over one thousand. Many of these people were good, zealous Catholics drawn by the existence of a church and a resident priest. By 1859 the stone church had become too small. Additions were started and completed in 1862.

In that latter year Mankato came spectacularly to the attention of both the state and the nation, for there, on December 26, thirty-eight Indians who had been convicted for their part in the Sioux Uprising of the previous August were executed. These Sioux had their choice of very

Execution of Sioux Indians at Mankato

capable and well-known Protestant clergymen or of Father Ravoux, who had once been a missionary among the Sioux. Ultimately thirty-three of the thirty-eight came to Father Ravoux. From December 22 to 25 he instructed them in the faith. On Christmas morning three of the thirty-eight, half-breeds under twenty, made their first communion. In the afternoon, at four o'clock, Father Ravoux with the help of Father Sommereisen baptized the other thirty. On the morning of the twenty-sixth, Father Ravoux said mass for them. Later he walked to the scaffold with them, remaining there until the execution was completed. His report states they went courageously to their deaths. Their names were entered in the baptismal register of the Mankato parish.

The people of Mankato soon felt the need of a Catholic school. Following a fruitless attempt in 1864 by a lay member of the School Committee to secure the School Sisters of Notre Dame, Father Sommereisen went to Milwaukee in 1865. He was successful, and on September 3 of that same year three Notre Dames and one candidate arrived in Mankato. The school they opened that same month, under the most trying conditions, is the oldest parochial school in southern Minnesota and the oldest in the present Diocese of Winona.

Father Sommereisen's pastorate ended in June of 1870 when he left to settle personal affairs in his native Alsace. It was an unplanned termination, for in Europe he was caught up in the Franco-Prussian War and was unable to return

to the United States until June, 1871. During his absence, expected to last only a few weeks, Father Anthony Holzer took care of the parish. Because Father Sommereisen did not return to his post within a reasonable time Bishop Grace appointed the second pastor of the parish, Father Augustine Wirth, O.S.B. He took jurisdiction on January 1, 1871. After his return Father Sommereisen spent a short time in Mankato before leaving to take charge of a new parish being formed in Yankton, South Dakota.

A new church which had been commenced in 1869 was completed under Father Wirth and dedicated by Bishop Grace on November 23, 1873. Until this date the parish had been St. Philip's. The dedication, however, was to Saints Peter and Paul, the name which the church bears today.

Father Wirth learned from experience that the duties of the pastor in Mankato were too numerous for one man. He recommended that the parish be given to the care of a religious order. It was in compliance with this recommendation that the Jesuits took over the parish. This they did on January 27, 1874, under Father Peter Schnitzler as pastor. They also cared for several missions, as well as places without priests along the railroad from Mankato to the Iowa border.

The foundation of the Mankato parish had fallen in pioneer times in the state of Minnesota. Many facets of its establishment are found in the histories of other parishes established in the fifties and sixties—the foreign origins of the great majority of the first parishioners, their modes of travel to the sites on which they settled, their efforts to secure resident pastors and to build the first churches and their occasional problems arising out of different ethnic backgrounds.

Winona Development

Winona, however, had something different about it. Perhaps this was because Winona was more completely a river town than Mankato. People seemed to arrive in Mankato as often by wagon and stagecoach as by steamboat, though they came down the valley of the Minnesota. Arrivals in Winona were chiefly by boat, though some came by stage. Departures however were practically all by wagon. More people came to Winona than to Mankato in the 1850's, but more people pushed on from Winona than from Mankato, for Winona was the gateway to the rich land of southern Minnesota. It was the first stop in the Territory for steamboats coming upriver, and it was a major stop for the stages that made their way up from La Crosse. Later on it became the eastern terminal for the railroad which finally penetrated the prairie lands in the western part of the state and of the diocese. Yet, it was more than a gateway. It was more than what it later became, viz., an outlet for the goods of the interior. It was a river town in its own right.

Founded in 1851, its growth at first was comparatively slow. Among the reasons which have been given for its slow start were the presence of the Sioux until 1853 and the general unattractiveness of the sandy prairie. Perhaps it did mean something that Fort Snelling provided protection against Indians in the St. Paul region and that Fort Ridgely, established in 1853, seemed adequate protection in the Minnesota River Valley. In any case, the latter valley proved far more attractive to settlers during the early fifties than did Winona.

Often overlooked is the fact that St. Paul, especially after 1851, was identified by potential settlers as the central spot in Minnesota Territory. This was due to publicity, some of it no more planned than letters to people "back home," but much of it was the result of intentional and organized effort. Some of it was the work of

Winona, looking east, 1870's

Bishop Mathias Loras in Dubuque and Bishop Joseph Cretin in St. Paul.

As far back as 1842 these two men had considered ways to advance the Church in the upper Mississippi Valley. They decided that a plan should be devised to attract immigrants to the lands west of the Mississippi and that in the area of St. Paul a new diocese should be erected. It seemed providential that the area of the new Territory of Minnesota was made a new diocese (July, 1850), and Father Cretin was appointed its first bishop. He proceeded to work on a plan similar to that which he and Bishop Loras had once worked out, but he soon discovered that the earlier work of Bishop Loras was bringing so many Catholics to his diocese each day that the Church in the Territory grew more rapidly than it did in Iowa.

In 1853 he began his own efforts to attract settlers with announcements in the *Freeman's Journal* (New York) that the soil, water, forests and climate in Minnesota made a happy combination and that some of the outlying settlements could count on the services of a priest. He wrote in March, 1855, that he expected the Catholic population to double in the next six months. Twelve months later he announced that it had tripled. At times half of the immigrants coming into the Territory were Catholics. When he died there were over fifty thousand of them in his diocese.

Inevitably some of this influx poured into the southernmost part of the Territory. Several developments attracted them. In 1853 the Sioux departed from the site of Winona. In early 1854 a railroad reached Rock Island, Illinois, a very important event since the eastern seaboard and the Mississippi Valley were now connected by rail. The occasion brought twelve hundred guests to St. Paul—by steamboat from Rock Island—and the press of the country accorded it wide coverage, giving much praise to the region of the excursion as well as to its accessibility. This had exciting consequences. In 1855, one-hundred steamboats arrived in St. Paul. The increase in population, which Bishop Cretin reported, is more understandable when we also read that one river line alone brought to St. Paul in the summer of 1855 more than thirty thousand people. In 1857 almost three hundred steamboats arrived at St. Paul and over one thousand in 1858.

Not every steamboat traveler went to St. Paul.

Steamboats at Winona levee

For we are told that the population of Winona estimated at eight hundred in December, 1855, increased to three thousand by December, 1856. In 1854 the former Sioux lands in the Territory had been opened to pre-emption of unsurveyed tracts. In 1855 land offices were opened in Winona and in nearby Brownsville. Although all who came to Winona in 1856 did not remain, that year was the first boom year in Winona's history. The depression of 1857 brought a serious decline, but by 1860, the population was back up to 2,443.

Many arrivals moved on into the interior. This penetration was aided by a network of roads which the territory created in this area, especially in the second half of the 1850's. Stagecoaches used these roads to carry both passengers and mail. (The J. C. Burbank Company ultimately built up a stage system covering 1,300 miles and pony express routes running to 300 miles.) In addition to a line from Winona to La Crosse, one operated from Winona to Chatfield (located on the road from St. Paul to Iowa), and another to the Minnesota River.

The majority of the immigrants to the interior traveled in ordinary wagons pulled often enough by oxen. One road surveyor on a road in 1854 counted thirty wagonloads of Norwegians on their way to Mankato, while on some occasions he counted two hundred wagons "on the road at the same time." There is evidence that as many as three hundred immigrant wagons passed through St. Charles on one day. Some settlers just walked. We read, for instance, that in 1858 Patrick Ryan and his wife, Johanna, walked with their small son from Read's Landing twenty miles into the interior to Hyde Park (where other Catholics were already gathered forming what later became St. Patrick's parish in West Albany). In 1859 Hugh Leonard, his wife Katherine and three children took that same long walk. In some instances the husband went on alone, returning as soon as possible with a wagon and oxen to pick up his family at Read's Landing. By 1855 there was a ferry operating across the Zumbro River on the road from Lake City to Rochester. By 1858 the traffic had increased so much that a hotel was opened near the ferry, followed very soon after by a shoe shop and a blacksmith shop.

Over seventy per cent of the states' population in 1860 was native-born American. Of the foreign born, the Germans and the Irish composed fifty-three per cent, and it was chiefly these who provided the people of the pioneer parishes in the diocese. We have already seen that Bishop Cretin

Local stage coach

visited Mankato in 1855. Either on this or another trip, he also visited Brownsville, Caledonia, Rushford, Chatfield, Winona and Buckley's Settlement. On such visits he customarily heard confessions, administered baptism and confirmation and offered mass. In Brownsville he refused to say mass in a room which was also used as a saloon, but did offer it in the home of a non-Catholic who acceded to his request to do so.

In Winona the first mass of record was said by Bishop Cretin in the home of Mr. and Mrs. Urell.

Immigrants moving west

Some writers state that he organized the Catholics there into a parish and that he appointed as pastor Father Michael Prendergast. However, the latter did not become a resident pastor until July, 1858. It appears that shortly after his visit the bishop gave Winona as a mission to the charge of Father Thomas Murray of Stillwater. In August of 1856, Father Murray purchased a site for the church and before the year was over had begun its construction. It was completed in the following year by Father Anatole Oster. This two-story frame structure, dedicated to St. Thomas the Apostle, was the third church erected in the present Diocese of Winona.

The church was located in what was then the southwestern part of the city because Father Murray deemed it the spot likely to be one day

the city's center. Father Prendergast did not wait for time to prove Father Murray right or wrong. But shortly after he became pastor in July, 1858, he purchased three lots on the corner of Center and Wabasha Streets, and there he relocated the frame church. During the pastorate of Father William Lette, April, 1864, to June, 1868, the foundation of the brick successor to the frame church was laid. The major portion of the structure was completed under his successor, Father Alois Plut, who was pastor until June, 1871. It was finished in 1872 under Father Joseph Cotter. This second church was, after 1889, the cathedral of the diocese until the present cathedral was built and dedicated to the Sacred Heart in 1952.

None of the pastors in the pioneer parishes of the diocese enjoyed much ease or bodily comfort. This was true of Father Prendergast and his successors. Until 1862 he was alone in taking care of the Catholics, not only in the city, but also in the County of Winona as well as those in Olmstead, Houston, Fillmore, Steele, and Mower counties. His two predecessors had cared for Wabasha County, but his duties there were short-lived since in October, 1858, Father Ravoux, administrator of the Diocese of St. Paul after the death of Bishop Cretin in 1857, appointed Father Felix Tissot as the first resident pastor of Wabasha. Father Tissot thus became the third resident pastor in the Diocese of Winona.

By the close of this very important decade (1850's) the Church in southern Minnesota had made its first foundations. It had seen established not only the first three permanent parishes of the diocese but the beginnings of others as well. Something of that growth may be caught from the following interesting facts.

Expansion Into New Areas

Father Tissot's appointment reflected the large number of Catholics, chiefly Irish and German, who had moved into Wabasha and Goodview counties during the decade. The city of Wabasha grew very rapidly. It received its postoffice in 1853, was platted in 1854 and incorporated in 1858. On October 13, 1859, Bishop Grace confirmed the first class in what Father Tissot had intended to be the first church actually built for that purpose. Deeming it too far from the center of the city, Bishop Grace refused to bless it, but a new one was ready and blessed in 1862.

In 1855 the first Catholics moved up the valley of the Zumbro to the site of West Albany where the parish of St. Patrick was later to be organized. In 1856 the first child born in West Albany was born to Catholic parents. In 1857 a road was run from Read's Landing to West Albany to Mazzeppa. In 1859 West Albany was platted and the plat recorded. The Catholics increased steadily, and the records at Wabasha preserve their requests for the services of a priest. The baptisms Father Tissot had administered from 1859 to 1864 increased from eighty-eight to one hundred ninety-four, or one hundred twenty per cent. Similar increases occurred in many other settlements.

Brownsville, on the military road leading south from Winona, was visited occasionally by Father Ravoux and had enough Catholics in 1856 to attract a visit from Bishop Cretin. While it is definite that Brownsville had a church in 1861, there is some opinion that it also had a small church in the 1850's.

Caledonia's St. John Baptist has been called the pioneer parish in Houston County. The concentration of Catholics there drew a visit from Bishop Cretin in the fall of 1856 when, it is written, "he organized a parish and blessed the cemetery." Recollections of pioneers in the parish mentioned "a little wooden building that was used for a meeting place and a church." It is rather definite that Father Prendergast came periodically from Winona and "celebrated Mass in private houses until a temporary place of worship was erected." We can be sure of these visitations after 1858. Caledonia received a new pastor in 1861 in the person of Father Edward Essing who built a large frame structure as a church in 1864.

The year 1856 marked several other beginnings. In that year Father William Tappert, pastor of St. Mary's parish in La Crosse, said the first mass in the present Crucifixion parish in La Crescent. He offered it in a small log schoolhouse located about five miles from the present church. This area, know then as Manton, fell to the care of Father Prendergast when he took over in Winona, and in 1858 he built the first church, a frame building 20 by 40 feet. Mass was not said there regularly every Sunday, however, and for a number of years the people had to travel to La Crosse or down to the chapel of the convent school in Hokah.

Near to Winona is the village of Rollingstone. By 1856 it had a large percentage of Catholics, and in 1857 Father Matthew Sturemberg, O.S.B., said the first mass in the home of Peter Stoos. In 1862 the first church, a frame building, was erected on the present church property. The cornerstone of the present church was blessed by Bishop Grace in 1869.

South and somewhat east of Rochester was Buckley's Settlement, located on the "Dubuque Road" running between that city and St. Paul. The first mass was celebrated there in the home of Michael Buckley in 1855. Bishop Cretin visited it, if not early enough to say that first mass, then in 1856. Father Prendergast cared for it between 1857 and 1864. In 1859 he directed the building of the church, which slightly remodeled and enlarged, is still the parish church of Simpson—St. Bridget's. In 1865 it became a mission of St. John's, Rochester.

West of Rochester was Owatonna. Once the hunting ground of the Wahpekute Sioux, the land attracted the attention of early settlers and in 1854 the village of Owatonna was established. It was located where the trail from Winona to St. Peter was crossed by the road from St. Paul and Faribault to Iowa. Perhaps that is some explanation of why the Catholic families, which began to arrive in 1856, were cared for by Father George Keller, made pastor of Faribault in the spring of 1858 and whose missions extended from there south to the state line. The first settlers were mostly Irish, but the Germans and Bohemians were not far behind them. It was in the house of Joseph Kiesel, a German tailor, that Father Keller said his first mass in Owatonna. We may assume this was before the end of the 1850's, but we know that he served Owatonna during much of the 1860's, always, however, residing in Faribault.

Beyond Owatonna, in Waseca County, another group of Irish settled in the years from 1855 to 1857. This settlement Father Keller also visited after his appointment to Faribault, saying his masses in the homes of Andrew Lynch and M. P. Fitzgerald. In 1860 they built their first church under his driving energy. He served it until 1866. One of the first settlers, John McCarthy, named it the Nativity of St. Mary. It was the first church in Waseca County.

Among the places which fell under Father

Keller's care was Germania, or as it was known after 1880, Johnsburg. Catholic settlers had come into the area as early as 1855 and the heavy preponderance of Germans among them, although there were also some Irish, gave the town its name. Located in Adams Township, it was the first Catholic center in Mower County, and the oak log church built there in 1859 was the first Catholic church in that county. It was named in honor of St. John the Baptist. In view of the fact that the Johnsburg parish originally served the Meyer and Staceyville area in Northern Iowa and in view of the relatively early date at which the settlers arrived in Minnesota, it is probable that they were among those known to have come into Minnesota from Iowa. In any case, Father Keller said mass for them in the little 18 by 28 foot log church until some time in the 1860's.

In 1856 Catholic settlers were moving into the sites of two other parishes—Danville and Madelia. Their growth was relatively slow. Danville, about three miles northeast of Minnesota Lake, where the parish was ultimately centered and named St. John the Baptist, did not have its own church until 1865. Father Sommereisen came down from Mankato to say mass there but it is probable that he visited the settlement and said mass in some private homes before the first frame church was built.

The records for Madelia show that it was also in 1856 that the first Catholic families arrived there. Although others came after them, by 1863 there were only about thirty Catholics in the settlement, and it was not until October of that year that Father Sommereisen offered mass—in the home of Mr. Francis Russell—for the first time within the confines of the parish. Accounts indicate that Lake Crystal, only twelve miles closer than Madelia to Father Sommereisen's residence in Mankato, was being cared for by him as early as 1856. If so, it would seem that it was not the distance from a priest that slowed Catholic growth in early Madelia. It became an important point in the Sioux Uprising of 1862. In that year a substantial blockhouse was erected there by a force under Judge Charles E. Flandrau, leader of New Ulm's second repulse of the Sioux and to whom Governor Ramsey had given command of the southwestern frontier from New Ulm to the Iowa line. At the end of 1862 there was one company of the Minnesota Seventh

Regiment at Madelia, one at Fairmont, one at Winnebago City, one at South Bend, one at the Agency and four at Mankato which was also the regimental headquarters. As late as July, 1865, there were still garrisons at Madelia and Fairmont. Such unsettled conditions may have contributed to delaying the construction of the first church in Madelia until 1872.

Mower County was included among those counties assigned to Father Prendergast's care. It was recorded that he said his first mass in the Austin area on November 2, 1857, in the home of Thomas Gibson, and returned in the following year to hold services in the home of Aloysius Brown. It was on this second trip, in 1858, that he said the first mass in Grand Meadow, which lay on the road from Austin to Winona. In view of the fact that Father Keller arrived in Faribault in 1858, that Austin is only half as far from Faribault as from Winona and that Father Keller soon began caring for Germania, south of Austin, it was but natural that he would also hold services in Austin. This he did every two months during the years 1861 to 1865. He also said mass periodically in Grand Meadow during the same years.

Before the close of the 1850's, Father Prendergast acquired the care of Freeburgh, located in Houston County. It is not far from Caledonia and Brownsville, both of which Bishop Cretin had visited in 1856. (Brownsville had been important enough as a center of settlement in 1855 to be made the site of a land office.) Father Prendergast began calling at Freeburgh in 1859. A few years later, probably in 1863, his duties there were taken over by Father Francis X. Neubrand, who had begun caring for Brownsville in 1861.

And so came the end of the 1850's. The opening of the 60's found three residential parishes: Wabasha, Mankato and Winona. Around each of them was a cluster of missions and stations, some of them with their small log or frame churches. Cutting southward across the western portion of this triangle was a line of missions roughly centered along the territorial road from Faribault to Iowa. In none of these first parishes had the beginnings been made without great effort and sacrifice on the part of both people and (the few) priests. It has been stated that the 1850's imparted to Minnesota the spirit and "air" which still prevades the traditions and institutions of the state. So too the spirit of sacrifice and of affection for the church exhibited by the pioneer settlers and their priests in the 1850's became part of the inheritance bequeathed by those first parishes to the Diocese of Winona.

During the 1860's the Irish and the Germans were joined by an increasing number of Bohemians and Poles in settling places within the diocese. Most of these moved into the locations near residential parishes, especially the ones established in the 1850's, although a large group of Bohemians settled in Owatonna. During the 1860's Father Sommereisen's name occurs often as responsible for helping settlers erect new churches in the missions served from Mankato. Father John McDermott, assigned to Austin in 1866, took over many of the missions or stations which had been in the care of Father Keller and also helped build additional churches. Considering the drain of the Civil War on the manhood of the state, it is not surprising that of the thirty or so churches built during the decade, only eight were erected between 1860 and 1865. Of these, six were in places served from Winona or Wabasha. In the central section St. Clair (Immaculate Conception) apparently replaced the Winnebago Agency after Chief Good Thunder and many of his Winnebagoes were removed from their reservation in 1863. It was cared for from Mankato.

It would have taken exceptionally brave settlers to go beyond the Mankato area after the Sioux Uprising in the summer of 1862. But while at first it looked as if this war would drive out all whites west of the posts erected along the line through the south central section of the state, by 1865 it was the Indians who had been driven out of southwestern Minnesota. Thus new rich farmlands awaited the thousands of settlers eager to push westward when the Civil War ended. Occupation of the far western portion of the diocese, however, had to wait until the seventies and upon the extension of the railroad into that area. Thus, while so many of the new settlers in the last half of the sixties were Catholics that twenty-two churches were erected, none of these churches was located west of Blue Earth.

A line drawn from Mankato south through Blue Earth would rather evenly bisect the area of the diocese. In the 1870's the western half was to see a great influx of settlers, many of them Catholics, so that by 1880 approximately fifty per cent of the missions and stations of the diocese were located in that area. However, of the new (first) churches erected during that decade only five per cent were erected in the west and seventeen per cent of the newly appointed resident pastors were in the west. Thus, one may see that the parishes in the eastern section were still enjoying most of the growth, although a substantial portion of it was taking place close to the Mankato-Blue Earth line.

Population throughout the state increased during the seventies at a more rapid rate than in the sixties in spite of the explosive growth in the five years following the Civil War. In 1880 it stood at 780,733 of whom about thirty per cent were foreign-born. By 1870 the Scandinavian group had moved ahead of the Germans and continued to do so in the succeeding decade. Nevertheless, the German increase remained notable. The rate of Irish increase fell off. These two groups were still providing most of the parishioners in the diocese at the end of the 1870's. The next two groups were the Bohemians and Poles (the latter numbering only 2,218).

Railroads and Colonization

Due largely to the availability of transportation, the majority of the first settlers had chosen to live in the southeastern part. This included the eastern part of the Winona diocese. Down until 1875 the center of wheat growing in Minnesota had been the eight southeastern counties, but after this date the western counties took the lead. It was not until 1870 that the Winona and St. Peter Railroad reached St. Peter, and it was not until after 1872 that the railroads could bring settlers out to occupy the lands of the western counties. Yet, by 1880 the tide of population had passed into Dakota and southwestern Minnesota was mentioned less frequently in publicity from the railroad offices. By 1880 the frontier had left Minnesota, and by 1885 the southwestern triangle of the state was filled with settlers.

Inducements to settle in Minnesota came from the state itself, from the railroads with large tracts of land to dispose of and from Bishop Ireland's Catholic Colonization Bureau. How many people came into the state in the seventies and eighties as a result of such publicity is not easy to determine. But records of the Minnesota

Avoca from the lake

State Board of Immigration show that forty thousand immigrants entered the state in eight months of 1879 alone. The estimated number of Catholic families who settled in the western counties between 1875 and 1885 as a result of Bishop Ireland's colonization efforts is four thousand.

His method was to have himself made the agent of several (ultimately five) of the railroads running through the southwestern counties. His contracts with the railroads specified certain of their lands would be made available for sale either through himself or through persons appointed by him. Some of these latter were priests who were at the same time appointed resident pastors of the same areas in which they were distributing the railroad lands. By publicity of various kinds he urged Catholics from the eastern states and Europe to settle in these several colonies. Altogether he became responsible for 379,000 acres of railroad land of which forty-four per cent lay within the present Diocese of Winona. On these lands ten Catholic settlements were developed, one-half of them—Adrian, Avoca,

Currie, Fulda, and Iona—being in this diocese.

The stories of one or two of these colonies make clear their contribution to the growth of the Church in the western counties in the late seventies. In 1877 Bishop Ireland contracted with the St. Paul and the Sioux City Railroad for seventy thousand acres of its lands in Nobles County. Within it was the village of Adrian, consisting of three houses and a railroad station. It was here that Bishop Ireland established Father Christian Knauf as official agent for the colony and as a resident pastor. Upon his arrival in Adrian in September, 1877, he found not a single Catholic. Yet, within seven months it was necessary to secure thirty-five thousand additional acres of land to care for the Catholic settlers who poured in. By May, 1880, only two farms were yet unsold. And two years later Father Knauf recorded that two hundred fifty Catholic families were living in the colony.

Avoca had a similarly rapid growth. In April, 1878, Bishop Ireland again contracted with the St. Paul and Sioux City, this time in Murray

County, for 52,000 acres. He appointed Father Charles Koeberl as his agent and as resident pastor. Father Koeberl platted the town and had a large immigrant house erected. By the end of the year ten thousand acres had been sold. Within two years thirty thousand acres had been sold. By this time two other nearby colonies, Iona and Fulda, the "offspring" of Avoca, had been started and Father Koeberl arranged for churches to be built there.

Meanwhile he had been attending to the needs of his own parish. On August 4, 1878, he said his first public mass in the Avoca House. This was also a private home. So, when it became possible, he secured half the space of the Immigrant House for use as a chapel. It was first used for the purpose on Easter Sunday, April 14, 1879. By 1881 this building was no longer needed for its original purpose and became the church of the parish. In addition to his own parish, Father Koeberl at first had to take care of some fifteen to twenty stations from Fairmont on the east to Flandreau in the Dakota Territory on the west, but with the arrival of Father Martin McDonnell in Iona as early as 1878, his work was lessened at once, at least in Murray, Nobles and Jackson counties.

Among the nearby settlements which Father Koeberl visited was Currie, at the foot of Lake Shetek. Settlers had come there as early as 1857, but the massacre of fourteen of them in the Sioux Uprising had frightened the others away. New ones came in after the Civil War, but few Catholics appeared among them probably because of the distance of Currie from any priest who might minister to them. With the arrival of Father Koeberl in Avoca in 1878, they were assured of such attention and his records of baptisms administered suggest that he had about a dozen Catholic families to care for there.

In June, 1880, some ten thousand acres of land around Currie were bought by a benevolent and well-to-do Irishman, John Sweetman, on which to settle a number of families suffering from poverty and famine in Ireland. In May, 1881, 191 of his colonists arrived. A second group of sixty-nine arrived in April, 1882. By this time, however, many of the first colonists had left, and Sweetman learned, as did other colonizers, that "assisted immigrants" were poor risks on which to build permanent settlements. He turned his efforts to attracting men possessed with a certain amount of capital and who sought what the western prairies had to offer. In later years he wrote: "As a scheme for helping Irish immigrants to settle on the land in America my work thirty years ago was a failure. *But as establishing a Catholic colony on the prairie it seems to have been a success.*" Currie still reflects his success today.

The western part of the diocese also reflects the efforts and varying success of other colonizers. They brought not only hopeful farmers; they brought Catholic people, people of the type that insisted upon having mass and the sacraments in their lives, but people who were also ready to make the sacrifices necessary to preserve that faith and even to extend it. Bishop Ireland's goal of establishing "self-supporting Catholic parishes in western Minnesota" was certainly fulfilled in respect of those founded within the present Diocese of Winona for they are today all residential parishes.

During the two decades following 1860, the churches in the counties making up the Winona diocese had enjoyed a rapid growth. Measured in terms of parishes, missions and stations, the increase from 1861 to 1880 was about 313 per cent. During the same period the population of the state increased 353 per cent. Insofar as these figures may be compared they suggest that parochial growth and services in the counties of the diocese kept pace with the over-all increase in population. While expansion continued in the 1880's, the rate of parochial institutional growth fell off somewhat and a comparison of statistics for 1880 and 1890 shows that of the churches, missions and stations which made up the diocese in the latter year, almost eighty-six per cent of them were in existence in 1880.

Winona Diocese Established

It was on November 26, 1889, that Pope Leo XIII issued the apostolic constitution erecting the Diocese of Winona and setting its boundaries. It was on the same day that he named Father Joseph B. Cotter, then pastor of St. Thomas church in Winona, as the first bishop. Ordained on May 21, 1871, in St. Paul by Bishop Grace, he was appointed pastor of St. Thomas in the following month. On October 11, 1877, Bishop Grace appointed him dean (vicar-forane) over the dis-

Bishop Joseph B. Cotter

trict including Winona, Rollingstone and St. Charles with a list of duties which indicated an intention to make him the representative of the bishop in a more immediate manner than a pastor usually is. Probably the choice of Father Cotter to be bishop was in part the result of the prominence he had won when, as National President of the Catholic Total Abstinence Union of America in 1885-86, he had delivered seventy-three lectures in the principal cities of the country. Certainly his devotion to this cause kept him a close friend of Archbishop Ireland, "The Apostle of Total Abstinence," and one may suppose that the choice of Father Cotter as Bishop of Winona fulfilled Archbishop Ireland's wishes and gave him great pleasure. It was he who consecrated Bishop Cotter on December 27, 1889, in the cathedral in St. Paul. It was also he who preached the sermon at Bishop Cotter's installation in the Procathedral of St. Thomas on January 5, 1890.

The Diocese of Winona was, according to Archbishop Ireland, "the first subdivision of the Archdiocese of St. Paul." Its territory embraces the twenty southernmost counties of the state, an area of 12,282 square miles extending from the Mississippi River on the east to South Dakota on the west. Under the circumstances Bishop Cotter had to devote time and attention to organizing the administration of the diocese as well as to providing for its continuing growth and the

needs of its people. By 1893 he had created a School Board for the diocese. In 1903 he promulgated "These Statutes and Regulations of the Diocese of Winona for the Good Government of the Temporalities of the Parishes." Within the next three years he divided the diocese into nine deaneries, each of them headed by a vicar-forane.

If the progress in the diocese was reflected by the increase of parishes, the appointment of resident pastors, the creation and disappearance of missions and stations, then the greatest growth from 1890 to 1900 lay east of the line south from Mankato to Iowa. During that decade seventy-one per cent of the missions and stations which were closed were located in the west, the remainder in the east. Of the new parishes, missions and stations, seventy-two per cent were in the east and central sections. It may be noted that the closings reflected local rather than diocesan-wide conditions, and some of them were only temporary. From the western area of the diocese a number of the people who had come there as colonists were leaving for St. Paul and Minneapolis. Difficult conditions there were also reflected in the burdens under which the few schools that existed tried to carry on. Tuition fees were often paid in produce and usually did not meet the expenses. Debts on churches and rectories were still being paid off so that, except at Adrian where the present school was erected in 1895, the other schools opened after 1900. Yet, the overall picture was one of progress. There were fifty per cent more openings than closings. Of the appointments of new residential pastors, thirty-three per cent were in the east, forty per cent in the center and twenty-seven per cent in the west.

In the second decade of his administration, Bishop Cotter set off two entirely new parishes, raised fourteen missions to residential parishes and established eleven new missions. Roughly forty-three per cent of these were in the west, thirty-six per cent in the central section and twenty-one per cent in the east. In the appointment of new residential pastors, only nineteen per cent went to eastern parishes. It would seem that at the time of Bishop Cotter's death parish lines were pretty well set in the eastern section of the diocese but were still being laid out in the central and western counties. By 1909 there had occurred an increase of but fifteen in the total number of parishes, missions and stations since 1889. The big increase came in the number of residential parishes, which in 1889 numbered forty-five, but in 1909 numbered seventy-two. This was made possible by the increase of the number of priests (secular and religious) from forty-nine to ninety-one. Obtaining them was one of the major problems which Bishop Cotter had to meet and which he resolved so well. He gave to his diocese a substantial parochial life and organization.

Institutions Created

In his involvement with these affairs, he did not neglect other matters and institutions which help to enrich any diocese. Not many new schools were founded during the first years of his episcopate, so that in 1900 there were twenty schools, or only one more than in 1890, although the number of children was increasing rapidly. This pressure soon reached the parishes and by the time Bishop Cotter died, nine more schools had been added to make a total of twenty-nine. From 1890 to 1910, the grade school enrollment jumped seventy-seven per cent.

Undoubtedly one of the most important academic foundations in the diocese during his episcopacy was the establishment in 1894 of the Winona Seminary for Ladies by the Sisters of St. Francis of the Congregation of Our Lady of Lourdes. The property they bought included a brick structure which had been opened as St. Mary's Academy in 1885 under the School Sisters of St. Francis of Milwaukee. It had operated as a school only until 1888. In that year it was converted to a hospital under the direction of the Sisters of St. Joseph. In 1890 Bishop Cotter acquired title to it. He in turn sold it in 1894 to the Academy of Our Lady of Lourdes in Rochester. This academy then moved to Winona and by August, 1894, was ready as the Winona Seminary for Ladies to receive its first students. The academy had been chartered by the state legislature to grant academic degrees, so in 1908 a year of college work was added to the Seminary curriculum and a second year in 1909. Three years later the name of the school was changed to the College of St. Teresa. Under this name it has attained prestige at home and abroad. It has been one of the glories of the Diocese of Winona and has sent out graduates who in all walks of life have brought honor to the College and its traditions.

In the very year that Bishop Cotter was consecrated, the same Franciscan Sisters opened St. Mary's Hospital in Rochester. It is known in the great medical and surgical centers of the world, largely because it has been inseparable from the careers and reputations of Doctors William and Charles Mayo. Yet it was Mother Mary Alfred, foundress of the Sisters of St. Francis, who first conceived of a hospital for Rochester and who, in the face of the cautious doubt of Dr. William W. Mayo, promised to erect a hospital if only he would agree to take charge of it. It was opened on September 30, 1889, as much the result of sacrifices on the part of the sisters as of planning by the Mayos.

This cooperation between the sisters and the Doctors Mayo continued through the years that followed. The two surgeons made the hospital their first clinic and worked there exclusively. Fame came quickly and the sisters provided the necessary additions to the building. Bishop Cotter, in 1892, encouraged the sisters to make the first addition. It was completed in 1894. He regarded it as the peculiar privilege of a bishop to look after hospitals, and he continued to manifest a keen interest in St. Mary's, watching with deep satisfaction three more buildings added to it (1898, 1904 and 1908) during his administration. Its reputation has grown with the passing years and the demands for its services continued to increase so that as this is written a new addition is being planned.

Of course it was the sick, not primarily the institutions for them, which concerned Bishop Cotter, so that when he could he arranged for hospitals in other parts of the diocese. In 1897 the Sisters of the Sorrowful Mother opened St. Joseph's Hospital in Mankato. In August, 1898, they received from Bishop Cotter property in Wabasha on which was a private home. This they enlarged and equipped for hospital purposes. St. Elizabeth's, as it was named, could never hope to equal St. Mary's in size, but it outgrew its first building by 1905. In that year a new structure was raised and to it there have been made three additions. Today St. Elizabeth's is a fine, fully equipped, modern hospital.

Bishop Cotter died in Winona on June 28, 1909,

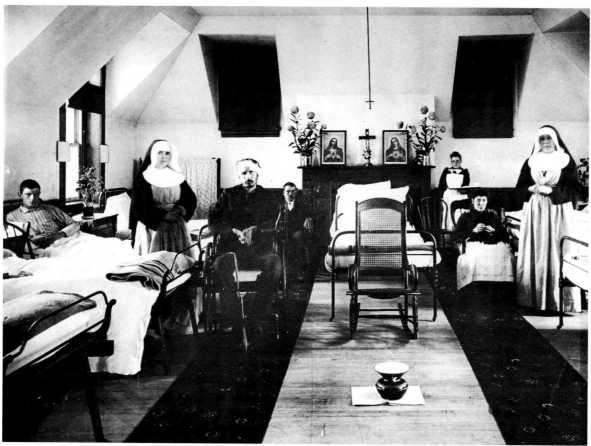

St. Mary's Hospital, Rochester

sincerely mourned not only by his own priests
and people but by the countless others who knew
him. The twenty years of his episcopate were
a period of quiet, steady development. He passed
on to his successor a diocese firmly established,
yet one in which the faith and the courage of
its founding settlers and their missionary priests
still flourished. He was a bond between the pioneers of the diocese and those who were to consolidate and enrich it in the twentieth century.

Progress continued under his successors, but
where the number of parishes was concerned
it was not startling. Under Bishop Cotter the
residential parishes, missions and stations had
increased by fifteen. Since 1910 they have increased by twelve. Under Bishop Cotter the
number of residential parishes increased by
twenty-seven. Since 1910 they have increased
by twenty-eight. But, after all, diocesan sub-

division can proceed profitably only to a certain
point. If, on the other hand, figures of active
diocesan priests are compared, the character
of diocesan progress becomes readily discernible. Under Bishop Cotter they increased by
thirty-seven; since 1910 they have increased by
ninety-two. Approximately one-half of this increase occurred under Bishop Patrick R. Heffron
(1910 to 1927), the other half under Bishop Edward
A. Fitzgerald (1950 to the present). While most
of the priests who became available to Bishop
Heffron were assigned by him to the care of
souls in the new parishes and to provide assistance in the larger parishes, a number of them
were involved in one way or another with education; under Bishop Fitzgerald at least sixty-
five of the active priests—or just about thirty-
three per cent—are engaged full time in teaching.

Education has always enjoyed respect and

93

support in the diocese. The causes have been several but perhaps the first organized diocesan emphasis came from Bishop Heffron. Educated and traveled himself, a onetime teacher—both as a young man in St. Bridget's Parish (Simpson) and later in the St. Paul Seminary— he was convinced that the future of both state and Church in Minnesota depended upon the education of youth. "Bishop Heffron saw the need for Catholic leadership in southern Minnesota, and the mid-continent in general, toward giving life and effectiveness to the Christian and American ideals which, without higher education, may lie dormant in the hearts of men of good will." He conceived of a well-developed educational structure in the diocese from grade school through college. He increased the number of grade schools by eight; meanwhile the number of pupils increased by fifty-one per cent. But the startling development was the appearance by 1928 of twenty-five parochial high schools where before there were none, or at least no record of them. Few of them had over one hundred pupils; in fact the average attendance was only sixty-three.

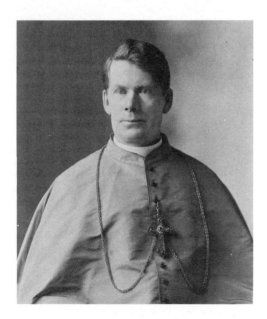

Bishop Patrick R. Heffron

But they did reflect his desire to make secondary education available wherever possible in the diocese as well as his hope that the graduates of these high schools would become students in the two colleges of the diocese. Of course such

operations were often uneconomical, though in the most important sense profitable, and today the number of schools has been appreciably reduced while the average attendance has increased by three hundred per cent.

No sooner had Bishop Heffron been consecrated, May 19, 1910, than he invited the Christian Brothers to open a high school in the diocese. On Thanksgiving Day in 1911 he dedicated that school, naming it after his predecessor. For several years he maintained his office in the brothers' residence.

Even before he had taken charge of the diocese the School Sisters of Notre Dame had been planning to erect in Mankato an academy for girls and a motherhouse for a new province. These sisters had first come to Mankato in September, 1865, and had begun in that year to teach some eighty-seven children in the parish school. In 1867 they had accepted charge of a school built for them two miles northeast of the village of Hokah. Intended as a boarding and day school and even as an orphanage, it never developed into a self-sustaining institution. Only by the sacrifices of the sisters was it kept open until 1904. By 1910 the Notre Dames were operating eight schools in the diocese and numerous others throughout the northwest. In that year, Bishop Cotter granted them the permission which they had ardently sought of him, and by September, 1912, the academy and the motherhouse of the new Northwestern Province were realities.

It would seem that the educational project which was closest to the heart of Bishop Heffron was the erection of what is now St. Mary's College, "an institution destined for the education of boys, a work that should be dear to everyone who has at heart the future welfare of the diocese. *It is a work that I love most dearly and to which I shall devote my best thought and strength.*" He wanted leaders in all walks of life, ecclesiastical and religious as well as lay. Therefore, he also conceived of St. Mary's as an institution "in which may be trained those youths whom God will call to the exalted vocation of the priesthood." Undoubtedly it was this practical expression of concern for priestly vocations which brought to the bishop before he died the pleasure of ordaining a number of boys from the diocese as well as an increase of forty-three, or fifty-two per cent, in the number of diocesan priests.

Priests of Winona diocese on retreat in 1903

1 C. Preis	12 C. Cavanagh	23 F. X. Mueller	34 J. Bartolome	45 R. Hughes
2 J. Schwartz	13 J. Schneider	24 J. N. Pivo	35 G. P. Murphy	46 P. Kiernan
3 F. B. Reichl	14 J. Mangan	25 H. Van der Berg	36 E. Madden	47 F. Freckmann
4 J. Meier	15 M. Wurst	26 A. Hechenberger	37 P. J. Fox	48 N. Schmitz
5 C. J. Knauf	16 W. Griffin	27 M. Borresch	38 D. Lavery	49 Caspar Kögl
6 Bishop Heffron	17 J. Doelle	28 D. Mangan	39 S. J. Condron	50 J. Trior
7 J. Campbell	18 J. Mikolai	29 E. Devlin	40 J. E. Donovan	51 S. Maddock
8 J. Coyne	19 J. A. Cummiskey	30 A. J. Walsh	41 J. Pacholski	52 F. English
9 J. J. Treanor	20 S. M. Sesches	31 M. F. Holper	42 H. Sherlock	53 V. Havlicek
10 W. Riordan	21 L. Gossman	32 S. Schels	43 J. Zahner	54 P. Ryan
11 V Schirr	22 M. O'Connor	33 R. Matousek	44 D. Coleman	

The college, which opened its doors in September, 1913, to boys on the elementary, secondary and college levels, became by 1929 a completely collegiate institution. In 1933 it was transferred to the Brothers of the Christian Schools. In the following year they established their scholasticate (house of studies) on the campus. The College never ceased to provide training for future priests of the diocese, but it was not until July 16, 1948, that Bishop Leo Binz (who had been named apostolic administrator of the diocese in November, 1942, after Bishop Francis Kelly had become incapacitated) formally erected the Immaculate Heart of Mary Seminary on the college campus. Bishop Edward A. Fitzgerald, installed as Ordinary on January 4, 1950, completed the erection of Kelly Hall for the seminarians in March, 1951. By 1963 there had occurred an increase of forty-five per cent in the ranks of active priests of the diocese (not including twenty-three religious priests), and today the largest proportion by far of priests in the diocese have

Bishop Francis M. Kelly

attended St. Mary's College. In 1959 the Congregation of the Sacred Hearts of Jesus and Mary established a seminary on the campus, and in 1961 completed their own residence building. During its half century of existence, St. Mary's College has increased in enrollment over one thousand per cent and in buildings from one to twenty. Its academic and spiritual life have grown apace. The vision and foresight of Bishop Heffron are bearing fruit.

On November 23, 1927, Bishop Heffron died in his home on the campus which he loved. During much of his time as bishop he had cancer of the face. Due to a strong determination, he worked up to the very end developing the program which he had laid out for himself. Before that, however, he needed help. On March 22, 1926, he consecrated as his auxiliary his chancellor, Reverend Francis M. Kelly. On February 10, 1928, Bishop Kelly was named successor to Bishop Heffron. And, on the following May 22 he was installed as the third Bishop of Winona.

Diocesan History Since 1928

Bishop Kelly was the first native son of the diocese to succeed to the see. Excellently educated, here and in Rome, he was a member of the faculty of St. Mary's College from its opening in 1913 until he took over his episcopal duties. He had distinguished himself at St. Mary's,

but it was also while he was there that the high blood pressure, which was later to strike him down, made its appearance. It was his added tragedy that he faced problems of a sort quite different from those which taxed his predecessors. Both Bishops Cotter and Heffron administered a diocese which, in one respect or another, was growing. It was only by efforts of which he was scarcely physically capable that Bishop Kelly prevented the great depression which struck in 1929 from becoming a time of serious retrogression for the diocese. One catches something of his burdens from a few statistics. During the years of Bishop Heffron's administration the Catholic population of the diocese increased by 19,585; from Bishop Heffron's death until Bishop Binz became Bishop Kelly's coadjutor in 1942, the increase was only 1,192. Baptisms fell off from 2,593 in 1927 to 2,226 in 1942, while deaths increased from 475 to 710. It is not surprising that there was also a falling off in the number of parochial schools and attendance at them, although the high school population held its own. Under such circumstances just to maintain the diocese at the level of development to which his predecessors had brought it required a special kind of courage. How much more his poor health cost him we can only surmise. He went about his work quietly, founding four new parishes but concerning himself more with the improvement of the ecclesiastical organization of the diocese and establishing such activities as the Society of the Propagation of the Faith, the Confraternity of Christian Doctrine and the Council of Catholic Women. In 1940 he suffered a severe paralytic stroke and was confined to the hospital. He never left it. For the last several years of his life, though completely conscious, he could utter no word nor leave his bed. His sufferings came to an end on June 24, 1950.

The shortest episcopal reign in the diocese was that of Bishop Leo Binz who was installed on January 6, 1943, as the coadjutor bishop of Bishop Kelly and apostolic administrator of the diocese. The modest increase in the population of the diocese during his administration was reflected by an equally modest increase in school enrollments. Baptisms, on the other hand, which had fallen off by 376 between 1927 and 1942, increased between 1942 and 1949 by 1,340, a warning that school space would soon become inadequate. While he knew the need for several buildings, Bishop Binz did not have time to launch an extensive program of construction. Thorough by temperament, he first set about gathering money for a needed cathedral, just as he did not first erect a seminary but established burses and a special fund to encourage ecclesiastical vocations. While he reorganized the finances of the diocese and improved its ecclesiastical organization, he showed a special interest in the promotion of the spiritual order. Vocations, the Enthronement of the Sacred Heart in the Home, the creation of a Committee for Religious Education in the Home, support for the Catholic Rural Life Conference—these areas of Catholic life received his greatest attention. Early in 1943 he established *The Winonan Edition* of *Our Sunday Visitor* as another religious influence upon the Catholic home. The time he needed to bring many of his plans for the diocese to fruition was not granted him, for on November 16, 1949, he was transferred to the Archdiocese of Dubuque.

Before this change occurred, Bishop Kelly had been transferred, October 17, 1949, to a titular see (Nasai). Three days later the Most Reverend Edward A. Fitzgerald, who had been auxiliary bishop in Dubuque since 1946, was named Bishop of Winona, its fourth. His installation took place on January 4, 1950.

Bishop Leo Binz at St. James in 1946

His immediate problems were material; they were the problems which practically all administrators of social groups faced after the Second World War—the problems created by an unprecedented increase in population and the consequent need for expansion. Since 1949 the population of the diocese had increased by 34,865 or forty-eight per cent. This has necessitated opening new parishes and increasing the number of churches, schools (or classrooms), parish halls, rectories and convents. The increase in active priests within the diocese has been fifty-eight, or forty-three per cent. Elementary and high school enrollment has gone up one hundred three per cent but for the 18,721 in these Catholic schools there are 11,749 more in the public schools who must receive special religious instruction.

Such needs as these are met by familiar institutions. But new needs have emerged—the need of hospices for the increasing number of aged, or other special institutions; of retreat houses, not only for adults, married as well as single, but also for high school and college students who, in ever-growing numbers, are making closed retreats. Several religious orders have settled upon the diocese for the location of their novitiates or houses of study—the Dominicans (1949), the Fathers of the Sacred Hearts of Jesus and Mary (1959), not omitting such congregations as the Sisters of St. Francis of Our Lady of Lourdes and the Christian Brothers, who have been in the diocese from earlier eras. Material edifices, they yet reflect the spiritual concerns of the bishop for the growth of the spiritual life, for sacerdotal and religious vocations, for the laymen's retreat movement and for the religious formation of the Catholic youth in the diocese including those in public schools.

The magnitude of Bishop Fitzgerald's task, particularly in view of the long distances in his diocese, made help a necessity. Rome named as his auxiliary the Most Reverend George H. Speltz, who had been Rector of the Immaculate Heart of Mary Seminary since its erection. He was consecrated by Bishop Fitzgerald on March 25, 1963, in the Cathedral of the Sacred Heart in Winona.

There is no doubt that the episcopate of Bishop Fitzgerald will go down as one of the great ones in the history of the diocese, but every consideration suggests that the final estimate wait upon time. Its dispensations are in the hands of God.

Provincial House of Our Lady of Good Counsel of the School Sisters of Notre Dame, Mankato

Motherhouse and Novitiate of the Sisters of the Third Order Regular of St. Francis of the Congregation of Our Lady of Lourdes, Rochester

Christian Brothers' Provincialate and Novitiate, Winona

RELIGIOUS IN THE DIOCESE OF WINONA _____

Brothers of the Christian Schools
Dominican Fathers
Fathers of the Sacred Hearts
Jesuit Fathers
_____
Benedictine Sisters of Pontifical Jurisdiction (St. Gertrude Priory)

Dominican Sisters (St. Dominic Province; Ilanz, Switzerland)
Dominican Sisters of the Third Order of St. Dominic
School Sisters of Notre Dame
Sisters of Charity of Our Lady, Mother of Mercy

Sisters of Guadalupe

Sisters of the Sorrowful Mother (Third Order of St. Francis)

Sisters of the Third Order Regular of St. Francis of the Congregation of Our Lady of Lourdes

DIOCESE OF CROOKSTON

by Reverend Gerald Foley

"KEEP YOUR EYE ON BUDDING CROOKSTON." By the time that the first bishop-elect, Timothy Corbett, gave this reply in 1910 to the condolences which his friends were offering in jest, the Church in northwestern Minnesota already had rich roots of history and heroism.

The beginnings of this history are shrouded in uncertainty. Of the bits of evidence which have appeared thus far, a large stone may hold the clue to the earliest Catholic history of the Diocese of Crookston. Many would deny its authenticity, but if this lone message from the past is true, Catholic Norsemen reached the central United States over a century before Columbus embarked on his famous voyage. Searching for Norse settlers who had moved west from Greenland, an expedition in a yawl boat traveled up the Nelson River and then continued their way up the Red River along the boundary of the present Diocese of Crookston. When they reached the Buffalo River, they turned eastward through a series of lakes and streams. At Cormorant Lake in Becker County the party stopped to fish. While half of the men fished behind a wooded island, Indians ambushed the ten men remaining in camp. Several days later a member of the expedition chiseled an obituary for his dead companions which, since its discovery in 1898, has been known as the Kensington Runestone. If it is true that Norsemen brought the Catholic faith into the Red River Valley, no trace of it endured when the Indians were next visited by white men nearly four centuries later.

The First Missionaries

During the eighteenth century Chippewa Indians from the St. Lawrence Valley pushed the Sioux southward and westward across the prairies. Through reports of the French fur traders and the Chippewa, French missionaries learned of Indian tribes further west who were thought to be ripe for missionary activity. An opportunity to Christianize the pagan Indians west of Lake Superior was offered to the Jesuits of New France in 1731. The French in Canada, interested in finding the Northwest passage to the Pacific Ocean, chose Pierre de la Vérendrye to build a fort on Lake of the Woods. With him came Father Charles Mesaiger, a forty-year-old Jesuit and veteran of nine years in the Indian missions, who is the first priest known definitely to have entered the area which is now included in the Diocese of Crookston.

By the fall of 1732, a stockade 100 by 60 feet had been erected on an island in Northwest Angle Inlet and named Fort St. Charles. There are no records to tell us whether or not Father Mesaiger baptized any of the large number of Indians in the area, but is is unlikely that he made much progress since the tribes were constantly moving. After one winter at the fort, Father Mesaiger's health was so broken that he could no longer endure the rigors of missionary life and he returned to Quebec an invalid.

Two years after his departure, Father Jean Pierre Aulneau arrived at the fort on his way to establish contact with the Mandan Indians living along the Missouri River. When these plans were postponed for a year due to lack of supplies and men, Father Aulneau decided to accompany a group of voyageurs to Michillimakinac so that he might consult other priests and have an opportunity to go to confession. On June 5, 1736, a party of twenty-one men left the fort heading for Rainy River. That night they were massacred on a small island about twenty miles from Fort St. Charles by a Sioux war party. Fort St. Charles was used as a western outpost for a few more years and then abandoned. When war broke out between England and France in the 1750's, the French voyageurs rushed to the defense of their country on the St. Lawrence, leaving the west deserted. The Indians who had been instructed by the missionaries died and new generations of Indians grew up in the polytheism of their ancestors. Nearly a century elapsed before another priest came to instruct them in Christianity.

Once the French lost control of Canada, British fur traders began to replace the French in the west. By the early 1800's competition in the fur trade forced the Hudson's Bay Company to build posts as far south as Minnesota. Beginning with Father Severe Dumoulin in 1818, missionaries from Pembina, the Earl of Selkirk's famous colony, ministered to the Indians and half-breeds in northwestern Minnesota for the next fifty years before other priests began to penetrate the area.

The Northwest was changing during the first half of the nineteenth century as settlers came up the Mississippi and spread northward over the fertile farmlands. Yet, when Bishop Cretin was assigned to the new Diocese of St. Paul in 1850, there were no priests living among the 10,000 Chippewa scattered throughout northern Minnesota.

When Bishop Cretin appointed Father Francis Pierz, already a successful Indian missionary at Sault Ste. Marie, director of Indian missions in the upper Mississippi region in 1852, he faced an overwhelming burden. The new religion had to supplant the old Indian religion which was ardently believed and interwoven with traditions of many generations.

Father Pierz made a tour of his missions in the summer of 1854, traveling the 1,200 miles through forests and swamps on foot. The chiefs at Red Lake begged him to establish a mission but he was unable to fulfill their request. Finally in 1858, Father Lawrence Lautishar, a Slovenian countryman of Father Pierz, came to help minister to the Chippewa. Father Pierz was then able to establish a mission at Red Lake, the very heart of pagan Chippewa country, where a few Catholic half-breeds had settled years before and kept their faith, although deprived of priestly ministrations. Father Pierz also chose Red Lake because these Indians were relatively civilized and therefore better disposed to accept religious preaching. Fathers Pierz and Lautishar arrived

Restored Fort St. Charles

at Red Lake on August 14, 1858, after a trip marked by many hardships. The next day mass was offered for the first time on the shores of Red Lake. For a time they labored together to build up a flourishing mission. Father Pierz spent his time visiting the sick Indians, while Father Lautishar gave instructions in the Catholic faith to both Catholics and pagans.

After six weeks Father Pierz returned to Crow Wing, leaving Father Lautishar to winter at Red Lake. The young priest lived at the home of a French half-breed fur trader, Joseph Jourdain, whose house served also as a chapel and school. When the missionaries arrived there were only ten Catholic families among a total population of 1,400 Indians at Red Lake, but the number of Catholics soon began to increase until his missionary labors came to a sudden and sad end. Father Lautishar received word that some pagan Indians at Obashing (north of Ponemah) were seriously ill and had asked to see him. He went to visit and instruct them on December 3, 1858, walking fourteen miles across the frozen lake on a bitterly cold day. On the same trip he had hoped to begin the conversion of this pagan settlement and met with the council in the afternoon to explain the chief teachings of the Catholic religion. The Indians urged the priest to stay with them for the night or at least to take nourishment before starting back. It was nearly sundown but he insisted that he must go because he had promised to return to the mission house that evening. The clear skies deceived the inexperienced traveler and in a short time the wind had swung to the north and a blizzard was raging. He was blinded by the snow, and his inadequate clothing could not keep out the intense cold. He had eaten nothing all day and fatigue gradually began to overcome him. Darkness descended as the snow began to fall. Joseph Jourdain had built a fire on the bank of the lake to guide him and after wandering about in the blizzard the priest finally saw it. But as he struggled toward the mission, his legs froze so that he could no longer walk. He crawled along the ice for some time, then froze to death when his strength gave out. His body was found the next day half a mile from shore.

There was sorrow among the Indians the next morning when they found the body of

Father Ignatius Tomazin

their beloved priest. With his death the process of conversion of the Red Lake heathen came to a temporary halt. Father Pierz visited the mission irregularly and there was no resident priest at Red Lake again until 1879.

By this time the Indians were being forced onto reservations by a series of treaties. In 1851 a treaty with the Sioux gave the government that part of the Red River Valley south of the Buffalo River. By another treaty with the Chippewa in 1855 the government acquired much of the timber land in northern Minnesota and opened pine logging around the headwaters of the Mississippi. The northern Red River Valley was ceded to the government in 1863. Four years later the government established the White Earth Reservation with the plan that eventually all the Minnesota Chippewa would be consolidated there. Indians on the reservation received help from the government to build homes and open farms. The first priest to visit the new White Earth Reservation was Father John Ireland who came as a member of a government commission to select lands for the Chippewa. Before he returned to St. Paul the Indians formally requested a permanent missionary. This request was honored by Bishop Thomas Grace of St. Paul in the person of Father Ignatius Tomazin of Crow Wing. He began to offer mass in homes on the reservation. The Church of the

Most Holy Redeemer was completed in 1874 and, after Father Tomazin was appointed full-time missonary to the Chippewa the following year, he began to make regular trips from White Earth to visit the Indians at Red Lake. Father Tomazin found his efforts partially blocked here by the Episcopalians who had control of the agency and school. Informed that neither a priest nor a Catholic mission would be permitted on the reservation, the fiery-tempered missionary refused to leave and obtained money for his work through the Catholic Mission Society of Austria. When government troops tried to remove Father Tomazin from the reservation in 1877, friendly Indians rallied to his aid. He reluctantly agreed to leave the mission, but was kidnapped by the Indians and held on an island in Birch Lake for two weeks. Then he was allowed to return to his work at White Earth. Father Tomazin was assisted in his work at White Earth by three men calling themselves Franciscan Brothers who taught in the school and traveled about the country begging funds for the mission.

Because he feared that Father Tomazin would stir up more trouble, Bishop Rupert Seidenbusch, who had been appointed Vicar Apostolic of Northern Minnesota in 1875, transferred him in 1879 to Red Lake where he built a church and opened a school immediately. Again the missionary was soon in trouble with government officials. This time his quick temper led to his removal from missionary work. In March of 1883 the Commissioner of Indian affairs demanded the Catholic Indian Bureau to replace the fiery Father Tomazin.

Benedictines

With the expulsion of Father Tomazin from Red Lake an era of missionary activity in northern Minnesota came to an end. Since that time the Indian missions have been staffed by monks from St. John's Abbey and by Benedictine nuns. Father Aloysius Hermanutz and Sisters Philomena Ketten and Lioba Braun arrived at the White Earth mission in November, 1878. They were destined to spend the next fifty years among the Indians on that reservation. The mission was in wretched condition. The small

log church was unplastered and the altar was only a rough plank box with another smaller box for a tabernacle. The small log house had been stripped by prowlers of all furnishings except two rusty stoves. The greatest hardship of the winter was the cold. Since the poorly heated buildings had many cracks through which the winter winds blew, leaving patches of snow on the floor, the missionaries were often sick from exposure, and Father Aloysius began to get discouraged. Sister Philomena retained her enthusiasm and began to teach classes in the barn. The little log church and school soon became too small and a better location was sought. As the sisters crowded more waifs into the small mission house, the

Father Aloysius Hermanutz

need for an orphanage became urgent. Indians living too far from the school also desired to have their children instructed and urged the priest and sisters to board their children. There was no money for a building project. Just when the cause seemed hopeless, Abbot Alexius Edelbrock appeared on a stormy January day in 1881 with plans for a new church and school for the Chippewa.

The blessing of St. Benedict's Church and

orphans' home in June, 1882, provided a grand climax to the early efforts of the missionaries as Indians gathered for a three-day celebration that closed with the confirmation of 230 Indians by Bishop Seidenbusch. The sisters opened an orphanage for thirty youngsters in the new convent building and a day school emphasizing the domestic arts in the basement of the new church. Father Aloysius was able to get a contract from the government for the care of ten orphans and managed to operate by many sacrifices and occasional charity. Sister Philomena undertook in 1882 to make a sixteen mile round trip daily on horseback to Buffalo River to instruct the children in that settlement.

Father Aloysius, the only priest among the Indians in northwestern Minnesota from 1883 to 1888, was frequently away from the mission, leaving the sisters to conduct the religious services and funerals and instruct the Indian children who did not attend their school. Unsatisfied with only an occasional visit of the priest, the Indians at Red Lake wrote to Abbot Alexius asking him to send a priest and to reopen the school.

Desiring to obtain the funds necessary to expand the Indian work of the Benedictines, Abbot Alexius wrote in 1886 to Katherine Drexel, a Philadelphia Catholic heiress noted for her gifts to the Indian missions, inviting her to extend her charity to the Minnesota missions. In 1888, Katherine, Louise and Elizabeth Drexel toured the White Earth and Red Lake reservations with Bishop James O'Connor of Omaha and Father Joseph Stephan of the Catholic Indian Bureau. Katherine was so impressed by the work of the Benedictine Sisters in the school at White Earth that she made arrangements for the erection of a new school building and dormitory large enough to shelter 150 orphan and dependent children. Touched by the plight of the Indians at Red Lake, the Drexel sisters promised Abbot Alexius that they would build a church and school if he would supply the priests and the Benedictines at St. Joseph would supply teaching sisters. In November, 1888, Fathers Thomas Borgerding and Simon Lampe and Sisters Amalia Eich and Evangelista McNulty arrived among the 400 Catholic Indians at the Red Lake mission and began plans for a new church, school, rectory and convent.

Soon after their arrival, the sisters opened a day school in an old Hudson's Bay Company warehouse. By the next April all of the children had left the school and the sisters realized that Indian children, because of their instability, were best educated in boarding schools. With the help of two more sisters, they opened a boarding school for thirty-five pupils at the end of May, 1889. A residence for sisters and girls and another for priests were completed during

HILL REFERENCE LIBRARY

Chippawa maple sugar camp

the first summer at Red Lake, together with a third building serving temporarily as a church and afterwards as a boys' residence.

With Catholic missons firmly established among the Chippewa, there was reason to hope that at least those Indians who embraced the faith would give up their roving life and accept the more settled ways of their white neighbors, but the Chippewa continued to be restless and without ambition. In 1889 Congress passed an act for the relief and civilization of these Indians, intending to lay the foundation for a better future. The bill provided that all the Indians living in northern Minnesota, with the exception of those living on the Red Lake Reservation, should cede their lands and move to the White Earth Reservation, where they would each receive a tract of land. The remaining land would be sold to settlers and the money placed in a fund, the interest from which would be distributed annually for supplies and schools. Few Indians accepted this plan. The Red Lake Indians agreed to take a diminished reservation but refused to take individual allotments of land. Other Indians refused to move and received allotments on their old reservations. At White Earth half-breed politicians became active and pine lands were distributed unfairly to the advantage of the more progressive element on the reservation while timber companies began to swindle unsuspecting Indians out of their pine stumpage.

During the last decade before the turn of the century the Benedictines' work among the Indians was quite productive. Mission churches began to appear on other parts of the reservations and additional priests and sisters entered into the mission work. Missionaries among the Indians found it took a number of years before they could do effective work because the Indians were instinctively suspicious of strangers and reluctant to open their hearts to them. But once they were certain that they could trust a person, the Indians were extremely loyal. Within a few years Father Aloysius and Father Thomas came to be universally loved and respected by the Indians and served as valuable intermediaries for the government.

The American Protective Association was instrumental in the federal government's withdrawl of aid for education of Indian children in 1899 on the grounds that congressional aid to such schools was uniting church and state. In their anxiety to stop the growth of Catholic mission schools, the non-Catholic groups were willing to give up their share of federal funds to sectarian schools. The Catholic mission schools were especially hard hit by this policy and were forced to turn to charity. Eventually support from the tribal fund set aside for Indian needs was obtained for the school at White Earth, but this required annual signatures of the Indians and made the missionary dependent upon the Indians for that part of the school support. Nevertheless St. Benedict's Industrial School was widely recognized for its outstanding work and was termed by a government official the "best Indian school in the country."

During the years that the Benedictine missionaries were striving to assure the continuance of their missions, the nature of their work was shifting because of the rapid changes which were transforming the reservations. While the government was making its futile attempts in the 1890's to consolidate the Chippewa, white settlers were filling the Red River Valley and spreading along the boundaries of the White Earth Reservation. There was much agitation to open the thousands of acres of fine farmland which remained on the reservation, but nothing was done about this until several congressional acts after 1900 allowed the Indians to sell their lands. In a very short time large timber companies and land prospectors swindled the Indians out of almost all their lands, leaving them impoverished as soon as their small payments were spent. In three years ninety per cent of the allotments were sold for ridiculously low prices. Indians had to seek manual work in the new villages springing up near the reservation or leave the area for employment, unless they chose to live on relief as many were forced to do. During these years of turbulence, the missionaries labored patiently and sometimes effectively to improve the conditions of the Indians. Efforts to interest the Indians in agriculture failed, however. Various attempts to develop the faith of the Indians, including annual Indian congresses to gather the Chippewa for a few days of intense spiritual activity, met with more apparent success.

With the influx of white settlers, Benedictine activity on the White Earth Reservation expanded in less than twenty years from a single mission to a total of six pastorates and almost a dozen churches. In 1928 the three original Benedictine missionaries completed fifty years of service among the Chippewa and then retired to make way for younger laborers.

Gradually conditions forced the Benedictines to change their boarding school program into day schools. During the depression years, St. Mary's School at Red Lake cared for about 200 pupils, but after 1938 concerted efforts were made to force the closing of the mission school as a means of reducing the influence of the mission in the community. Fewer children and only the most destitute were allowed to board at the school. To stem this opposition, and in response to the requests of many Indian parents, the school was changed to a day school in 1940. At St. Benedict's Industrial School the sisters and their 135 charges were also undergoing great

Lumber camp and crew

privations and 200 local Catholic Indian children were either attending the public schools or not going to school at all. As the Indians exchanged their nomadic way of life for a more settled one, the government advocated district day schools instead of the boarding schools which had been set up to isolate the Indian children from their primitive surroundings. Schools were also needed for the children of white settlers on the reservation. Finally tribal funds for the support of the school were cut off in 1945, making the change to a day school necessary. With the end of the boarding school era, the sisters found themselves battling against the wretched home life of the Chippewa Indian children.

Settlement in Northwestern Minnesota

While the Indians in northwestern Minnesota were being cared for, white settlers began to enter the area in greater numbers. One hundred years ago the Red River Valley remained a lonely waste crossed here and there by poorly marked trails connecting settlements further north along the river with southern Minnesota. In 1857 the Hudson's Bay Company abandoned the difficult water routes to Lake Superior and adopted the shorter Red River Trail to St. Paul. Two years later the company put a small steamer on the river to haul supplies between Georgetown and Fort Gary. After 1870, what started as a trickle of pioneers swelled into a flood of settlers, so that within a few years almost all of the valley was under cultivation. Chief causes of this sudden change were the railroad, which made land accessible to settlers and connected the new wheat fields with flour mills, and the Homestead Act of 1862, which made land available free of charge.

Towns sprang up rapidly throughout the Red River Valley as the railroads penetrated the region. The railroads were quick to build stations and start towns at frequent intervals for the convenience of the people. Encouraged by government and railroad agents, large numbers of Norwegians started to open farms throughout the valley; these were soon followed by Scotchmen, Frenchmen and settlers of several other national groups. Just as this influx was reaching a peak, the Panic of 1873 retarded immigration for a number of years. But this change of events also created opportunities for financial gain to James J. Hill, known as the "empire builder," who not only brought in settlers but also helped them to learn better methods of agriculture and to improve their communities.

Scandanavians were predominant among the immigrants prior to 1877, but from this time on a large number of French Canadians migrated southward into the valley. Within several years there were over 5,000 prosperous French settlers in Polk County. Meanwhile the eastern fringes of the valley began to attract immigrants, mostly Scandanavians, who worked in the lumber camps or patiently developed farms out of the cutover timber land. The eastern pine-forest region of the present diocese still remained an almost untrod wilderness, not destined to see activity until the logging enterprises began just prior to 1900.

While the Red River Valley was showing these signs of new life, Catholic missionaries arrived upon the scene to minister to the struggling pioneers. These first priests were hardy itinerant missionaries who claimed one town as their permanent abode but spent most of their time visiting the scattered settlements, where they offered mass in private homes for the Catholics in the neighborhood. They were welcomed by the frontiersmen as friends and advisors. The priests were strong men—strong in their beliefs, incapable of disappointment,

combining vision and practicality. Unfortunately many of them were men of fiery temper who found it difficult to remain in any established parish for more than a short time.

Years of the Vicariate

The first priest to reside in the Red River Valley settlements of Minnesota was Father Jean Baptiste Genin, a former Oblate missionary from Canada, who built a house at Holy Cross in 1867 and a church in 1872. The Vicariate of Northern Minnesota was established in 1875 and was to last until such time as the area's population warranted the establishment of a diocese. Vicar Apostolic Rupert Seidenbusch, former abbot of St. John's Abbey, resided at St. Cloud. The forty-five-year-old prelate traveled throughout his vicariate presiding over the spread of Catholicism in the area, organizing parishes, encouraging priests and people. He provided means for the maintenance and extension of the work by appeals for money outside the vicariate. At the time the vicariate was formed, Father Ignatius Tomazin was the only priest living in the area which is now the Diocese of Crookston. Residing at White Earth, he attended the missions at Red Lake, Detroit Lakes, Audubon, Glyndon, Hawley, Crookston and Sand Hill. Moorhead and Holy Cross were occasionally visited by Father Genin who had settled in Duluth. In a short time additional priests were sent to care for the spiritual needs of the Catholics moving into the valley. Bishop Seidenbusch replaced the old itinerant missionaries with resident pastors. In 1879, Father Aloysius Hermanutz, O. S. B., was at White Earth, Father Tomazin at Red Lake, Fathers Lawrence Spitzelberger and James McGlone at Moorhead, Fathers Andrew Straub and J. Fortier, O.M.I., at Crookston, and Father Pierre Champagne at Red Lake Falls. That fall, the Sisters of St. Benedict of St. Joseph, Minnesota, opened a parochial school in Moorhead. Settlers continued to push northward, occupying almost all the available land in Marshall County in the four years after the railroad penetrated this area in 1878. Catholic churches continued to spring up in the new towns which were now dotting the prairies.

Bishop Seidenbusch searched constantly in

Europe and America for priests who would volunteer to staff his vast mission field. Father Pierre Champagne, who came to Minnesota from Quebec in 1879, is a typical example of the men Seidenbusch found. In seven years he directed the erection of churches in Red Lake Falls, Terrebonne, Lambert, Crookston, Gentilly, Fisher and Louisville. And in fourteen years the clergy of the vicariate increased from eight to thirty-seven. With the additional help which the Benedictines could provide, mass was offered in most of the larger settlements at least a few times each year.

Diocese of Duluth

Bishop Seidenbusch suffered a serious heart attack in 1885. Soon after the ailing bishop sent his resignation to Rome in 1888, the northern Minnesota vicariate was divided into the Dioceses of St. Cloud and Duluth. The first Bishop of Duluth, James McGolrick, had the entire northern half of Minnesota under his jurisdiction. Still mission territory, the entire diocese had only fifteen secular priests and five regulars, of whom over half were stationed in the Red River Valley: Sebastian Schells, Barnesville; Etienne Fayolle, St. Anne's in Crookston; Edward Lawler, St. Mary's in Crookston; Clement Gamache, Detroit Lakes; Elie Theillon, Gentilly; Augustine Brockmeyer, O.S.B., Moorhead; L. Arpin, Red Lake Falls; Louis Fiege, Terrebonne; Thomas Borgerding, O.S.B., and Simon Lampe, O.S.B., Red Lake Reservation; and Aloysius Hermanutz, O.S.B., White Earth Reservation.

The gradual movement of settlement into the fringes of the valley and finally into the more heavily timbered regions continued. During the first years after the establishment of the Diocese of Duluth, most of the churches were either along the Red River or along the railroads spanning the western regions of the valley. After 1900 the northern and eastern sections became the center of activity. Bishop McGolrick did not have sufficient priests to staff the increasing number of new parishes so he appealed to the Benedictines for help. The building program advanced in earnest after 1895 as the effects of the recent depression started to disappear. There was abundant evidence of prosperity in the val-

ley at the turn of the century, due mainly to the extensive logging and the rich farm land which continued to attract settlers from the East and from Europe. Many national parishes served as the principal agencies for the maintenance of the language and cultural traditions of the homelands, and thus they perpetuated the insulation of the immigrant groups from the native-American society and culture.

The settlement and prosperity of the individual communities in the valley were often connected in some way with the Church or with an ingenious pastor who encouraged and guided his parishioners to a successful means of livelihood. Father Elie Theillon, pastor for forty-seven years among the French-Canadian farmers at Gentilly, is a good example. Faced with the prospect of losing his entire parish within a few years, the young priest began to study agriculture and to teach practical farming to his parishioners so that they might learn to diversify their crops. After a short time he formed a dairy association and personally helped the distressed farmers buy cows. In 1895 they borrowed money to build a cheese factory which was organized on a cooperative plan to assure the farmers a good return for their milk. The farmers adopted this project enthusiastically under the leadership of the energetic priest, were quickly satisfied with it, and the exodus from the farms came to a sudden halt. By 1910, what had once been the poorest township in Polk County was one of the most prosperous, and Gentilly's First Premium Cheese was widely acclaimed for its excellence.

During these years of growth, enterprising sisters pioneered throughout the diocese, adding much to the success of the Church's work. Benedictine Sisters from St. Joseph, Minnesota, taught in the schools at White Earth, Red Lake, Moorhead and Barnesville. A daughter community established in Duluth in 1892, Villa St. Scholastica, opened hospitals at East Grand Forks (1897), Bemidji (1898) and Crookston (1902), and schools at East Grand Forks (1900), Argyle (1901), and Red Lake Falls (1902). Bemidji, a young booming community in the heart of a logging district, had only one store, a small post office, and six houses when the Benedictine sisters leased the second floor of the store for temporary use as a twenty-four bed hospital. To assure a basic income and to help defray expen-

Bemidji in 1897

ses for the care of those with more serious and prolonged illnesses, the sisters started their own insurance plan for the local lumberjacks. An insurance ticket selling for $7.50 entitled the purchaser for one year to ward accommodations, medical and surgical care and nursing services in the Bemidji hospital or any other hospital operated by the sisters.

The failure of the parochial school at Argyle brought another congregation of religious into the area. When Father Joseph Barras found his Argyle parish, complete with a new school and convent, on the verge of bankruptcy, he appealed to the Sisters of St. Joseph of Bourg, France, to staff his school. Five sisters arrived from France in 1903 to buy the school and convent for a boarding academy. The Sisters of St. Joseph had been in Argyle only two years when Bishop McGolrick urged Mother Marie Jeanne to found a house in Crookston. In March, 1905, she rented a small house near St. Anne's Church and opened a school which in the fall of 1906 enrolled seventy-one students. That year a new brick residence replaced the original building. Here a few years later St. Joseph's Academy was founded.

The future of the Church in northwestern Minnesota, however, was not totally unclouded. Most of the parishes along the Red River suffered a decline in membership between 1905 and 1908 due to crop failures, while those farther east were hard hit when sawmills closed. Nevertheless, the optimistic pioneer spirit prevailed in most of the parishes and the Catholics who remained accepted the added sacrifice necessary to keep their churches open. In many cases it was impossible to build a church without outside help. One of the notable donors was James J. Hill, whose gift of several hundreds or a thousand dollars often made the existence of a church possible. Since its establishment in 1905, the Catholic Church Extension Society has contributed money to help almost every parish in northwestern Minnesota.

The New Diocese

Within the first ten years of the twentieth century almost all the open land in northern Minnesota was taken by settlers. After this, immigration decreased rapidly. But the Diocese of Duluth had expanded in population and in Catholic

109

Bishop Timothy Corbett

activities to such a point that Bishop McGolrick found it difficult to carry out his episcopal duties satisfactorily. Consequently the bishops of the Province of St. Paul recommended to the Apostolic Delegate in August, 1909, that a new diocese be erected in northwestern Minnesota. The recommendation was favorably acted upon when Pope Pius X established the Diocese of Crookston on December 31, 1909. The fifth diocese in Minnesota, previously the western half of the Diocese of Duluth, comprised the territory west of the eastern boundaries of Hubbard and Beltrami counties and north of the southern lines of Clay, Becker and Hubbard counties. This division was a high tribute to the Catholics of the Red River Valley but many people doubted its advisability. Several years of rapid progress were needed to assure its success and to remove the last lingering doubts.

Timothy Corbett, the first bishop of Crookston, was born in 1858 at Mendota, Minnesota, and grew up in Minneapolis. After his ordination for the Diocese of St. Paul in 1886, he was assigned as assistant to Father James McGolrick at the parish of the Immaculate Conception. Three years later he became pastor of Sacred Heart Church in Duluth where, by the time of his elevation to the episcopacy in 1910, five large buildings stood on the hill above the city as testimony of his constant activity. In Duluth he gained such titles as the "Bishop's right arm" and the "thundering orator." The choice of

Corbett as first head of the Diocese of Crookston was a natural one in view of the fact that his duties as chancellor of the Diocese of Duluth for fifteen years had demanded of him a thorough knowledge and a sympathetic appreciation of the problems and needs of the Red River Valley.

The new diocese had less than 20,000 Catholics scattered over 17,000 square miles. There were only thirty priests working in the entire area— seventeen secular and thirteen regular. St. Mary's Church, the new cathedral, was poor and run-down. On one occasion after his arrival in Crookston, the bishop pungently expressed his outlook by saying that he "found nothing in sight but the sunshine and the rolling prairie." From the beginning of his labors in Crookston, Bishop Corbett benefited by the constant assistance of Father Joseph Wurm who was rector of the cathedral and chancellor.

No time was lost in starting the organization of the new diocese. Bishop Corbett wrote appeals for help for his "poor and struggling diocese" to dignitaries throughout the world and to almost every priest and mother superior in the country. In a short time he was known throughout the county as the begging bishop through his letters asking not only for cash donations and mass stipends, but also for vestments, chalices and other goods for the parishes and missions of his diocese. Bishop Corbett reported that the diocese had twenty-nine churches with resident pastors, twenty missions, twenty-two stations, seven chapels, Catholic hospitals at Bemidji and Crookston, academies for girls at Argyle and Crookston, industrial schools at Red Lake and White Earth, and parish parochial schools at Moorhead, Barnesville and Red Lake Falls. Less than eleven per cent of the people in the area were Catholics.

Just after his installation Bishop Corbett told Father Wurm that "he who has the children has the future, and we must build a school for the children. We may not get a Cathedral for years to come, but we must have a school." In less than two months excavation was started for the construction of Cathedral School. Since the building fund was still small, the bishop feared that even this first building might not materialize, but his appeals for help drew an enthusiastic response.

From the outset of his episcopate, education

was the bishop's main concern. To extend this work throughout the diocese, he saw that there would be a need for religious communities to provide teachers for the schools which he planned to build. With this thought in mind, he encouraged the Sisters of St. Joseph of Bourg to erect a large convent and academy which opened in Crookston in 1913. After repeated invitations, the Sisters of St. Benedict from Duluth consented to the establishment of a house in the diocese. In 1919 forty-two sisters under the leadership of Mother Eustacia Beyenka volunteered to found the new community which became independent in 1921. The Benedictines owned two hospitals and provided teachers for four schools. At first the outlook for the new community was dim, but with the encouragement and financial assistance of Bishop Corbett, it became firmly established in a short time. During their first summer in Crookston the sisters remodeled St. Vincent's Hospital and added an eighty thousand dollar wing with funds raised by the bishop. He also provided most of the money for Mount St. Benedict Academy which they opened in 1923.

New parochial schools were opened at East Grand Forks, Detroit Lakes, Thief River Falls, Bemidji and Mahnomen under Bishop Corbett. But the bishop was not satisfied to have Catholic doctrine taught only in those cities which were large enough to support a Catholic school. He was one of the first to urge the instruction and preparation of catechists to aid the priest in teaching religion to children who attended public schools. When a movement for the organization of religious vacation schools in rural areas began after 1920, Bishop Corbett was one of the initial supporters. At the request of his clergy, he asked the sisters in 1924 to begin teaching two weeks of summer vacation religion classes in those parishes of the diocese that did not have schools.

Since it was impossible for the Benedictines to maintain their schools and to staff two hospitals adequately and since St. Vincent's Hospital needed a larger staff to provide a nurses' training course, the sisters closed St. Anthony's Hospital in Bemidji in 1924. Four years earlier the Sisters of St. Francis from Little Falls had purchased Northwestern Hospital at Moorhead.

KEN R. JOHNSON STUDIOS

Early Crookston

Growth of the Diocese

It is possible to get some indication of the faith of the sparsely distributed Catholics and of their willingness to support their new ordinary by noting the increase in the number of churches after 1910. Several factors helped to make this possible. One of these was the continuing settlement in certain areas of the diocese, especially along its eastern edge. At the same time the area was developing materially through an increase of productive farmland and the growth of new industries. Bishop Corbett approved erection of mission churches in many of the smaller communities. By 1919 the diocese had forty-two churches with resident pastors, thirty-seven mission churches and thirteen stations. Due to the shortage of priests occasioned by the rapid parochial expansion, Bishop Corbett also found it necessary to rely strongly on St. John's Abbey for help in staffing the parishes.

The growth in population slowed down after the First World War and there was less institutional construction in the early 1920's and practically none immediately before the depression. Farmers had a hard time earning a living in the years after the war. These difficulties caused a population decline of almost 9,000 in the diocese between 1920 and 1930.

Corbett's last building project was St. Joseph's Boys' Home in 1931 for which he personally raised the money from sources outside the diocese. This institution was soon used by the cathedral parish to accommodate the increased enrollment in the school.

Soon after he took charge of the diocese, Bishop Corbett began to draw up the first book of diocesan statutes, summarizing the disciplinary regulations for both temporal and spiritual affairs. In 1921 he convoked the first Diocesan Synod to approve the second revision of these statutes. To unify the educational system in the parochial schools, the bishop published in 1921 "An outline of Studies for the Catholic Schools of the Diocese of Crookston." By reason of his firm stand on Catholic education the enrollment in the Catholic schools rose from 793 at the time of his installation to 2,007 by 1922.

Many of the bishop's ideas were presented to the people through his pastoral letters. Annually during Lent he sent these letters to his priests to be read in parts on three successive Sundays in every church of the diocese. These masterpieces of solid thinking, the result of many days of reading, study, writing and revising, dealt with modern social, religious and educational problems.

Bishop Corbett was always in closest touch with his people and especially with his priests. He loved to have his priests call on him. The priests knew that their ordinary would not tolerate shoddy performance and made heavy demands upon them. He made it clear that he would tolerate no interference on the part of the laity with the work of the Church or its priests. Sometimes he talked to troublemakers privately; at other times he waited until confirmation was conferred to chastise the people in a parish for their actions. It was an awesome sight to see the bishop walking up and down the aisle in a church threatening the people in a loud voice with many dire things unless they conformed. But this brusque exterior concealed a fatherly heart and the bishop always regretted the necessity of being hard on some people for the good of his diocese. Students in the Catholic schools feared their ordinary's visits to distribute the report cards and trembled as he read off their marks with appropriate comments.

Because Bishop Corbett did not feel that public appearances were necessary to promote good relations with his fellow citizens, both Catholics and people of other denominations, he rarely accepted invitations to speak at official gatherings. He was seen in public very seldom.

While the bishop sincerely loved all his flock, he took a special interest in his Indian charges. He was delighted to be among them and mingled with them as a father with his children. The Indians called Bishop Corbett the "Big Horn," a well-chosen title and one that pleased him very much. Whenever the annual Catholic Indian Congress was held in his diocese, he attended the meetings and preached to the Indians, mixing humor with serious words in a manner the Indians greatly enjoyed.

As the depression years progressed declining health and advanced years caused the bishop to lose much of his initiative. He suffered a broken hip in 1934 while hospitalized for diabetes and arteriosclerosis. He began to confirm again in 1936, but during Holy Week the next year he was again hospitalized with a broken hip. He

112

continued to perform his routine duties from his hospital bed, but he realized that the diocese would suffer unless someone could fulfill all the episcopal duties soon. After lying bedridden for more than a year, he finally asked to be relieved of his office on May 23, 1938, citing his declining health and his advanced age as the reasons for his decision. The retired prelate spent his last year in St. Vincent's Hospital, where he continued to take an active interest in all that concerned the diocese until his death on July 20, 1939, a week after his eighty-first

Bishop John H. Peschges

birthday. During Bishop Corbett's tenure the Catholic population of the diocese rose to 28,000 and the clergy more than doubled. The construction or enlargement of over sixty churches, forty rectories, and fifteen parochial schools scattered about the diocese stood as monuments of his energetic episcopate.

Second Bishop of Crookston

Shortly after the resignation of Bishop Corbett, John Hubert Peschges was appointed as the second Bishop of Crookston. Born at New Ulm on May 11, 1881, he was ordained for the Diocese of Winona in 1905. After a year as pastor at Geneva, he worked with various mission bands until he became pastor at Easton in 1910. When St. Mary's College at Winona was organ-

ized in 1913, Father Peschges joined the initial faculty and five years later became president, an office which he held until the college was turned over to the Brothers of the Christian Schools in 1933. He became a domestic prelate in 1925. After his departure from St. Mary's College, Monsignor Peschges served for five years as pastor of St. Augustine's Church in Austin and Rural Life Director for the diocese until his consecration on November 9, 1938.

In his sermon at the installation of Bishop Peschges, Bishop Aloisius Muench of Fargo pointed out that "it is a token of the Church's interest in the farmer that Bishop Peschges was called by the Holy Father to a see which lies in one of the most important agricultural areas of our nation." The rural problem in 1938 was a serious one. Farmers were still suffering from the effects of the depression, large surpluses were building up and government legislation was limiting acreage and trying to resettle farmers living on submarginal land. From the start of his episcopate, Bishop Peschges gained renown for his interest in agriculture and his first-hand knowledge of rural problems. He participated in farm shows and rural meetings and discussed agricultural matters with farmers of all faiths. Much of his time was devoted to the development of the program for the Catholic Rural Life Conference which he had helped to organize in 1923. Under his direction, a Farm Placement Bureau was organized in Crookston in 1939 to keep farm people on the land and to bring more Catholic farmers into the area. Although the constant flow of young men and women from northwestern Minnesota into the cities was necessary, the bishop hoped to attract more young people to country life by altering rural conditions. In 1941 he was appointed as a member of the Farm Security Administration Committee for Minnesota, an agency whose aim was to raise the standard of living among low income farmers.

Both the FSA and the Catholic Rural Life Conference faced the problem caused by thousands of migrant workers moving about the country to supply the wartime demand for farm laborers. Bishop Peschges was aware that only a few of the children among the thousands of Mexicans who were coming into the Red River Valley each summer to work in the sugar beet

Migrant workers' children welcomed at school

and onion fields had received any schooling and that all of them were deficient in a knowledge of religion, hygiene and English. As a remedy for this situation he organized summer schools in which the Benedictine Sisters and several seminarians taught.

Toward the end of Bishop Peschges' short episcopate, the economic condition of the northwestern farmer was becoming less critical. Farm income doubled between 1940 and 1943 and, although the simultaneous rise in the cost of labor and farm supplies absorbed much of the increase, there could be little doubt that farmers were more prosperous than at any time during the past generation. The bishop continued to devote much of his time to agricultural problems and to the work of the Catholic rural life movement. He formulated plans for the postwar era which he was not destined to see.

This attempt to solve the agricultural crisis is only one of several means by which Bishop Peschges provided for his flock. From the beginning he recognized the need for an apostolic organization which would provide religious instructions for those outside the reach of the Catholic schools and encouraged the growth of the Confraternity of Christian Doctrine in the diocese to meet this need. He had the care of

several groups of the faithful in mind. His chief objective was to provide religious instructions to the youth in the rural districts through release-time instructions and religious vacation schools, but he also felt that the adults of the diocese had not received adequate training in Catholic doctrine. He asked that the Confraternity be active in every parish and inaugurated an annual Christian Doctrine Congress in 1939 to bring CCD members together for a day of spiritual emphasis. Feeling some obligation to the more than eighty-five per cent of the people who were not Catholic in the diocese, he organized a three-week street-preaching campaign in 1940. He supplied Father Joseph Lilly, C.M., and his assistants with a public address system and a large supply of Catholic literature for a series of outdoor meetings in some of the more predominantly Protestant towns.

Bishop Peschges was also an active supporter of the national and state organizations of the Catholic Central Verein and of the Catholic Aid Association of Minnesota.

There was a very limited amount of material growth in the diocese during the short episcopate of Bishop Peschges. The fact that Bishop Corbett had developed most parish plants to a

Instructing migrant workers' children

114

satisfactory status, the recession of the late thirties and finally the war effort contributed to make construction unnecessary or difficult. Five new churches were opened during these years. But while the material progress was almost at a standstill, the spiritual activity was intensified. In his talks to Catholic groups the bishop constantly stressed the need for strong Catholic action. A series of annual regional clergy conferences was introduced to foster study among the priests.

Amid such a variety of activities, Bishop Peschges' success was due largely to a character and personality which endeared him to every acquaintance. A tireless worker, he often labored late into the evening. A man of somewhat retiring manner, he spoke more as a teacher than with the eloquence of an orator, but his wisdom and zeal placed him frequently in demand as a speaker for diverse groups. He often addressed national conventions and other large assemblies, yet he also found time to deliver numerous talks at farm meetings and communion breakfasts and before other small groups. No audience was insignificant in his estimation, so that he would brave a blizzard to talk to a handful of 4-H members.

The labors of the episcopate wore heavily on the active prelate. On August 5, 1944, he suffered a heart attack which led to his death on October 30 at the age of sixty-three. Because of his short episcopate, many of his carefully laid plans were not realized during his lifetime.

Bishop Schenk's Administration

Monsignor Joseph Wurm, the faithful old pastor of the cathedral, served as administrator of the diocese during the vacancy after the death of Bishop Peschges as he had done previously after the resignation of Bishop Corbett. Five months elapsed before the selection of a successor. Then on March 16, 1945, it was announced that Father Francis Schenk had been appointed as the third Bishop of Crookston.

Francis J. Schenk was born April 1, 1901, at Superior, Wisconsin, grew up at Gaylord, Minnesota, and was ordained for the Archdiocese of St. Paul in 1926. After serving briefly as the secretary to Archbishop Austin Dowling, he was sent to the Catholic University of America to earn the degree of Doctor of Canon Law. He then served as vice-chancellor of the Archdiocese until he became professor of moral theology at the Saint Paul Seminary in 1934. He taught at the seminary for seven years, and then became vicar-general of the archdiocese and rector of the St. Paul Cathedral. This background—scholar, teacher, administrator, orator and parish priest—combined with a kind and

Bishop Schenk becomes Chief Red Golden Eagle

fatherly demeanor, was to prove invaluable in his role as bishop of a small diocese.

Bishop Schenk came to Crookston at a very critical time. Less than four months later, the Second World War ended and the United States was faced with the postwar readjustment. Even in his small diocese the bishop confronted many social and economic problems which affected the religious life and morals of his flock. Demobilization meant the return of veterans and wartime workers who needed housing and employment. At the same time family farms were yielding to large commercial organizations which caused a decline in the number of parishioners in rural parishes. A higher marital rate and a sharp rise in the birth rate in postwar years caused a critical shortage of classroom space in the parochial schools.

Convinced that it was important to establish a spirit of diocesan unity and to inform the people of his plans for the Church in the diocese, Bishop Schenk among his first projects established a diocesan newspaper, *Our Northland Diocese,* which first appeared in October, 1946, under the editorship of Father John O'Toole. In 1950 the *OND* staff launched a daily radio news broadcast and added a full-time radio editor. This venture, one of three news broadcasts under Catholic auspices in the United States, proved for over ten years a useful means for informing Catholics on matters of local and general interest.

Diocesan Administration Building

Among other things, these media reported Bishop Schenk's concern about current social problems facing the nation and the diocese. Soon after the war, by appointing priest-directors for various projects, he enlisted the resources of the diocese in the relief work of the Church. Nor did he overlook the pressing needs of the poor in his own diocese. The Catholic Social Service Association was organized in 1947 to provide child welfare and family counseling services with Father Arthur Lemire as director. The schools established by Bishop Peschges to provide elementary religious and secular education for children of migrant workers were expanded and improved. This expansion included the establishment of summer boarding schools at Moorhead in 1945 and Crookston in 1949. These latter schools attracted national attention as the only such schools for migrant children in the United States. As the number of migrant children in the education

program rose to about 500 and additional work was done with the migrant families, the Sisters of St. Joseph and a number of diocesan priests took an active role in the work.

Fostering Spiritual Advances

Although Bishop Schenk showed great concern for the temporal welfare of his flock, he primarily endeavored to develop the spiritual life of the Catholics under his care. He launched a campaign early in his episcopate to have the rosary recited publicly every day in the churches of the diocese. To further this devotion and to bring the rosary into the daily lives of more Catholics, he asked Father Patrick Peyton, C.S.C., director of the Family Rosary Crusade, to conduct a crusade in the diocese in 1950 and again in 1958. The bishop placed special emphasis on the Confraternity of Christian Doctrine as a means for advancing the Catholic education of residents in this rural area and encouraged the work under the leadership of Father Joseph Mulvey, diocesan director after 1951, in frequent letters and speeches. Radio broadcasts served as another instrument for promoting the religious education of the laity. To further the use of this medium for religious purposes, Bishop Schenk appointed a committee of five priests to supervise the radio apostolate.

Youth activities received considerable attention under Bishop Schenk. A diocesan Catholic Youth Council was organized in 1950 under the direction of Father Leonard Weber, which in the ensuing years engaged in numerous meetings, conventions and rallies on the parish, deanery and diocesan levels. In 1952, the Catholic Youth

Oak Island Camp, Laketrails

Organization launched a wilderness camp for high school youth on Oak Island in Lake of the Woods. The only Catholic wilderness camp in the United States, Laketrails Base Camp, directed by Father William Mehrkens, started as a boy's camp and two years later added an additional camping period to accommodate girls. Newman clubs were organized at Bemidji State College and Moorhead State College with local priests appointed as chaplains to the Catholic college students.

Bishop Schenk gave renewed emphasis to the parochial school program. The Crookston Diocesan Educational Association, organized in 1950 by the two motherhouses in Crookston and expanded two years later to include priests and laity, focused on current trends and problems in education at its annual meetings. Because of the growing Catholic population, much-needed replacements for some of the original buildings and building opportunities of the postwar era, Bishop Schenk approved the construction of nine new parochial school buildings.

Many other building projects were also undertaken at this time. To facilitate the administrative work of the diocese, a diocesan administration building providing necessary office space, chapel and living quarters was constructed in 1950. Noting that the sisters in the diocese had largely concentrated on education, Bishop Schenk encouraged them to train more sisters for hospital work and to build hospitals. The Sisters of St. Joseph opened their first hospital at Park Rapids in 1945 and another at Baudette five years later. The Benedictines opened their third hospital at Mahnomen in 1945 and their fourth at Red Lake Falls in 1951. In addition they opened in 1950 St. Francis Hospital in Crookson, the largest and most modern hospital in northwestern Minnesota at the time, and added a large wing to St. Mary's Hospital in Detroit Lakes in 1959. St. Vincent's Hospital in Crookston was converted into a nursing home. The Franciscan Sisters completed a new St. Ansgar's Hospital at Moorhead in 1959, cited then as the only hospital in northwestern Minnesota to provide psychiatric care and the most modern hospital facility in the Red River Valley. When St. Joseph's Novitiate became too small for the increasing number of girls aspiring to the community, a new provincial house was built to care for larger classes, provide offices for the provincial superiors and house St. Joseph's Junior College.

An indication of the prosperity which the people living in the Red River Valley enjoyed during the fifteen years of Bishop Schenk's administration was the construction of the many new churches in all sections of the diocese. The shortage of building materials after the war checked the construction of churches for some time, but several parishes converted other buildings into temporary churches. Materials gradually became available and by 1949 there were seven churches under construction. In all, more than thirty parishes completed new churches during the postwar years.

To commemorate the fiftieth anniversary of their founding in Minnesota, the Knights of Columbus began a project to reconstruct old Fort St. Charles. In 1951 a marble altar was blessed on the site and the property was turned over to the Diocese of Crookston. Soon the Knights built cement palisades at the original corners of the old stockade and a chapel of cement logs. In 1960 they constructed out of cedar logs the walls, blockhouses, powder magazine and gates of the fort. Though accessible only by boat or airplane during the summer months, Fort St. Charles has become a top tourist attraction in Minnesota.

Father Aulneau, who had lived briefly at old Fort St. Charles before his death by the hands of Indians, was honored in 1949 when the bishops of Minnesota decided to note the centennial anniversary of the Minnesota Territory by erecting at Warroad a monument and commemorative church to him. The result was the construction of the largest log church in the United States, designed by the noted architect, Ursa Freed, who also gave one of the largest donations.

Several other activities in the diocese contributed notably to the spiritual growth during these years. The retreat movement received the bishop's encouragement, with the result that retreats became available to almost anyone of high school age or older. In 1955, two priests seeking quarters for the first new chapter of the Congregation of the Servants of the Paraclete, a young community which had started only seven years before, opened Our Lady of the Snows Retreat House for priests on Fifth Crow Wing Lake near Nevis. Coincident with the arrival of the Paracletes the death or illness of several parish

St. Mary's Church and Rectory, Warroad

priests made it necessary for Bishop Schenk to ask that the community accept several pastorates. Although parish work is not strictly part of their apostolate, this group gave valuable service to the diocese by caring for parishes and by providing priests for substitute assignments.

Bishop Schenk devoted considerable attention to an apostolate among the nurses working in the Catholic hospitals. In 1947 delegates from the Catholic hospitals formed the Catholic Hospital Association and Father Arthur Lemire was appointed the bishop's executive secretary for this organization, the first of its kind in Minnesota. This organization met quarterly to discuss hospital problems. A Diocesan Council of Catholic Nurses was organized in 1958 to promote professional competence and to encourage spiritual excellence. To meet the demand for more nurses in the Catholic hospitals throughout the Red River Valley, St. Francis Hospital added a school of practical nursing in 1957.

Bishop Schenk inaugurated a Diocesan Development Fund in 1959 to "establish the necessary reserve to permit the Diocese to meet the ever pressing demands of those who require our care and our charitable enterprise." Funds collected in this annual drive were intended to eliminate a number of special collections and assessments, to support the Catholic charities agency and the diocesan newspaper, to pay for the costs of diocesan administration and to subsidize the education of priests. Other diocesan projects, such as the establishment of new parishes and missions, building of Newman centers at the secular colleges and radio programs, were also to be included. Part of the funds from the first drive helped to pay for a $100,000 renovation of the cathedral for the golden jubilee celebration of the diocese in 1960.

On February 3, 1960, Catholics in the diocese learned of the transfer of Bishop Schenk to the Diocese of Duluth and the appointment of the Most Reverend Laurence A. Glenn as Bishop of Crookston. Bishop Schenk was loved by everyone, but in a special way by minority groups. He was honored on a number of occasions by Mexican migrant workers, whose spiritual and temporal welfare he had promoted. At the forty-second Catholic Indian Congress, held at Red Lake in 1954, Chief Peter Graves made the bishop an honorary member of the tribe for his great spiritual interest in the Chippewa and, in this honor rarely given to anyone, named him Chief Red Golden Eagle.

The Fourth Shepherd

Bishop Glenn, who was installed in Crookston on April 20, 1960, was born in Bellingham, Washington, in 1900 and was ordained to the priesthood for the Diocese of Duluth in 1927. After receiving a Master's degree in sociology from the Catholic University of America in 1928, the young priest became director of Catholic Charities in Duluth, an office which he held for twenty years. Until 1947 he served also as assistant pastor of the Church of St. John the Evangelist, and from 1947 to 1958 pastor of St. James Church in West Duluth. In 1951 he was consecrated as the first auxiliary bishop of Duluth. After the death of Bishop Thomas Welch on September 9, 1959, he served as apostolic administrator of the diocese until his appointment as the fourth Bishop of Crookston.

During these first years of Bishop Glenn's administration, educational facilities have been expanded. The Sisters of St. Benedict embarked upon a $2,300,000 building project. The result was a new Mount St. Benedict high school plant, opened in 1963, which included a residence hall for 200 girls, a seventeen room classroom building, a library, a gymnasium and an administration building. At the same time the sisters expanded Corbett College, a junior college begun in 1957 for members of the Benedictine order, to allow the admission of lay women. This was the first Catholic college for lay persons in the Diocese of Crookston. The Benedictines also agreed to staff Colegio San Carlos, a college in Bogota, Colombia, as their first foreign mission. With facilities expanded at Mount St. Benedict, Cathedral High School was converted into a boy's high school and opened for students from the parishes surrounding Crookston. With funds from the Diocesan Development Drive, Bishop Glenn was able to devote more money to Newman work on the secular college campuses. A $95,000 Newman Center was opened at Bemidji State College in 1963. At Moorhead State College, a house was purchased to provide facilities for the Newman work until a larger structure could be provided when funds were available.

Urbanization has affected the Red River Valley just as deeply as it has other rural areas in the Province of St. Paul. Mobility is high, and the annual loss to the area of young adults is staggering. Catholics form a small minority, only about fifteen per cent, of the 217,000 persons living in the diocese. The overall Catholic population has very gradually increased to 38,590 in 1962. While some rural communities have lost so many Catholic families that it is hardly possible to maintain a church building, the Catholic congregations in several of the larger towns have grown rapidly. If such a growth trend continues in some of the towns, facilities for worship and education must be expanded.

An area composed of farms and small communities cannot retain a large proportion of its young people. The number of available jobs remains relatively stable or may even decline with modern technology, and this situation forces the surplus youth to migrate to the cities or to form a restless subgroup at home. With few large communities in the Diocese of Crookston, many young people must leave northern Minnesota, and many of those who acquire an advanced education do not return because the number of jobs for college graduates is very limited.

Actually the northern forested area acts as a sponge, absorbing population in bad times and releasing it in economically good times. When non-farm employment is available, the tendency is for farmers to rent out their land and seek full-time jobs, and sometimes to leave the area entirely. When non-farm employment is not available there is a damming up on farms of people who would otherwise leave. This instability effects the life of the small rural parish.

The history of northwestern Minnesota can never be fully understood without a knowledge of the labors of the Catholic missionaries and pioneers who helped develop the spirit of this state. Mass was offered on makeshift altars before the forts and homes of the white men appeared. From the arrival of Father Mesaiger in 1731, the civilization and culture of this area have deep Catholic roots. The early explorers were Catholic and so were the French fur traders. Priests were teaching Christian doctrine to the Indians before white settlers penetrated into the Red River Valley. The first settlers brought their Catholic faith and sometimes even their own priests with them. Well rooted in Catholic heritage, "budding Crookston" continued in this pioneer optimism under four bishops. The spirit continues to permeate the work of the clergy and laity after more than fifty years of gradual growth.

Mount St. Benedict Motherhouse, Crookston

St. Joseph's Provincial House, Crookston

RELIGIOUS IN THE DIOCESE OF CROOKSTON —————————————————

Benedictine Fathers (St. John's Abbey)

Oblate Fathers of Mary Immaculate (Central Province; Assumption Province)

Servants of the Paraclete

Society of the Precious Blood

————————————

Benedictine Sisters of Pontifical Jurisdiction (St. Gertrude's Priory)

Benedictine Sisters of Pontifical Jurisdiction (St. Benedict's Priory)

Franciscan Sisters of the Immaculate Conception

Sisters of St. Joseph of Bourg, France, of Pontifical Jurisdiction

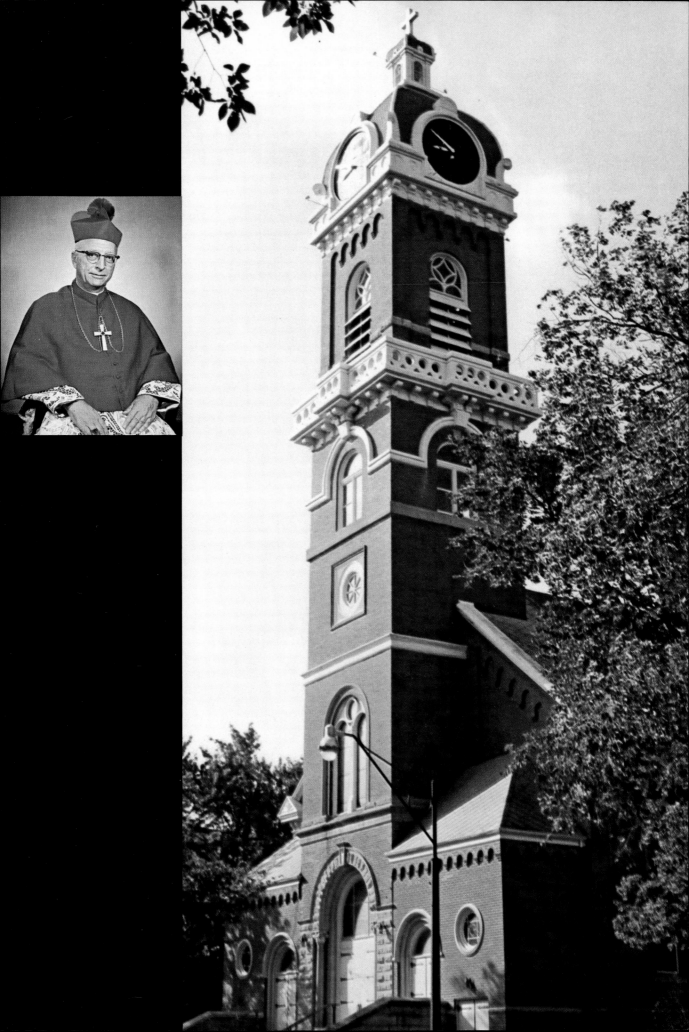

DIOCESE OF NEW ULM

by Reverend Germain Kunz

A S MEN STEP OFF their lives on the face of the earth, each takes his own trail and leaves his own marks behind. Some marks are shallow and others are deep; a few become more vivid with time. The marks that endure are the focus of succeeding generations in man's endless search for guidance and inspiration. Speculation about the future does not have the same universal appeal, but planning and dreaming have always been an important part of human thoughts also. The early decades of the twentieth century saw a good deal of both types of thinking in regard to the territorial boundaries of the Archdiocese of St. Paul.

A great deal of conjecture was finally ended on December 4, 1957, when Pope Pius XII made public his apostolic constitution of November 18, 1957, establishing the Diocese of New Ulm. The fifteen western counties of the metropolitan see (Big Stone, Brown, Chippewa, Kandiyohi, Lac Qui Parle, Lincoln, Lyon, McLeod, Meeker, Nicollet, Redwood, Renville, Sibley, Swift and Yellow Medicine) formed the territory of the new diocese. And with 9,863 square miles, the new offspring was to be territorially larger than its mother. New Ulm, in Brown County, was named the see city and the Church of the Holy Trinity in New Ulm was designated as the cathedral.

Ten days after establishing the new diocese Pope Pius XII appointed Monsignor Alphonse J. Schladweiler, then pastor of the Church of St. Agnes in St. Paul, as its first bishop. On January 29, 1958, Monsignor Schladweiler was consecrated in the St. Paul Cathedral by Archbishop William O. Brady. On the following day the diocese was canonically erected and Bishop Schladweiler was installed in the Holy Trinity Cathedral. The trails were blazed; New Ulm now faced its own future.

Early White Travelers

The territory of southern and western Minnesota remained in the possession of the Indians until the 1851 treaty signed at Traverse des Sioux. As a result of this treaty 21,000,000 acres of land were ceded to the government by the Sioux. All the territory of the present New Ulm diocese was included with the exception of a ten-mile strip of land on each side of the Minnesota River from Lake Traverse to Little Rock Creek about eight miles northwest of the city of New Ulm. In 1858 the Sioux Indians signed another treaty giving up the land north of the Minnesota River.

But even while the land was still Indian territory, it had been penetrated by explorers, fur traders and missionaries.

The first recorded explorer to reach the territory of the present New Ulm diocese was the Frenchman, Pierre Charles Le Sueur. In his earlier explorations of the Northwest he had heard reports among the Indians which led him to believe that copper deposits existed near the

122

Signing of Treaty of Traverse des Sioux, 1851
(oil by Millet)

Jonathan Carver

southernmost bend of the Minnesota River. During the month of September, 1700, he started his journey up the Minnesota River and by the end of that month had reached the mouth of the Blue Earth River near the present site of Mankato. Here he built a fort at which he spent the winter. In spring of 1701 he made the return journey with samples of earth from that region.

Though there is no evidence to indicate that Le Sueur traveled up the Minnesota River beyond the mouth of the Blue Earth, a map with a fairly accurate charting of the Minnesota River was drawn by a French geographer in 1703. The very existence of this map would seem to indicate that, if not Le Sueur, someone else probably explored the upper Minnesota River at that time.

In November, 1766, Jonathan Carver began his Minnesota River explorations. He traveled up the river as far as the future New Ulm where a hard freeze made further water travel

123

impossible. He wintered there with the Sioux and made his return trip in April, 1767.

An expedition of scientists guided by Major Stephen H. Long started up the Minnesota River on July 9, 1823. Professor William H. Keating of the University of Pennsylvania was the geologist and historian on the expedition. There were also twenty-one soldiers, with Joseph Renville as a Dakota interpreter and William Joseph Snelling as assistant guide and interpreter. On July 13 the expedition reached Traverse des Sioux. From there they moved westward past Swan Lake, crossing the Minnesota River and following the southwest side of the river valley to Lac Qui Parle, Big Stone and Traverse lakes.

In the summer of 1835 G. W. Featherstonhaugh and William Williams Mather traveled up the Minnesota River to Big Stone and Traverse Lakes.

Two years later artist and explorer George Catlin, accompanied by Doctor Robert C. Wood and an Indian guide, traveled to the Pipestone quarries following the normal route along the Minnesota River to Traverse des Sioux and then overland to New Ulm through Brown, Redwood and Lyon counties. Approximately the same route was followed by Joseph Nicolas Nicollet and John C. Fremont during their extensive Minnesota explorations between 1836 and 1843.

In 1844 an expedition headed by Captain J. Allen explored the territory around the present sites of Marshall and Redwood Falls.

Among the earliest and best-known Indian traders of Catholic background were Joseph Renville at Lac Qui Parle (1826), Louis Proven-

St. Peter in the 1850's

calle at Traverse des Sioux (1834) and Joseph La Framboise at Little Rock (1841).

Thomas S. Williamson and Stephen R. Riggs, Presbyterian ministers who established an Indian Mission at Lac Qui Parle in 1835, were probably the first Christian missionaries in western Minnesota. Father Augustin Ravoux made several missionary journeys to evangelize the Sioux at Traverse des Sioux, Little Rock and Lac Qui Parle between 1841 and 1847.

More than 150 years would pass between Le Sueur's original journey and the establishment of the first permanent settlement. The trails of history seemed to be advancing in slow motion.

Early Settlements

Once the land in western Minnesota was opened for white settlement, pioneers gradually arrived following the waterways of the Minnesota and other rivers. The first settlement in the present New Ulm diocese was located at St. Peter. As early as 1853 Catholic settlers had come up the Minnesota River to establish homes in and around the townsite of St. Peter. That same year a military base, Fort Ridgley, was established on the Minnesota River a few miles north of present New Ulm. With soldiers in the area, the newly opened Indian lands seemed protected sufficiently for settlement.

The Chicago Land Society, which had been formed in 1853 for the purpose of establishing a German colony in the American Midwest, sent scouts to the Minnesota Territory to select a suitable site. They returned with enthusiastic reports about the land at Swan Lake in Nicollet County. A second fact-finding party, sent to check the report of the earlier group, preferred a site near Le Sueur to Swan Lake.

A group of thirty settlers (fourteen of them Catholic) was then sent by the Chicago Land Society. They had authority to make a definite decision concerning a site and to begin the work of building a settlement so that other members of the society could soon follow. This group arrived in St. Paul in September and before the end of the month they left for Le Sueur. But they were disappointed with the Le Sueur site, so ten of them moved on to Swan Lake only to experience the same disappointment.

New Ulm, 1856

Quite discouraged, six of these men returned to the main group at Traverse des Sioux while the more determined, Ludwig Meyer, Alois Palmer, Athanasius Henle and Frank Massapust, made their way toward Fort Ridgley. On the way they met Joseph La Framboise who told them about the good land at the site of the present New Ulm. They visited the spot, found it to their liking and then returned to the main group.

Encouraged by the new report, the band set out for the New Ulm area the very next morning. On their arrival all were pleased with the sight that greeted them. The land was rich, and a plentiful supply of water was available in the Minnesota and Cottonwood rivers.

There was, however, one serious drawback which they could not ignore. This was a lack of timber for fuel and shelters. Since it was already October, they left the site and went to a wooded area nearby in what is now Milford Township. A few of them crossed the Minnesota River into West Newton Township (present St. George parish). Here they prepared for the coming cold season.

During the winter the settlers became more and more impressed with this new location— so much so, in fact, that they were ready to

forget about the New Ulm site and make this the townsite of their colony. However, Ludwig Meyer strongly opposed this decision and his wishes prevailed.

On May 16, 1855, another twenty members of the Chicago Land Society arrived. With them was a surveyor named Volk who, according to instructions from the society's president, Frederick Beinhorn, laid out the townsite of New Ulm.

On May 30, 1855, official approval of the New Ulm site was received from Chicago and that very day the settlement was given a name. Since most of the settlers had come from Erbach (Schwabenland) near Ulm, Württemberg, the new community was called New Ulm.

In 1856 a Father Brady was sent to organize the parish at St. Peter. Shortly after his arrival he died a victim of typhoid fever. Later that same year, construction of the first Catholic church in what would become the New Ulm diocese was begun in St. Peter under the supervision of Father Valentine Sommereisen of Mankato. But due to the inability of the parishioners to meet the church payments, it was closed during the panic of 1857, and services were temporarily held in the courthouse. (Later during the Indian Uprising the church was used as a storehouse and a place for the wounded. It was finally redeemed by Father Valentine Venn.)

The first church in the immediate New Ulm area was begun at St. George in the fall of 1857, but due to a severe winter it was not finished until the spring of 1858.

Father F. X. Weninger, S. J., preached a mission at a farm home just outside the city of New Ulm in the fall of 1856. Shortly thereafter plans were discussed for building a church but work was not begun until February, 1857, and it was not yet finished at the time of the Sioux Uprising in 1862.

Father Sommereisen visited the New Ulm Catholics and said mass in a farm home five miles southwest of New Ulm. A church dedicated to St. Joseph was built there in 1861.

During these early years settlements began to spring up along the rivers and Catholics were among the early settlers in most cases. On the banks of the Crow River in Meeker County, the village of Forest City was founded, and a large number of Irish settlers brought the Catholic faith to this community early in 1856. Later that year and again the following year more Irish Catholics arrived. Benedictine monks from St. John's attended to their spiritual welfare.

In the spring of 1856 the first Catholics arrived in Glencoe on Buffalo Creek. Others soon followed and the first mass was said there in 1858. These settlers were cared for by Benedictines residing in Shakopee.

The upper Minnesota Valley (northwest of Fort Ridgley) was not accessible for white settlement until 1858 when the Indian reservation north of the river was ceded by the Sioux. Previous to this, it was illegal to settle in the Indian reservation without special permission of the government and the consent of the Indians. Hence only a few missionaries and traders were found in the reservation during these years.

Sioux Indian Uprising

The Indian action against the white settlers during the Sioux Indian Uprising of 1862 is normally considered as savage, cruel and inhuman, and yet this very cruelty can be shown to have substantial precedent in the inhuman treatment

Sioux traveling

of Indians by the whites. The pages of history seem to consider any Indian victory in battle as a massacre and a white triumph as a triumph of justice. Though the atrocities of the Sioux Uprising of 1862 cannot be justified, the guilt of the Indians can be greatly lessened, and most of the causes can be laid at the doorsteps of the white settlers and representatives of the federal government. The widespread shedding of blood could have been avoided by the whites.

What caused the uprising on the Minnesota frontier? The answer can be found in a combination of reasons, some stemming from past events, some immediate and peculiar to the time.

The coming of the white man to Minnesota brought a gradual acquisition of Indian lands through a series of treaties. The treaties were signed not because the Sioux preferred cash to their lands, but rather out of fear that the land would be snatched from them without reimbursement if they refused to sign. So they chose the lesser of two evils. The most important treaty was signed at Traverse des Sioux in 1851. There the Sioux gave up 21,000,000 acres of land for $1,665,000 in cash and annuities to be paid over a fifty-year period.

The Sioux were now restricted to two reservations along the upper Minnesota River, each about seventy miles long and twenty miles wide. The Upper Sioux occupied the northern reservation and the Lower Sioux the southern reservation. Two Indian agencies were established by the federal government as administrative centers. The Upper or Yellow Medicine Agency was located at the mouth of the Yellow Medicine River near present-day Granite Falls. The Lower or Redwood Agency was located about thirty miles down the Minnesota River near what is now Redwood Falls.

Much of the trouble between Indians and whites stemmed from misunderstandings over amounts and methods of payments. The Indians were tricked into signing traders' papers which gave to the white and half-breed traders about $400,000 of the cash payments.

In 1858 the Indians signed away the half of their reservation north of the Minnesota River, more than a million acres, thinking that they would receive increased annuity payments, food and hunting supplies. Again the traders' claims absorbed most of the benefits. Disappointment and bitterness grew as the Indian invariably found himself with less land and no noticeable increase in benefits.

Usually payments of cash and supplies were made simultaneously at the Indian agencies about the end of June. In 1862 the tardy action of Congress in appropriating the funds followed by a month-long discussion in the treasury department as to whether to pay in paper currency rather than gold delayed these payments. (Coincidentally, the $71,000 in gold arrived in St. Paul on August 16, the day before the first bloodshed.) The need of prompt payment that year was more important than ever before because the crop failure of 1861 was having its effect on the Indians, and they were in dire need.

In July, 1862, about five thousand hungry Indians appeared at the Upper Sioux Agency at Yellow Medicine demanding that the food supplies in the warehouse be issued to them. The Indian Agent, T. J. Galbraith, did not want to change the normal procedure of making payment of cash and provisions at the same time, but to avoid an outbreak he did issue some food to the demanding Indians. Day by day the Indians grew more impatient. On August 4 five hundred of them returned. They broke into the warehouse and carried off some flour. Conflict was avoided only by assurance of more supplies, and a conference was arranged for August 6. The Indians attending the meeting agreed to return to their villages and wait for the annuity payment if more food supplies were given to them.

Meanwhile, at the Lower Agency at Redwood,

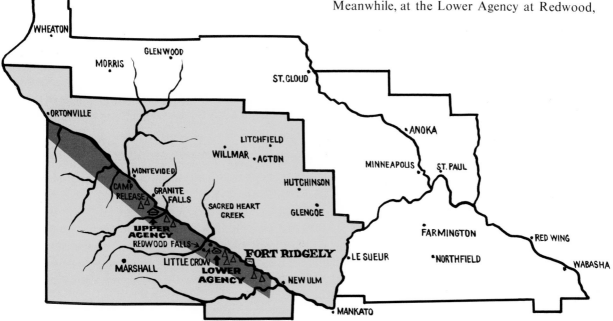

Sioux War fought principally in New Ulm diocese

Sioux War panorama

a payment of supplies had been made in June with another promised in August. But this promise was not kept. At a meeting on August 15, a chief named Little Crow asked the traders to extend credit. The traders refused. One of the store-keepers, Andrew J. Myrick, callously aggravated the situation and added to the tension by stating in the presence of several hundred Indians, "If they are hungry, let them eat grass." History repeated itself by echoing the sentiments of Marie Antoinette's much more publicized "Let them eat cake," spoken just as imprudently in similarly troubled times.

The first bloodshed was not actually planned in advance. On Sunday, August 17, four Indian hunters were returning from an unsuccessful hunting trip in the Big Woods near Kandiyohi. In passing a white farm in Acton Township, Meeker County, one of the Indians found a nest full of eggs. A companion warned him that the eggs belonged to the whites and this angered the first Indian. He dashed the eggs to the ground and said, "You are a coward. You are afraid of the white man. You are afraid to take even eggs from him, though you are half-starved." To show that he was not a coward he stated that he would kill the white man and dared his companions to come along.

But it wasn't that simple. The farm held five whites, three men, a woman and a girl. The Indians killed them all. Then, in fright at their deed, they stole some horses and raced home to their village. When they reported what they had done to Red Middle Voice, the leader of the Rise Creek village, he took them to Chief Shakopee. He in turn decided that a council of chiefs should be held at Little Crow's village that very night.

Though Little Crow was not the principal Sioux leader, it was felt that his support and leadership would be essential to wage a successful fight against the whites. The pros and cons were aired at the meeting. The Indians felt certain that they

128

would all be punished for the white killings and their lands taken away. Others still maintained, and at first Little Crow was among them, that chances for a successful uprising were non-existent because whites would follow whites until the Indians would be overcome.

Finally Little Crow, probably hoping to regain the prestige he had lost among the chiefs when he was defeated in an election for the speaker of the Lower Sioux, agreed to lead the Sioux in battle. The decision of the chiefs in favor of a general uprising was by no means unanimous. But the dissenters were overruled and eventually most of them felt compelled to go along with the general feeling. Before the Indians disbanded, an attack on the Lower Indian Agency was planned for the following morning.

The fact that the United States was then engaged in the Civil War might have led the Indians to believe that the white men were too preoccupied in the South to make any concentrated effort against their uprising. At any rate, the hour had come to release the bitterness that had arisen.

Shortly after sunrise on August 18 a large party of Sioux appeared armed and in war paint at the Lower Agency. The braves forced their way into the stores and trading posts. The storekeepers who had refused to extend credit to the hungry Indians were chosen as their first victims. At a signal, the slaughter began. After the first encounter was over, thirteen whites had been killed fighting, seven more in flight; about ten were captured and some fifty escaped. The number of escapees was large because the Indians soon directed their attention to plunder. Found among the dead was Andrew J. Myrick, his mouth stuffed with grass.

From this point the uprising spread like a wind-swept prairie fire. Until word of the war could outdistance the warriors, the whites were all taken by surprise, for they had been on friendly terms with the Indians up till the outbreak. Probably the greatest loss of lives occurred in Brown and Renville counties. In Brown County's Milford Township about fifty were killed before nightfall.

A tragic note of surprise and horror pervaded the reminiscences of the survivors of the uprising. The following are some of the details related by Maria Hartman-Bobleter, a survivor of the Milford Township slaughter:

My husband, Florian Hartman, was on the 18th of August engaged with another man, John Rohner, in binding wheat near our house. When I had their dinner ready for them I heard some noise, and on looking out I could see houses on fire, and also thought I could see them at work trying to save the buildings. At the same moment I heard a cry "Nippo" (Kill) and the reports of several rifles. Thinking the Indians were killing some cattle, I ran out to see what was going on. An Indian came close up to the house, stared at me and then ran away. Full of fear I hurried toward my husband who was about forty rods from the house, and on crossing the road I noticed a man lying on the ground and thought he was asleep. It was Hartman's hired man, Rohner, and he was covered with blood. Looking for my husband I found him about thirty steps away from Rohner, lying on the ground. He motioned to me to keep quiet and to drag him into the cornfield, because he was shot. Stricken with fear, I was powerless to do it. I cast myself down beside my husband and in my excessive grief knew not what to do. Soon after, two Indians came up to the dying Rohner and fired two more shots at him. My poor husband then begged me to hide in the cornfield, because I could not do him any good where I was. I ran and hid as he told me, digging a hole in the ground with my hands to creep into. I remained there till toward evening. Two Indians passed close by me, but did not notice me.

About eight o'clock I heard someone weeping bitterly, but did not dare to leave my place, thinking it might be an Indian. After a while I crept toward my husband, and found him cold and stiff in death. I took some hair from his head as a remembrance, and fled into the woods. Even the animals seemed to realize what was going on. Under a large oak, in the vicinity of a spring, I remained all night, and toward four o'clock in the morning I hurried toward the Minnesota in order to escape across the ferry into Nicollet county. But the boat was on the other side of the river. I tried in vain to get across on the rope, and so I had to hide all day in the woods, and suffered greatly from the mosquitoes. About eight o'clock in the evening I went back to our house and passed five Indian tepees on my way. I went into the house to take some clothing, and in picking up some of the bedding that was lying on the floor I noticed a wounded Indian lying thereon, and immediately ran away. When I passed the barn in my flight an Indian fired at me, but missed me on account of the darkness of the night. During the whole of that night and the following day I remained in concealment. On the fourth day it rained heavily. I was very tired and completely worn out. Such sadness overcame me that I was almost sorry for not having found death at the hands of the Indians. The rain continued to the fifth day, and being completely drenched, I ventured back to the house; but on going in I found everything gone. However, I felt happy to find some dry underclothing to put on. The hogs were in the pen and screaming from hunger. I had compassion on them and gave them some corn. I was lucky enough to find a loaf of bread, and with this I went back to my hiding place. But I was sorry to have betrayed my presence through my compassion for hungry animals. On the sixth day I wanted to go to the house, but noticing some Indians

First Battle of New Ulm, August 19, 1862
(painting by Anton Gág)

near the place I hurried back. During this and the next day I heard continual shooting. On the evening of the eighth day my dog came to me and was overjoyed to see me. I, too, rejoiced as if I had met with a friend in my terrible loneliness. I shared the remainder of my bread with him. He seemed so very hungry. But at the same moment the thought struck me that he might betray my hiding place and in order to remove that danger I took my apron and strangled him with it. But he fought so fiercely, that it was with the greatest exertions that I succeeded in killing him.

On the morning of the ninth day I heard a great noise which seemed to come nearer and nearer; but I soon felt relieved when I found it to be only a few hogs. I remained two more days in my concealment, and hardly dared to go a hundred steps farther. In my terrible condition, living on a little bread and wild berries, life seemed to have new charms. I enjoyed the

singing of the birds, and thanked my Creator and prayed for the preservation of my life.

A strange presentment made me leave my hiding place on the twelfth day. I went to the homes of my brothers, and to that of Cassimir, but found them all empty. A terrible sight presented itself to me in Zettel's house. There I found the bodies of the father and his four children, and between them a loaf of bread. I was very hungry and greatly desired to take the bread, but the odor of the corpses was so repulsive that I could not eat it. In Pelzyls' house I found the dead bodies of his father and of a woman. A short distance from the house I found the bodies of old Messmer and of a girl. In Anton Henle's house lay the body of one of the children. The air was everywhere filled with the stench of the corpses.

I now determined to go to New Ulm, six miles distant. In the cemetery I noticed a white flag, which filled me with courage and hope. But when I came near town and noticed that many buildings had been burned down and the town was deserted, new fear and anxiety came over me. I did not go farther, but returned immediately to my hiding place because I was afraid I might meet Indians in town. At seven o'clock in the evening I was again at my brother Anton's house, from which I could hear a great noise. I went in because I thought I would have to die anyhow. The noise, however, was caused by all sorts of animals that had gathered in the house.

From there I went to my own house, and to bed, and reproached myself for having gone so far. On the following day I searched for some potatoes; but it was only with great difficulty, and after going to two houses, that I could find a match. As soon as I had found some matches I returned to my house, feeling rich and happy, and prepared a soup. I had two matches left, and for fear that I might lose them I kept up a fire at a stump nearby.

On the fourteenth day I found some eggs and a sack of flour, but could not make use of the flour. After that I remained indoors most of the time. An ox came up to the house with an ugly wound. I washed the wound and the animal got well. I then began to gather plums and nuts and dig potatoes, because I had lost all hope of being rescued, and wanted to provide for the winter. I was under the impression that all the settlers had been put to death.

On the seventeenth day I went to look for the body of my husband, and, on my way thither, I heard some shooting and the barking of dogs. I almost fainted on looking up and seeing eight men coming toward me. One of them leveled his gun, and now I thought I would after all have to die. But the cry "Oh, sister!" roused me again, and in a moment I was in the arms of my brother, Athanasius, who had taken me for a squaw on account of the changes made by sufferings and anxieties. Fortunately, I knew of an old wagon nearby which had been left by the Indians. My brother had only a sled for his horse. The wagon was fixed up and he went to town in it, where I again enjoyed the society of human beings, of which I had been deprived for more than a fortnight.

Maria Hartman-Bobleter was a sister of two of the first Catholic pioneers in the New Ulm area, Athanasius and Anton Henle. On the first day of the uprising twenty-one of the Henle relationship were killed.

The toll of the first day was staggering to the small settlements. A military detachment from Fort Ridgley was ambushed at the Redwood Ferry and almost wiped out. Farmers and their families throughout the entire Minnesota Valley were killed or captured; their homes were pillaged and burned. Those who received a warning and managed to escape fled in haste to Fort Ridgley, New Ulm, Mankato, St. Cloud—even as far as Fort Snelling and St. Paul.

At midnight the attack on the Upper Agency began. The fighting was strictly one-sided, and as word of the uprising spread many of the settlers joined together in groups as they fled. This made the slaughter all the easier for Indians who overtook large, panic-stricken bands of whites.

The loss of white lives was great, but it would have been even greater had it not been for some friendly Indians who warned some whites and even led them to safety. Indian John Other Day guarded a group of sixty-two whites at the Upper Agency one whole night and then guided them for three days until they were beyond the reach of hostiles.

Resistance eventually began to form as troop reinforcements from Mankato, St. Peter and Fort Snelling arrived, and citizens of village and farm became organized. New Ulm and Fort Ridgley were the whites' greatest strongholds and several attacks on each were warded off successfully. New Ulm suffered great losses in the second attack. One hundred ninety buildings were burned. The town was abandoned for fear of another attack and the possibility of epidemics. There were over a thousand refugees in New Ulm at the time.

But the whites managed to hold at this point. With surprising speed they organized a military force and with army help they took the offensive. But, although the tide had turned, hostilities were not over. Indians still attacked white settlements, and the soldiers suffered losses in ambushes and direct engagements. The victory of Sibley's forces at Wood Lake on September 23, 1862, marked the end of organized Indian fighting, and on September 26 the first of the white and half-breed prisoners were freed at Camp Release. A total of 107 whites and 162 half-breeds were eventually given up by the Indians.

Reports on the total number of lives lost in the Sioux Uprising of 1862 vary from about 500 to 1,400 soldiers and civilians. President Lincoln figured the number at 800. But even by the most conservative estimates the loss of life was great in western Minnesota.

The fighting of the Sioux Uprising was confined almost completely to the territory now comprising the New Ulm diocese. The area was almost totally depopulated. Some of the terrified settlers never came back to the ruins of their homes and villages, but many were willing to dare again.

They returned to clear the rubble and rebuild their homesteads as soon as the danger seemed past. Life went on, but an indelible mark was left on the state.

The Role of Father Berghold

By the end of the Civil War, in the spring of 1865, there was no further danger of Indian uprisings. An era of prosperity and rapid growth began.

Since waterways were almost the only means of bulk transportation, the settlers naturally continued to establish settlements on rivers and tributaries. Oxcart travel, the only other possibility, was slow and not suited for rushing a harvest to market.

New Ulm was among the Catholic communities experiencing rapid expansion during this period. From a commercial point of view, it had the advantage of being located on the Minnesota River; from a religious point of view it had the good fortune of securing as pastor Father Alexander Berghold whose foresight was only exceeded by his zeal.

In the summer of 1866, Father Berghold visited New Ulm while he was preaching a mission at Mankato. He was so impressed by the town and

Father Alexander Berghold

its people that he told Bishop Thomas Langdon Grace of his desire to be stationed at New Ulm when he returned from a visit to Europe.

Back from Europe in December of the same year, Father Berghold again called on Bishop Grace in St. Paul. He had not changed his mind about New Ulm, and the bishop forthwith appointed him pastor. Unannounced and quite unexpected, Father Berghold arrived at New Ulm on December 26, 1868, to take up his duties. His congregation numbered sixty Catholic families.

Shortly after his arrival Father Berghold converted an old barn into a rectory which would serve him until a more fitting dwelling could be provided in 1869. He did most of the work with his own hands. He also labored with the construction crew on the completion of the church which had been already building in 1866 when he had first visited the town. This church was dedicated by Bishop Grace on September 12, 1870.

As soon as the church was dedicated Father Berghold began to agitate for a new Catholic school. In 1872 a convent was built which would also serve as a boarding school until 1881 when a new school was built and dedicated.

On July 15, 1881, a devastating tornado struck New Ulm. It completely destroyed the new school. Only the four walls of the church remained standing; the steeple and bells were hurled into the street. The roof was blown off the convent and damage was done to the rectory roof. Extensive damage was done the rest of the town also and many people were injured. The boarding school addition to the convent was turned into a temporary hospital.

When the crisis passed, Father Berghold began to push for a hospital and home for the aged. In 1883 this dream, too, became a reality.

By this time the church had been outgrown by the congregation and an addition was built. Finally, in 1888 Father Berghold began to raise money for building a new church. On May 4, 1890, the cornerstone was laid by Bishop Joseph B. Cotter of Winona.

But Father Berghold was not destined to see the completion of the Romanesque structure destined to become the cathedral. A difference of opinion with Archbishop Ireland over Americanization of immigrants and the teaching of English in the parochial schools led to his sudden resignation as pastor of Holy Trinity Church. On December 7, 1890, Father Berghold sadly walked from the rectory to his carriage bidding his final farewell to the people and parish he had loved and served so well.

During his pastorate at New Ulm, Father Berghold's work involved something deeper and richer than the material construction of buildings. He brought the teaching and culture of Christianity to the people among whom he worked.

Father Berghold ministered not only to the people of New Ulm but to the entire population of an area almost coterminous with the New Ulm diocese. He brought the comforts and benefits of religion to St. George, Swan Lake, Sleepy Eye, Fort Ridgley, Leavenworth, Springfield, Lamberton, Wabasso, Walnut Grove, Redwood Falls, Birch Coulie, Sacred Heart, Lake Benton, Marshall, Big Stone Lake and Kranzburg, South

Homesteaders on the prairie

132

Dakota. Tales of his efforts to bring the sacraments to the sick and dying are many. He established, in all, eleven churches in this mission territory during his twenty-two years at New Ulm.

Railroads and Colonization

When Bishop Joseph Cretin arrived in his infant Diocese of St. Paul in 1851, one of his foremost interests was to increase the Catholic population of his territory by settling his coreligionists on the fertile lands of the area. His integrity forbade him to extol the oft-proclaimed virtues of the soil to prospective settlers until he had firsthand evidence that the land could live up to the claims being made. Even after the land advertisements had been investigated and found accurate, Bishop Cretin did not actively encourage colonists to settle in his diocese because an acute shortage of priests made it impossible to promise religious care. Bishop Grace followed the same course.

By this time the railroads were vying with one another to settle the lands along their respective lines. The railroads' interest was simple enough: more settlers meant increased passenger and freight revenue. The railroads made large tracts available to settlers and financed them at reasonable rates. The plan was quite successful.

When Father Ireland became coadjutor bishop of St. Paul (Dec. 21, 1875) he immediately adopted the already successful plan of colonizing railroad lands. On January 22, 1876, he announced that he had obtained land rights over 75,000 acres of railroad lands along the St. Paul & Pacific (later to become part of J. J. Hill's Great Northern line) and was ready to locate 2,000 Catholic immigrant families on these lands in Swift County. The towns of De Graff and Clontarf were soon platted there fourteen miles apart.

The initial project proved to be so successful that Bishop Ireland soon had to obtain additional lands. Within three years the colony comprised 117,000 acres of railroad land in Swift County and probably an equal amount of government lands.

Bishop Ireland invariably began a new colony by assigning a priest to advise and help the colonists as well as to minister to their spiritual needs. Next he arranged for the erection of a church around which the life of the colony would center, and also for the building of an immigration house which would afford temporary accommodations for the families of the settlers while they were selecting their farms. Father John McDermott was assigned to this task in the Swift County colonies.

Early in 1878 Bishop Ireland commissioned Colonel Josias R. King, a surveyor, to select a suitable townsite in Big Stone County. He obtained 200 acres for the townsite of Graceville, which was named after Bishop Grace. The railroads had not yet arrived in Big Stone County and no railroad lands were available. So the first settlers took up homestead and timber-culture claims.

Under the Homestead Act, a maximum of 160 acres of government lands could be claimed without charge by settlers who agreed to live on the land for a period of five years. Timber-culture claims required settlers to plant ten acres of trees for every 160 acres of government land claimed within a period of two years of the time the claim was made. Government lands were also available under a pre-emption claim which allowed the purchase of additional lands other than homesteads.

Bishop Ireland shipped five carloads of lumber by rail to Morris, then overland to Graceville with orders to build a church. Father A. V. Pelison was named resident pastor. Settlers arrived in March and April, and before winter seventy houses dotted the prairie surrounding the church.

In December, 1879, Ireland obtained control of 50,000 more acres of indemnity lands from the St. Paul, Minneapolis and Manitoba Railroad.

Indemnity lands were sections of land given to the railroads to compensate for the lands in the alternating railroad sections which were unsuitable for farming, such as lakes and alkali flats, and lands which had already been claimed as homesteads before the railroad lines were determined.

Within the year 100 Catholic families had arrived in Graceville. By September, 1881, the colony consisted of 400 Catholic settlers.

On July 12, 1879, Bishop Ireland announced the opening of 45,000 acres for settlement in Lyon County. Most of the lands near Minneota were taken by Irish settlers in 1879 and 1880. Father Michael J. Hanley was placed in charge. In 1880 Canon Peter VanHee, a Belgian priest, saw some of the brochures on Minnesota land. He interested his brother Angelus, a wealthy farmer,

Graceville at the turn of the century

and together they visited the Lyon County colony. The brothers were quite impressed. Angelus purchased 320 acres and returned to Belgium to tell his fellow countrymen of his find. Some fifty families came to America with Angelus in the spring of 1881. But all except a dozen families decided to settle in Illinois when they heard about the great blizzard of 1880. However, the success of VanHee soon brought the rest of the original group to Ghent, Minnesota. Father Louis Cornelius accompanied the Belgian farmers and was appointed pastor of the Minneota parish with Ghent six miles away as a mission.

In the spring of 1883, about fifty French-Canadian Catholics bought farms in the Lyon County colonies. That same year Father Cornelius returned to Belgium to recruit additional settlers. Soon seventeen families from Belgium and Holland arrived with Father Jules Emile DeVos who was named pastor of St. Eloi's parish in Ghent.

Because of their previous agricultural training and love for farming, the Belgium farmers made Ghent and Minneota the most successful of Bishop Ireland's colonies. Although at the start in 1880 they numbered only a handful, today their descendants own and operate almost every farm near Ghent and Minneota as well as many farms near Marshall, Green Valley and Cottonwood.

Although Bishop Ireland's colonization efforts were, on the whole, exceedingly successful, his final attempt to establish a colony ended in complete failure. Unfairly, all of his colonization work is often judged in light of the one failure.

The story of this unfortunate experience began in Ireland where the 1879 crop failure made it-

self felt in 1880. It was brought to Father James Nugent's attention in Liverpool that many of the Irish in Connemara were destitute. When a collection of alms was not sufficient to improve the situation, Father Nugent felt that emigration might ease the pressure on those who were left. So he appealed to Bishop Ireland to accept fifty families in his colonies. Against his better judgment, but filled with compassion at the suffering of fellow countrymen, Bishop Ireland agreed. He collected $5,000 and arranged for free railway passage to Big Stone County. He had sent orders to his agent in Big Stone County to reserve 50 farms of 160 acres, construct a frame house on each farm and break five acres of sod for immediate tillage. In addition, Bishop Ireland gave each family an issue of clothing, household furnishings, farm tools, sufficient seed for the year's planting and credit for a year's supply of food at Graceville.

The indigent settlers arrived in Graceville at spring planting time. However, the Connemaras were content to hire themselves out to other farmers during the summer rather than plant and harvest crops. Many even sold the seed and farm implements given them by Bishop Ireland.

A severe and early winter in 1880 soon brought reports of the great suffering of the Connemaras. An on-the-scene investigation by Dillon O'Brien and non-Catholics from Morris, showed that the hardships of the Connemaras were much their own doing. They had been warned about the severe winters and told to sod the exteriors of their houses. They neglected to do this. Their potatoes were frozen because they failed to dig cellars to protect them. They refused to collect free flour because they claimed the snow was too deep for their horses. Other farmers purchased it and hauled it away by hand on sleds. Their suffering from lack of fuel was shared by colonists, not only in Big Stone County, but all over the state of Minnesota. Some of the complaining settlers were even discovered to have hidden extra food and clothing in order to prove the acuteness of their suffering. Bishop Ireland personally provided $600 a month and he appealed to the St. Paul people for additional funds to help alleviate the suffering.

Since Bishop Ireland had provided them from the very beginning with everything they needed, the Connemaras felt that he would always continue to do so. When asked for an explanation of their slothful and imprudent conduct, one retorted: "The bishop brought us here and he must care for us." Seeing that the Connemaras had neither the inclination nor the ability to stay on the land, Ireland paid their return transportation to St. Paul and secured jobs for them there.

Bishop Ireland freely admitted that the Connemara experiment was the greatest grief of his life. The Connemara experiment failed because Father Nugent had chosen, not the competent but the incompetent, not the industrious but the shiftless. They had no experience whatsoever in tilling the soil and they had no inclination to learn.

The Irish settlers in Ireland's other colonies had at least some farm experience. Most of them had been operating small farms in the East before coming to Minnesota. All of his other colonists had incentive to succeed: they were protecting their own money which they had invested in their claims. The Connemaras did not have a cent of their own invested. Others came to the Minnesota colonies because they could foresee a good; the Connemaras came to escape an evil.

Bishop Ireland's colonization efforts ended at this point, not because of the Connemara failure, but because the frontier moved into Dakota Territory and no more railroad lands were available in Minnesota.

While the colonization efforts were going on, individual settlers were arriving and establishing farms elsewhere. The railroads had by now pretty well checkered the Minnesota frontier and it was possible to get the harvest to market.

Sod hut east of Madison in 1870's

Life on the Prairie

Accustomed as we are to our present standards of living, life on the western frontier may seem a little too challenging and harsh to us. But the pioneers accepted these challenges with the confidence that their freedom was worth it and that perseverance would soon bring better times.

One of the immediate problems facing any settler was the construction of a home. In most instances the dwelling, hurriedly assembled, was intended to be only a temporary shelter to be replaced by something more adequate and permanent as soon as possible. Since most of the New Ulm diocese was on the open prairie where trees were a rarity, lumber was simply not available locally. Before the coming of the railroad, transporting it to the frontier was almost impossible. Often the pioneers had to settle for a sod hut as their first protection from the elements.

The absence of wood presented another and even more serious problem, that of fuel for the long and cold winter season. Twisted slough hay and flax straw was the only fuel available for many settlers.

After the hurried construction of a temporary shelter, the most urgent need was tilling the soil so that a crop could be harvested the first year. Although the lack of trees was a hardship in many ways, it did have one advantage for the farmer. It spared the prairie settlers the agonizing and endless work of clearing the land before it could be tilled. But breaking the sod was still a slow and arduous task. Few farmers were fortunate enough to have anything better than a wooden plow to accomplish the task. About five acres were all that a settler could plow the first year.

The settlers in Bishop Ireland's colonies were fortunate in that these first two hurdles were cleared for most of them. When they arrived to claim their lands almost all of them already found a small, but wooden, frame house and five acres of tilled soil.

Though the pioneers knew nothing of our current standard of living, they were also spared today's problems of inflation, the ever-increasing operating expense of farming and the high cost of living. With the profits of their first few crops of meager acreage, the industrious farmers were able to replace their impoverished tem-

Breaking sod

porary homes with spacious comfortable homes as well as pay for their land.

Even as today, the forces of nature were not always on the side of the farmer. The prairie winds, unhindered by hills and groves, swept fiercely across the open lands damaging both homes and crops. Hail storms all too frequently cut down a promising harvest. Drought was a not infrequent visitor and certainly there are few who have not heard of the intensity of a Minnesota blizzard.

Among the pioneer disasters, the grasshopper (locust) plagues from 1873 to 1877 are perhaps remembered as the most devastating. Fortunately the entire area was not infested by them every year during this period, but few sections of the New Ulm diocese escaped their ravages completely.

They arrived suddenly in great clouds, so numerous that the sun was at times obscured. Once they landed they attacked almost everything green in sight and leveled it to the ground.

The many efforts to disperse and destroy them all seemed futile. "Hopperdozers," drags made of sheet metal and wood covered with tar, were dragged over the ground trapping some of the hoppers in the sticky tar. Ditches were dug and the grasshoppers were driven into them to be burned or buried. Scoop nets were used also, but nothing did much good.

The damage done by the grasshoppers was so extensive and so repeated that state and federal aid to provide seed was given to the most stricken areas. Bounties as high as $1.00 per bushel were paid for the capture of the grasshoppers, and often the bounty payments exceeded the farmers' crop income.

In answer to popular request, Governor John S. Pillsbury set aside April 26, 1877, as a day of fasting and prayer. Religious services were held throughout the state asking for deliverance from this scourge. These prayers and penances were heard. A snowfall at the end of April prevented many of the grasshoppers from hatching. A heavy rain killed many more in June. On July 1, the grasshoppers formed a swarm, rose into the air and disappeared.

Though these hardships discouraged some of the pioneers and caused them to leave their farms, the majority grew in determination to conquer, and most of those who persevered were eventually rewarded with better things. Economic improvement, however, was not the only incentive bringing the settlers to the Midwest. The Catholic in particular had another motive, a religious motive, in settling in this particular section of the west.

The Irish had since the penal days developed a deep loyalty to their Catholic faith. The Germans fled religious tyranny under Bismarck and the French Canadians had been unfairly rated as second-class citizens. After enduring much for the sake of their religion, none of them was about to jeopardize it for the hope of mere economic gain. In moving westward, it was their uppermost concern to locate in a place where they would have the assurance of being able to assist at mass, receive the sacraments and raise their children in the same Catholic tradition. Midwestern Minnesota provided them with these opportunities.

On arrival their deep faith was again evidenced not only by sacrificial financial contributions for the erection of churches and schools, but also by their time and physical efforts in the actual construction of these edifices—all this even before they had established themselves financially and when every hour could have well been spent in breaking additional sod for the coming planting season.

Each Sunday morning the countryside came to life as the seasonal oxcarts or sleighs came almost out of nowhere and fell into the caravan heading to the church. With their very existence depending so totally upon the generosity of nature, they could not be unmindful of the providence of God, and in most parishes prayers for a good harvest were said at Vespers each Sunday. From their weekly worship they seemed to receive a renewal of spirit and courage to face the hardships once again.

Since traveling by oxcart was tedious and slow the weekly journey to church was normally the only trip to town each week, so it also afforded a limited opportunity for social activity among the settlers.

Rural Trends

The future New Ulm diocese maintained a slow but steady pace of growth and development. By the turn of the century there were approximately 55,000 Catholics (235,322 total population) served by 67 parishes and perhaps an equal number of priests.

When the diocese was established the Catholic population had grown to 68,094 (285,394 total population). It could boast of 86 parishes and 9 missions served by 98 priests. There were 37 primary schools, 7 secondary schools, 2 hospitals and 1 home for the aged.

The New Ulm diocese is strictly a rural diocese. Most of the parishes in the diocese are predominantly rural and some are totally rural. There are only two cities (New Ulm and Willmar) within the diocesan boundaries with a population over 10,000 (1960 census). Four of the diocese's fifteen counties (Lac Qui Parle, Lincoln, Renville, and Sibley) do not have any urban population. (The U. S. Census Bureau considers any community under a population of 2,500 rural.)

Being so thoroughly rural the modern trend towards larger farms, caused by greater farm mechanization, has made itself felt in the New Ulm diocese. From 1940 to 1960 every county in the area except Kandiyohi has decreased in rural population. During this time the rural population in the diocese decreased from 226,806 to 201,538. Though the urban population in most of these counties increased during this period, in most instances the urban increase was not sufficient to offset the rural decrease. Ten of the diocese's fifteen counties decreased in total population. Only five counties (Brown, Kandiyohi, Lyon, McLeod, Nicollet) showed an increase in total population, but this increase did surpass the loss of the other ten counties, and the total diocesan population grew from 282,183 in 1940 to 286,772 in 1960.

With its strongly community-oriented parishes whose members share the love of the land as the common denominator, the New Ulm diocese is as parochial as it is rural. There are no academies, colleges or seminaries in the diocese. Nor are there any priories or motherhouses of religious communities.

Threshing near New Ulm

Chancery and bishop's residence

Diocesan Expansion

When Bishop Schladweiler began his administration he rented a building from the city of New Ulm to serve as a temporary chancery and as his residence. Plans were soon underway for the construction of new and adequate diocesan facilities. On November 10, 1960, a multi-purpose building with diocesan offices and living quarters was dedicated. This stone structure is located on a bluff overlooking the cathedral.

Another parish plant, three elementary schools, two homes for the aged and one hospital have also been constructed. One hundred nine priests are now active in serving the 71,823 Catholics.

The Diocese of New Ulm is young in years, but it has demonstrated a remarkably mature grasp of the universal Church's needs in a rapidly changing world. As early as 1958 Bishop Schladweiler announced publicly that he planned to tithe his priests—that is, to send volunteers from his diocese to serve as missionaries in Latin America. By 1962, the bishop made good on his promise: in August of that year the first New Ulm priest was dispatched to serve in the Diocese of Solola, Guatemala. He was joined a year later by a second priestly volunteer. Today they staff the parish of San Lucas Toliman, where they serve 10,000 Guatemalans and bring to them God's Word and Sacraments as well as the latest techniques in medicine and dentistry. Surely there could be no finer flower of the seed planted by the Catholic pioneers.

The footprints of our predecessors have led us to the present via the scenic route of centuries. At times the panorama may not have been as detailed as we would have liked, but we must be grateful that the trail did not vanish completely. But even as we pause at this point, time continues and the trail is slowly being lengthened as we, in turn, leave our marks on the course of history.

RELIGIOUS IN THE DIOCESE OF NEW ULM _____

Benedictine Fathers (St. John's Abbey)
Third Order Regular of St. Francis
_____

Benedictine Sisters of Pontifical Jurisdiction (Crookston; St. Paul's Priory; St. Benedict's Priory)
Daughters of St. Mary of Providence

Missionary Benedictine Sisters
Poor Handmaids of Jesus Christ
School Sisters of Notre Dame
School Sisters of St. Francis (Milwaukee)
Sisters of Christian Charity
Sisters of Most Precious Blood

Sisters of the Presentation (Aberdeen)
Sisters of St. Joseph (Crookston)
Sisters of St. Joseph of Carondelet (St. Paul)
Sisters of the Third Order Regular of St. Francis of the Congregation of Our Lady of Lourdes (Rochester)

THE DAKOTAS

by Reverend Patrick H. Ahern

NORTH AND SOUTH DAKOTA were admitted to the Union on November 2, 1889, as the thirty-ninth and fortieth states without designation as to which was admitted first. Because the area in which they are located is in the center of the North American Continent, the Europeans engaged in the hazardous occupation of exploring the large continent did not penetrate that far into it until the eighteenth century. For the same reason settlement in the region was delayed until the more accessible parts of the continent began to fill up.

The early history of the twin states is quite similar. In the historical sketch that follows, therefore, they are considered together until settlement in each state began. Moreover, the present boundaries of the sister states in the upper Missouri Valley are, for purposes of clarity, considered to have existed throughout the period described.

White men first entered North Dakota in 1738. They were members of an expedition led by Pierre Gaultier de Varennes, Sieur de la Vérendrye, who was seeking a water route across the continent as well as new areas in which fur traders could operate. Some members of this party traveled south without their leader to the center of South Dakota where they buried an inscribed lead tablet, dated March 30, 1743, on a mound near the mouth of the Teton or Bad River on the west bank of the Missouri River. (This visitation

of South Dakota came sixty years after Pierre Charles Le Sueur's men first trapped along the Big Sioux). La Vérendrye's group then left the Dakotas, and they never returned to trade with the numerous Sioux (Dakota) bands and other Indian tribes who lived off the great buffalo (bison) herds in their Dakota domain. But the path they had made into the region was soon followed by French and half-breed hunters and trappers. By the end of the century many adventurous men had roamed widely in the two states to collect pelts and hides.

The Dakotas became part of Spain's colonial empire in 1763 when France ceded to her the vast area west of the Mississippi River. In that same year France lost her possessions north of the United States to England. British trading companies with posts south of Hudson Bay then provided the merchandise for the fur trade in the Dakotas. This encroachment of British subjects on territory claimed by Spain irked that government's colonial officials at St. Louis, but they were powerless to prevent it. However, during the last two decades of the century they issued licenses to trade and gave commissions for exploration to a number of Spaniards and Frenchmen who used the Missouri River entrance from the south to carry out their objectives in the southern part of the lower twin. Nonetheless employees of British companies were still the principal traders in the Dakotas when Spain retroceded the trans-Mississippi area to France in 1800, and when France sold it to the United States three years later.

In the first years that the twin states were under American sovereignty the famous expedition of Lewis and Clark took the Missouri River route through them, and American traders began to gather furs and hides in parts of South Dakota. Until the end of the War of 1812, however, the representatives of British companies continued to carry on a thriving business with the Indians in northern South Dakota and in North Dakota. When the war ended in 1815, American fur-trading interests quickly established friendly relations with all the Indians in the area and gained exclusive benefits from trade with them. In less than twenty years American companies had erected numerous small trading posts on the eastward flowing tributaries of the Missouri River and on the Big Sioux, Vermillion and James rivers in eastern South Dakota. Fort Union at the confluence of the Yellowstone and Missouri rivers and Fort Pierre at the mouth of the Teton or Bad River were then the principal posts. In 1831 steamboats began to deliver trade goods to the main posts on the Missouri and to carry on the return trip to St. Louis cargoes of buffalo products, including robes and tongues, and the skins of other animals. The bulky buffalo products and light pelts collected in northeastern North Dakota were transported from the Red River of the North in oxcarts over trails that ended in St. Paul. By mid-century the most active years of the fur trade in the Dakotas had ended.

When the fur trade was reaching its peak in the 1830's, Joseph Nicolas Nicollet directed a survey of the area east of the Missouri River. The first accurate maps could then be drawn for that region which was included in Minnesota Territory created in 1849. In the next decade reliable information about the physical features of the Black Hills and the surrounding country was obtained by army officers, and the first military posts (Fort Pierre and Fort Randall) were established in the Dakotas. By that time settlers moving relentlessly westward and advancing steadily up the Missouri River were poised for the penetration of South Dakota.

Settlement In South Dakota

The Indians yeilded to pressure from the whites and relinquished their land south of a line from Fort Pierre to Big Stone Lake and east of the Missouri to the Minnesota and Iowa borders by the treaty of Yankton in 1858. Settlers then rushed into the area to claim choice land and to develop townsites at Yankton, Vermillion, Bon Homme, Elk Point and Sioux Falls. Many of the early settlers fled the region when the Sioux War that began in Minnesota in 1862 created an Indian menace in South Dakota that lasted for several years.

Migration to the state was resumed as soon

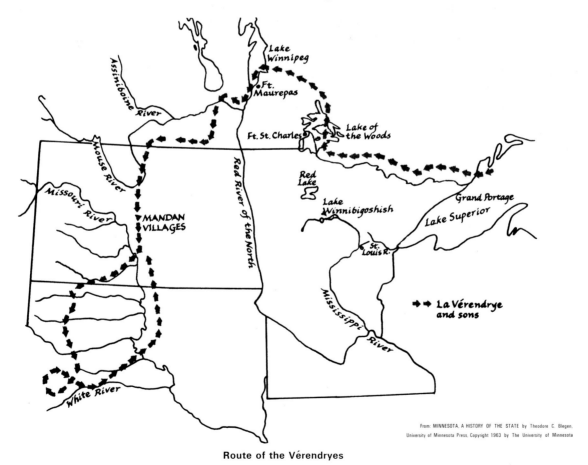

From: MINNESOTA, A HISTORY OF THE STATE by Theodore C. Blegen, University of Minnesota Press, Copyright 1963 by The University of Minnesota

Route of the Vérendryes

Deadwood, 1876

as homesteaders were convinced that garrisons at newly established military posts and roving troops could protect them. The homeseekers drove their wagons and stock along trails to the state from railheads in Iowa and Minnesota and settled along the Missouri River as far as Yankton, in the valleys of the Big Sioux, Vermillion and James rivers and on the prairies in the southeast. Although most of the approximately ten thousand settlers living in the Yankton cession in 1870 were from older communities, immigrants from Norway, Sweden and Denmark were already playing an important role in the advance of settlement in the region. German-Russians began to arrive on the first trains to Yankton in 1873. They and the Bohemian immigrants, who arrived just a little earlier, occupied land in the unsettled area west and north of Yankton where many of their compatriots joined them within a few years. The first of several Mennonite and Hutterite communities were also established in the early seventies.

While the farming communities in the southeastern part of the state were being hard hit by the depression following the Panic of 1873 and by grasshopper plagues that began at the same time and lasted for several years, gold was discovered in the Black Hills. More than twelve thousand people from every part of the nation rushed into the mining region during the two years before it was ceded by the Indians in 1877, and opened for settlement. By that time the clusters of tents, cabins, saloons, gambling houses and hotels in the Hills had been named. Custer, Hill City, Deadwood, Spearfish, Crook City, Lead City and Rapid City were settlements in the areas in which prospectors first found placer and quartz mining to be profitable and where the lumber industry began to flourish. By the year 1880 farmers and ranchers were using most of the land in the fertile valleys and the foothills to produce some of the provisions needed by the sixteen thousand people then living in the region and by twice as many a decade later. The inauguration of rail traffic to Rapid City in 1886 lessened considerably the cost of food and equipment that had previously been freighted in by wagons over long distances. Because it was the only town in the Hills served by a railroad, Rapid City enjoyed for many years a privileged position as a provisioning center for the area as the population continued to grow.

Meanwhile, similarly swift development was taking place in the southeastern counties. In a ten-year period, beginning in 1878, twenty-four million acres were occupied by landseekers. In fact, nearly all of the land available to settlers east of the Missouri River was occupied by the end of the boom period. The white population in the region had then risen to about 250,000.

Considerable impetus was given to the boom by railroads. Early in the period tracks were laid by several companies from railheads in Iowa and Minnesota to or through Milbank, Aberdeen, Ipswich, Mobridge, Watertown, Redfield, Volga, Arlington, Lake Preston, De Smet, Iroquois, Huron, Pierre, Canton, Mitchell and Chamberlain. As railroad companies extended their lines within the region and as settlers streamed in, towns and villages varying in size were established principally along the rights of way.

To the three railroads that connected it to the nation's markets and to the settled district in eastern South Dakota during the boom years Sioux Falls owed its rapid growth and emergence as the trading center and main distributing point for a large area. The city had supplanted Yankton as the principal city in the state by 1889 when its population was over ten thousand and when it was designated as the see city of the first diocese in the state.

In the year that the Diocese of Sioux Falls was created, South Dakota was admitted to the

Steamboat on the Missouri

Union. The white population was then about 325,000. The majority of the inhabitants were American-born farmers from Iowa, Wisconsin, Minnesota and Illinois. From the same states had come a considerable number of foreign-born Scandinavians, Hollanders and Welshmen. Russo-Germans were the largest group of immigrants in the state directly from the Old World.

When statehood was attained the federal government concluded negotiations with the Indians for about nine million acres of the Great Sioux Reservation between the Black Hills cession and the Missouri River. Cattlemen and sheepmen extended their operations into the ceded region making it principally their domain for about a decade. To serve the range industries railroad companies flung lines across the plains

New settlers heading for the Black Hills

143

and cow towns sprang up. For a brief period Belle Fourche and Mowbridge were important cattle-shipping centers.

The open-range cattle industry was doomed when homesteaders started a procession westward into the range country that increased the trans-Missouri population from 57,575 in 1905 to 137,687 in 1910. The newcomers forced cattlemen to fence their grazing land at the beginning of the next decade and the colorful era of the open range ended abruptly.

The region that was the scene of the roundups of great herds of bawling cattle and of the last land boom in the state had become a part of the Diocese of Lead established for the care of Catholics in the western half of the state in 1902. The see city of the diocese was changed in 1930 to Rapid City on the eastern edge of the Black Hills which has replaced Aberdeen as the second most populous city in the state.

Steady growth in the state's population was recorded until the high mark of nearly seven hundred thousand was reached in 1930. Depression and drouth in the thirties and the attraction of manufacturing centers in other states during the Second World War caused an exodus that reduced the number of inhabitants by about two hundred thousand. In the last fifteen years most of those losses have been regained.

Settlement in North Dakota

Pembina in the northeast corner of the state is the oldest settlement in the Dakotas. In 1812 a group of dispossessed Scotch and Irish peasants, sent by the Earl of Selkirk to occupy

STATE HISTORICAL SOCIETY OF NORTH DAKOTA

Main Street, Bismarck, 1873

land granted to him for colonization purposes, established the colony. They and other immigrants who joined them in the early years led a precarious life in the isolated community until they obtained a supply of seeds suitable for the region and three hundred head of cattle at the beginning of the next decade. Thereafter, the settlers who had remained during the difficult years were less inclined to leave their colony.

Further settlement in North Dakota was delayed because there was little pressure from homeseekers to have the area opened to them and because the Indians there had not been convinced that the whites could take the land that provided their livelihood. To protect settlers in western Minnesota from hostile Dakota tribes, Fort Abercrombie was constructed in 1858 on the west bank of the Red River about thirty miles south of Fargo. After the Sioux Uprising in Minnesota in 1862, the year after the Territory of Dakota was organized, hostile Indian forces in the state were augmented by the Minnesota Sioux fleeing before military units on punitive expeditions. To end the depredations of hostile bands and to intimidate the Indians who were still friendly, a line of forts was erected across the state. Garrisons at Fort Rice north of Bismarck and Fort Abraham Lincoln south of Mandan on the west bank of the Missouri River, at Fort Ransom sixty miles due west of Fort Abercrombie, at Fort Totten on the south side of Devils Lake and at Forts Stevenson, Buford, Pembina, McKeen, Lincoln and Cross gradually brought the Indians under subjection, herded them into reservations and made the eastern part of the state safe for settlers. Because the Pembina area was secure during the period of Indian unrest most of the twenty-five hundred settlers in the state in 1870 were concentrated there.

After the Indian menace had been eliminated in a major portion of the state, railroads became the most important among the factors contributing to the growth of its population. The first rail line entered from the east at Fargo, reaching Jamestown in 1872 and Bismarck the following year. A national panic in 1873 halted railroad construction until the end of the decade, but the movement of people to the state continued during these years, raising its population to 37,000.

In the eighties railroad companies finally built a network of roads that made the great

Laying Great Northern tracks

agricultural region in the eastern, central and northern parts of the state available and attractive to settlers. The Great Northern entered the state at the ten-year-old town of Grand Forks in 1880 and crossed the state through Devils Lake, Rugby (the geographical center of North America), Minot, Berthold and Williston in eight years. At the same time the company crossed the Red River at Wahpeton and built two lines the length of the Valley, constructed feeder lines at regular intervals north of its main line and laid tracks across the southeastern corner of the state. During the same decade the Northern Pacific completed its road west of Bismarck to the western border, entered the northern part of the Red River Valley and constructed a line to the southwest from Fargo. The Soo Line had also penetrated as far as Oakes during the decade and early in the nineties the company laid rails from Hankinson in the southeast diagonally across the state through Valley City, Carrington, Drake, Minot and Kenmare.

As these and a few other railroad companies were expanding the transportation system, there was a land boom in the eastern, central and northern counties which by the middle eighties were liberally dotted with towns and with farms varying in size from a few hundred acres to huge bonanza farms of wheat growers.

When statehood was attained and the Diocese of Jamestown was established in 1889, there were about 190,000 people in the commonwealth. The settlers had come from Canada, the northern states and many European countries. Most

numerous among the residents born outside the United States were Norwegians, Canadians, Russians and Germans. The majority of the inhabitants had been attracted to the state during the boom period between 1876 and 1885 when above-normal rainfall made the fertile soil produce bumper crops of wheat. Expectation of similar rewards from tilling the earth was uppermost in the minds of the majority of newcomers to the state in the nineties when the population increased steadily, reaching the total of 319,146 by the turn of the century.

During the first decade of the twentieth century there was a great influx of settlers into the southwestern part of the state. They homesteaded or purchased a considerable amount of the land that had supported the cattle-ranching industry there from the late seventies until the extremely cold and snowy winter of 1886-1887 ruined many ranching enterprises. Although cattle production continued to be important in the economy of the area, wheat farming supported the majority of the newcomers.

The number of residents in the western half of the state having greatly increased by the end of 1909, when the total population numbered 577,056, that region was detached from the first diocese in the state, whose see city had been changed from Jamestown to Fargo in 1897, to form a new diocese with Bismarck, the state capital, as the see city.

North Dakota, like her sister state, counted nearly seven hundred thousand citizens in 1930. As also happened in her twin, a decreasing trend in the population developed in the thirties and continued until 1950. Since then the number of residents has gradually increased. However, the decline in farm population that began before the great depression and drouth of the thirties has not been reversed, but the size of farms has increased steadily.

While the rural population was decreasing, many towns and cities were growing. Fargo, Grand Forks, Bismarck, Jamestown, Dickinson, Mandan, Valley City have a record of steady growth over the years, and towns in the Williston Basin have benefited from the oil boom that began early in the fifties.

Oil derricks in the northwestern part of the state, herds of cattle on large ranches in the southwestern counties and grain elevators in most towns and cities reveal to the casual observer the bases of the economy of North Dakota.

A typical western grain elevator

Oil well in Williston Basin

Roundup in North Dakota Bad Lands

BISHOP CAMBERT A. HOCH — *St. Joseph's Cathedral* ▶

DIOCESE OF SIOUX FALLS

by Right Reverend Monsignor Leonard J. Sullivan

A RICH, BLACK SOIL covers the entire area of the Diocese of Sioux Falls. It is a land where the rivers run south, and even the Missouri runs south to form the western boundary of the diocese, and then turns obligingly to fix the southern boundary too, and pick up the rivers that flow south to find it. Ours is land, once ice covered, and now rich in its deposit of glacial soil.

Our country was once the bed of a sea, and even after the glacial ice had melted, a large part of the land was covered by a huge lake and many lesser ones. Now it is a land of corn and wheat, of cattle ranches. Cereal grains, sorghums, beets, flax, all manner of vegetables, fruits and berries, these are the bounties of our soil. Trading towns dot the countryside. Fine highways intersect the land, and airlines put us in close communication with all the world. Sometimes parts of our land cry out for moisture, and hot winds wither the stunted crops in the rich black soil.

Led by the Bishop of Sioux Falls, almost two hundred priests, twenty-four brothers, a few less than a thousand sisters, and over ninety-one thousand people now comprise our diocese which lives a vigorous Catholic life, in step with the times in which we live and committed to the deposit of faith that came from the mind of God.

We are so close to our beginnings that the oldest of our cities have stood little more than one hundred years. The story of those beginnings is a fascinating one.

The First Tribes

Our land, indeed our very name, would suggest that we are the land of the Sioux, the Dacotahs, and so we are. But the penetration of the Sioux into this land was coincident in time with the penetration of the white man. Both were intruders, coming at much the same time. The difference was in the volume of those who came.

Before the coming of the Sioux, the Omahas, who were themselves of Siouan stock, lived in the valley of the Big Sioux. The first white men to enter our state found these people. La Salle had just discovered the mouth of the Mississippi, and his countryman, Pierre Charles Le Sueur appreciated that by this route he might escape the tax on furs levied in Montreal. He came to the Omahas on the Missouri in 1683, and in the spring his men came trapping up to the falls of the Big Sioux. Their pelts were sent by raft down the Sioux to the Missouri and hence by way of the Mississippi to the Gulf and then to

England. Later, when Le Sueur was established on the Blue Earth River near the present site of Mankato, Minnesota, his men followed an Indian trace to the west to the Omaha villages, and perhaps even to the Missouri.

But it was the Arikaras who were numerous in the land. Ancient mounds tell us of a still earlier people, but they are not really known to us. The Arikaras were a people who lived in villages and farmed the land. They lived in large huts built of willows and mud. They grew corn and beans, squash and tobacco in their river gardens. Their villages were fortified and highly defensible. But they deserted their own palisades for frequent hunts during the summer, and to wage war on their enemies, always returning for the harvest and to spend the winter.

These villages were an overweening attraction to the white man from the moment he found them. The Sioux were always on the move, to be found where they might be—but the villages of the Arikaras were landmarks. Somehow these people seemed more akin to the white man who often found winter sanctuary with them. The once numerous Arikaras, having at one time perhaps as many as thirty-two villages, were reduced to one by the time the white man had become an annual visitor to their land, and this village was located near the present city of Pierre.

The Adventurous Vérendryes

The coming of the white man to the Missouri region began in North Dakota, with another tribe of village-dwelling Indians, the Mandans. These Mandans must have been startled beyond belief when on the third day of December in 1738 they heard three volleys of musketry near their village. They rushed out of their huts to watch the approach of twenty men bearing the flag of France. The leader of the band was Pierre de Varennes, Sieur de la Vérendrye of Montreal, adventurer, patriot, trapper, dreamer extraordinary. His dream had led him across Canada, and had now driven him here in an effort to find a way to the Western Sea. He had heard that the Mandans knew the way and he had come to seek their guidance. The gifts he had brought for the Indians were promptly stolen by them, but he and his band were welcomed and feted. Vérendrye intended to winter with the Mandans, but his health made it necessary that he return home to La Riene. He intended to come back again to the Mandans and he left two men with them to learn their language.

The elder Vérendrye was not able to fulfill this intention. His health was no longer equal to that, but he was strong in his sons. In 1738 the Mandans had fired his imagination with

Indian camp
(Drawing by Carl Bodmer)

stories of white men who lived a summer's journey away. These men lived in iron suits that arrows could not pierce. The two men who had remained behind came nine months later to La Riene saying that in the spring several Indian tribes came to camp on the west side of the river. They had crossed over to visit them. These Indians had many horses, and their chief claimed to speak the language of the white men who lived in houses of brick and stone; men who had beards and prayed holding books before them and the leaves of the books were like the husks of Indian corn. They spoke of Jesus and Marie as they prayed. The Frenchmen could not understand the language, but it was quite probably Spanish, and the Indians spoke of the Spaniards of California.

So Vérendrye sent his son, Pierre, to the Mandans in 1740, but the young man was unable to find guides to the Western Sea and he returned.

In the spring of 1742, other of Vérendrye's sons, Francois and Louis Joseph, were with the Mandans. They waited for the Horse Indians to guide them. Perhaps they meant to await the men who had come in the spring of 1739 and camped on the other side of the river and had spoken of the white men by the sea. Perhaps these were Cheyennes, perhaps Arikaras—we do not know.

The Vérendryes set out finally, without guides, but in the hope that they would come upon them in their journey to the west. They did find Indians who told them that the Snake Indians farther to the west had spoken of white men by the sea who had horses. There were soldiers and priests among them. The Vérendryes listened to Spanish words, and they remembered that in 1720 an expedition of Spanish had set out from Santa Fe, most of them never to return. They were massacred, perhaps as far north as the state of Nebraska.

Much wandering and many adventures brought the company as far west as the Black Hills. Here their Indian friends who were going west to fight the Snake Tribe were suddenly seized with fear that the Snakes had slipped past them and would strike their own defenseless camp, and they began a disordered retreat to the east. The Vérendryes were compelled to come east with them. Nearing the Missouri they came to a band of Indians whom they called the Choke Cherry Indians. Bishop O'Gorman, second bish-

op of Sioux Falls diocese, said of these in 1903: "I believe that they were a band of Sioux who lived along Cherry Creek and had an encampment on the Missouri." The Vérendryes came to the Missouri with these Indians to the Arikara village there. Here they found a man who had been reared among the Spanish and spoke their tongue. He had been baptized and knew his prayers. He said that these Spanish were but twenty days away on horseback; that they worked in iron and had a great trade. He also spoke of a Frenchman, who had been established many years, only three days journey away. The Vérendryes did not think their horses fit for the extra travel, so they sent word for the man to come and see them, but the man did not come. This strange bit of information is strengthened by a letter of Jean de Bienvelle, Governor of Louisiana, to the Minister of Marine, in which he says: "A Frenchman who lived many years with the Panimaha, established on the Missouri, having been with the savages to the Ricaras who inhabit the upper part of the same river, and who have

Lead plate buried by the Vérendryes

never yet seen a Frenchman. . . . Two voyaguers setting out with him verify this report." This letter bears the date of April 22, 1734.

The Vérendryes buried a lead plate on a bluff near the river to commemorate the event. It lay undiscovered for almost two centuries until some school children came upon it on a Sunday stroll in 1913.

The Traders

We have little record of men who came to our part of the country in the decades that followed the visit of the Vérendryes. The Hudson's Bay Company did have a post at Elk Point in 1755 and another one at Flandreau, both of which were discontinued in 1763. Were there others here? It does seem probable, but we have no record. In 1787 a youth of twenty-three years and his companions, however many they were, came to the upper Missouri. They settled at the Arikara village and the young man, Joseph Garreau, remained there many years, as much as twenty years. Three years later Jacques D'Eglise went up the river as far as the Mandans, and in 1794 a schoolmaster from Saint Louis came with seven men to make his fortune in the fur trade. He was Jean Baptiste Truteau.

Truteau had little success as a trader. He and D'Eglise wintered with the Arikaras at Pierre. Garreau was there too, and he and D'Eglise seemed always to have the best of the trade with the Arikaras, leaving little for Truteau. In the spring D'Eglise took his own and the furs of Truteau down to Saint Louis. Truteau trapped along the river that summer. Going down as far as the Sioux, and coming back north again, he fell in with a band of Teton and Yankton Sioux who compelled him to trade at a loss. Arriving at the mouth of the Cheyenne, he learned that the Arikaras had abandoned their homes near Pierre and moved up to the Grand River or Mobridge area. He turned about and near the site of the Wheeler townsite he built a cabin and he and his men wintered there. They were joined in midwinter by some of Jean Monier's men who had been living near the mouth of the Sioux and were short of provisions. The Omahas, with their infamous chief, Blackbird, found Truteau's house and they made the winter miserable for the trader.

The next spring Truteau and six of his men went up to the Arikara village on the Grand. Garreau and his companions were there, as was D'Eglise and a man named Lauson. Truteau eventually returned to Saint Louis and to his teaching. The fur trade had not been good to him.

The years 1725 to 1775 were in the main the years of the migration of the Sioux. They had come from the east, from the headwaters

Mounted Sioux

of the Mississippi, and had been pushed into western Minnesota and then into our land. In the 1760's they were still a people on foot, hunting the buffalo, and returning to trade in their old land near the head of the Minnesota River. By comparison the Sioux found the Arikaras a strong people and indeed came to them in the manner of suppliants. The Sioux were warriors and by 1786 the Arikaras were reduced to five villages, these being the consolidations of smaller villages that could not stand against the new enemy. It was not until 1795 that the Arikaras were driven northward from their villages at the mouth of the Cheyenne.

The big difference between the Sioux of Minnesota and the Sioux of the Dakota country was the horse. It seemed right that the Sioux and the horse should be brought together. The soldiers were to say later that the Sioux were the finest light cavalry in the world, and in this they may have been right. With a horse to ride and with a gun in hand, the Sioux was indeed formidable. It was the Sioux that struck terror to those who would come up the river in the nineteenth century.

The Arikaras had come upon bad days. The depredations of the Sioux and the anger of the United States combined to drive them finally out of the state. They went first to their kindred people in Nebraska, the Pawnees, from whom they had separated centuries before. But this proved no solution, and they went into the land of the Mandans and there found conditions tolerable to themselves. Disease, too, had played a part in the destruction of this people. Smallpox was a disaster to these town dwellers, but with the advance of the Sioux they needed no other foe.

The fur trade was the moving force during the first thirty years of the nineteenth century. These were the days of the Missouri Fur Company, the Columbia Fur Company, the American Fur Company, the Chouteaus, Manuel Lisa and many more. Registre Loisel had a post on a beautiful cedar island, below Pierre. Manuel Lisa had a fort up near the boundary of the state. Fort Tecumseh, later Fort Pierre, was built by the half-breed Joseph La Framboise. Pierre Dorion had been with the Yanktons for twenty years at the time of the Lewis and Clark Expedition. Jean Valle was near the Cheyenne in 1804 and had three men with him. He claimed that he had trapped all the way up the Cheyenne to the Black Hills, and this might well be true. In 1803 ten of Registre Loisel's men trapped on the Cheyenne and Belle Fourche rivers all the way to the Hills, and another of his men, Guennville, was back to the Hills with a party of Cheyennes in 1804. The Picottes, Honoré, Joseph and Henry, were at Tecumseh. Honoré married a Teton, and his son, himself married to a Yankton, owned the section of land on which the city of Yankton was to be built. Recalling that a trader often had as many as a hundred trappers associated with him to supply his post, there were many whites in the country in the first quarter of the nineteenth century.

Early Catholicism

Significant to our purpose is the fact that almost all of the men in our part of the country during these years were Catholic. They were, of course, French. One cannot discount the impact of the famous trip of Lewis and Clark. Spain having

The *Yellowstone*

retroceded the Louisiana Territory to Napoleon and he in turn having sold it to the United States, this official journey of Lewis and Clark that carried even to the Pacific, with its attendant publicity, did much to open the country. But the men who lived in the land were largely Catholic. Their arduous journeys into the wilderness, their prolonged absence from home and from their own kind, were indicative of men of heroic cast and men of strange desire. Many of them felt that their lives would always be lived on the frontier, and they had no hesitation in finding an Indian wife who could live that life with them. Many of these marriages were sound and a genuine love of family followed. There were, of course, casual unions, and the Indian concept of sexual morality between themselves and between themselves and the whites did little to prevent these. But we remember too that the Indian wives and the half-breed children were those most certain to receive the ministrations of the Church when the priests did arrive on the scene.

It was the lay Catholic who came first to the territory which now makes up our diocese. The priest came next, the itinerant priest who traveled over vast expanses of territory to attend to the needs of the widely scattered people. These priests were under the jurisdiction of distant bishops and of necessity the training that must follow baptism had to be left to the parents who in most cases must have been poorly equipped to give it.

152

The decline of the fur trade, beginning as far back as 1830, could be considered an accomplished fact by 1855. The change of fashion which made the once popular beaver hat a thing of the past had a lot to do with this decline, for the beaver pelt was the heart of the trade; indeed, almost the coin of the frontier. The fur trade continued, but it lost importance, and when the American Fur Company sold its post at Fort Pierre to the government in 1855, it might be said to be over.

The Missouri did not look like much of a place for a steamboat. Most men had said that the sandbars, the varying currents, the ever-changing channel precluded any thought of steam traffic. But in 1831 Pierre Chouteau, Jr., had completed a boat of shallow draft and was ready to try the river. Until this time all goods had to be transported up the river in pirogues, canoes and keelboats. Such boats were certainly no blessing to the outward journey. Men toiled with poles, oars, ropes, sails to bring their boats up the treacherous Missouri. They were menaced by sandbars, currents and shallows, gnats and mosquitoes, to say nothing of the occasional danger from animals and the always present threat from Indians. So in 1831 the ascent of the *Yellowstone*, built for Pierre Chouteau, Jr., was an event of significance. His was the first on the upper Missouri, and he got as far as Fort Pierre in 1831. The next year he got as far as the Yellow-

stone for which his boat had been so hopefully named. Here was the first of that large fleet of boats that would now ply the river, boats that were said to "walk on the prairie." They and the boats on the Mississippi would soon make Saint Louis the third port in the land, surpassed only by New York and New Orleans. On her first trip down river the *Yellowstone* carried five tons of buffalo tongues and thousands of hides. But then, the descent of the river by canoe, pirogue, keelboat or raft had never been a problem.

The Jesuits

The earliest ministrations of the sacraments in our diocesan territory must be attributed to the Jesuits from Saint Louis. Bishop Du Bourg had given them a farm at the confluence of the Missouri and the Mississippi in exchange for a promise to send four or five priests to the upper Missouri within two years. It was twelve years before this promise was fulfilled and a few more before they could ascend the river to our part of the country.

In 1839 Father Pierre De Smet, whose name must always be associated with the upper Missouri, came up to visit the Yankton Sioux in the vicinity of the Vermillion. The Potawatomis, to whom he was then assigned, were particularly impoverished at that time and were further bedeviled by clashes with the Sioux. Father De Smet came on a peace mission, though he said later that he baptized a large number of Sioux children on this occasion.

Father Christian Hoecken, who replaced Father De Smet at Council Bluffs, freeing De Smet for a mission to the Flatheads, came up to visit the Yankton Sioux in 1840. He recorded baptisms at Yankton in June of that year, and still others at Fort Pierre and at Fort Vermillion later in the summer. These are the first baptisms recorded within our state—Father De Smet seems not to have made a record of his of the earlier date.

The steamboat had made the ascent of the river comparatively easy and now De Smet and others were on the river almost annually. De Smet stopped to reproach the Yankton Sioux in 1840 for their infidelity to their promises of 1839. He was back in 1841 and in 1846 and again in 1848 he was in Fort Pierre.

Father De Smet

Meanwhile, in the summer of 1845, Father Augustin Ravoux came to visit the Sioux at Vermillion. He came by way of the Pipestone country and down the valley of the Sioux. As an old man he recalled that he had offered mass in the Sand Lake area on the upper James River in 1847. This is often regarded as the first time mass was celebrated within our diocese, but it is quite probable that the Jesuits had celebrated mass here before this time, though they have left us no specific record. It is quite certain that Father Ravoux crossed the state in 1847. He made the crossing in the company of nine men, three women, and two or three children, and arrived at Fort Pierre exhausted, having been tortured by thirst on much of his journey. He spent over two months in the state, at the fort and with the Indian encampment there. He went down to Fort Bouis on the great bend, and then by steamboat to Vermillion. He baptized, solemnized marriages and gave instruction.

Father Christian Hoecken was back in 1850 at the mouth of the Big Sioux. He continued up to Fort Pierre and then back down to Fort Vermillion. He came back again that year to the French Settlement between the Big Sioux and Vermillion, spending three days there and baptizing fourteen children. The godfather for all these baptisms was Theophile Bruyere, who was himself married to the daughter of White Eagle, a Sioux Chief.

The year 1851 was a memorable one. The Indian Commissioner had called the Indians of the upper Missouri to assemble at Horse Creek Valley, near Fort Laramie. De Smet was asked to be there by reason of the great respect and friendship between himself and these tribes. He and Father Hoecken started upriver on the *St. Ange.* Cholera broke out among the passengers and both priests were stricken. De Smet recovered but Hoecken died and was buried near the mouth of the Little Sioux. On the return trip the *St. Ange* stopped to disinter the body, and it was taken to Flourissant to be buried. The council was judged a success, and its most amazing statistic must have been the 1,856 baptisms performed by Father De Smet among the assembled tribes.

During these years many army posts had been established for the protection of trade and travel. Randall, Thompson, Sully, Bennett and Wadsworth were among them. These posts brought many men into the country, and still more, the Indians, who as wards of the government were associated with the posts, made the supply of these outposts big business. Many of the soldiers were Catholic. Father De Smet speaks of the Irish, German and French who made up Fort Thompson, and he says of them that they were "all Catholic."

Father Trecy and his Colleagues

In 1855 a priest of the Diocese of Dubuque, a young Irishman, Father Jeremiah Trecy, only four years ordained, came into our country. He was engaged in the establishment of an Irish colony at Saint John's City (now Jackson) on the Nebraska side of the river in the Sioux City neighborhood. In August of that year he crossed the river to visit White Bull's Village, a settlement of Canadians, Indians and half-bloods, some fifteen miles from his projected colony. Here he offered mass for three hundred warriors. In September he visited Smithy Bear's Camp, where he baptized fifty-two children, and Strikes-the-Ree's Camp, baptizing thirteen half-bloods there.

In 1856 Father Trecy was pastor of Saint John's City, and on October 2 he paid a visit to Fort Randall. There were six hundred Catholics there at the time, most of them Irish. He heard five hundred confessions and the next day offered mass for these men. He went on up to the post on the White River and there he baptized eight half-breeds and three Negroes. This generous priest had an enduring interest in the Indians and the Army posts. In one of his accounts, he is describing the rather bleak terrain in the Fort Randall area and he says: "I have never yet, and I have ten or twelve times been to the post, seen a single quadruped save a wolf, and of fowls, none." It must be supposed that he ministered to the French colony more than the one time on record, since he went so often to the distant post at Fort Randall.

Father James Mary Ryan, who was at Saint John's from 1861 to 1866, served Vermillion and the French Settlement during those years. Fathers Felix McLaughlin, E. P. Walters and Edward Dillon were there too, and they visited

Fort Thompson on the upper Missouri, 1865

a colony on the James River and went up to Fort Randall. Fathers Erlach and Keenan were at Saint John's in the years until 1873 and they too took care of the settlements across the river. Still these people along the river were French speaking, and in 1868 Father John Curtis, administrator of the Vicariate of Nebraska during Bishop O'Gorman's absence, wrote to De Smet to remind him of his promise to spend a week in the French Settlement and hear confessions. "They are anxiously awaiting you," he said. "Their new frame church is in the process of construction." This was Saint Peter's, now Jefferson, which was dedicated in that year. This request seems strange since Father Boucher should have been there at this time. But be that as it may, the busy Father De Smet did not come. De Smet made his final trip up the river in 1870, three years before his death.

These were the years when families were coming into the territory to establish homes. Some effort had been made by land speculators to bring in settlers before the enactment of the Homestead Act of 1862. Settlements were made at Sioux Falls, Medary, Flandreau, Fort Pierre, Yankton and Fairfax, with varying degrees of success. The uprising of the Sioux in Minnesota in that year and the scare that followed this did not make the land of the Sioux look like a suitable place for homeseekers, and it was not until 1868 that homesteaders began to come in numbers. There were only five hundred settlers along the river in 1860, and ten years later the number was only ten thousand.

155

The Indian Invaded

Until this time the Church had worked with the trapper, the Indian, the soldier and the children of these. No priest made his home in the country until 1867. The Arikaras were driven from the state, and the Sioux were in constant negotiation with the government in matters that they could not comprehend. Despoiled of their land, despoiled of the buffalo on which they depended, invaded by men whose ideas of private property and marriage were alien to theirs, the Indian saw the end of a way of life and saw no way in which he could easily accommodate himself to the new way. For a people who regarded theft from an enemy as a form of bravery, a people accustomed to kill the women and children of the enemy with the same enthusiasm as they would a warrior, a people who had no tradition of daily labor, it is to be wondered at that their brushes with the whites were as few

as they were. They could have been more formidable than they were. But they had too little capacity for organization to fight a campaign. Their fights were at best raids, and there could be but one conclusion to the matter.

Between 1851 and 1873 all of the land east of the Missouri in South Dakota except small reservations at Yankton, Sisseton and Crow Creek was ceded to the United States. The Indian could not have understood these land transfers, but they were the steps that made possible the colonization of the land. On the reservation, the Indian would know the ministrations of the priest, and an effort would be made to educate him for his place in the new society. Much government incompetence, mistakes in policy among missionaries and interference on the part of the government, notably by President Grant, would make the Indian problem one that is not fully solved even in our day. But the land was now to be the land of the whites. The Indian fell into a

New sod for the roof

Indians receiving provisions at Fort Sully

state of dependence, and his voice was not loud in the councils of the future.

The French colony that settled along the Missouri at Jefferson marks the true beginning of permanent settlement. These people came overland from Canada, driving their stock. They are not to be confused with the mixed bloods who were already there and who comprised an earlier "French Settlement." The French colony came to make homes and their descendants are still here. They came in 1862 but it was not until 1867 that they had a priest of their own. As pastor of Saint Peter's, Father Pierre Boucher, appointed by Bishop Thomas Langdon Grace, O.P., of Saint Paul, was the first resident pastor in the diocese. He was of such value that he was also missionary apostolic to the entire Dakota Territory, which had been created by act of Congress in 1861.

In the summer of 1871 Father Valentine Sommereisen came to Yankton and built the church and rectory there. Yankton, together with the James River settlement, and sometimes Vermil-

lion had been attended by Father Ferdinand Lechleitner from Saint Helena across the river. Father Lechleitner had attended the forts on the Missouri too and in early 1871 had gone up as far as the Grand River collecting money from the soldiers for the building of his church at Saint Helena. Father Sommereisen and Father Boucher were the only priests within our present diocese at that time, and up through 1876 there was only the addition of Pierre J. Bedard.

Bishop Marty

The summer of 1876 was the summer of Custer's defeat in the battle of the Little Big Horn. Any chance that the Sioux might have had of continuing for a time their free way of life was lost in their victory there. Now they were to be reservation Indians, and the presumption was that that was what they ought to be. In that same summer, only a little more than a month later, Abbot Martin Marty, O.S.B., arrived at Fort

157

Yates to begin his work with the Sioux. Marty had been abbot at Saint Meinrad, Indiana, for the past five years. He was answering a call for Indian missionaries to the Sioux. His labors at Fort Yates, the schools he founded there, the priests and sisters that he brought there to carry out the work are not properly a part of our story. He passed through our region on his way to and from the fort many times.

On February 1, 1880, Martin Marty, O.S.B., was consecrated as titular bishop of Tiberias and on the fifth of the month he was named Vicar Apostolic of the Dakota Territory. This territory then comprised the present states of North and South Dakota. In this vast expanse Bishop Marty had but twelve priests, and only four of these were stationed within the present limits of our diocese. Within this diocesan area, there were only the small and contentious city of Yankton, a few national communities of Catholic people, the forts along the river and some baptized Indians. Before 1870, if one were to exclude the river forts and Wheeler, all of the people within the area of our present diocese lived within a small triangle of land, beginning at the confluence of the Sioux and the Missouri rivers, along the Missouri to Bon Homme, up the Sioux to the

Bishop Martin Marty, O.S.B.

falls, and then in a diagonal from the falls to Bon Homme. Ten years later the settled area reached into the state perhaps eighty miles, a little beyond the Bohemian settlements, then running north for about fifty miles and narrowing abruptly to about thirty miles and continuing north as a strip about thirty miles wide, narrowed to twenty miles by the time it arrived at the boundary of the present state.

This was not an impressive extent, but it was one to excite imagination and inspire zeal. There were established parishes only at Yankton, Jefferson, Bon Homme, Tabor and Wheeler. The priests of these parishes served stations at Maxwell and Olivet in Hutchinson County, at Smetland and Wanari in Bon Homme County, at Bloomingdale in Clay County and at Turnergale in Turner County. They also took care of a station at Bijou Hills and Forts Randall and Sully.

The five years from 1880 to 1885 were fabulous ones in Dakota. The population leaped from 135,000 to 250,000. In 1882 there was a veritable flood of immigrants. By this year there were nineteen priests serving within the limits of the present diocese. A study of the towns in which they lived reveals that only six of these parishes were properly ethnical communities.

The arbitrary peace policy of President Grant had given the Crow Creek Reservation to the Episcopalian Church, much to the disappointment of the Indians, who were either pagan or Catholic. When this policy was abandoned in 1881 the bishop wanted to send priests to the reservation. However, it was five years before he could do so. Then he asked Father Willard, the pastor at Yankton, to select a site and establish a mission. Father Willard did so, but he had to continue as pastor at Yankton, so Fathers John Brogan and J. Sullivan opened the little school for him in the fall of 1886. In January of 1887 Father Pius Boehm, O.S.B., came to take charge of the mission. He labored here until his death forty-eight years later.

The twofold task of the mission was to bring the Indian into relation with the white civilization in which he now must live and to teach him the doctrine and practice of the Catholic faith. In the first years much seemed possible, for the Indian showed surprising adaptability. The children, loveable and docile, responded well to the opportunities given them. The mission had great expectations for the reservation Sioux.

Stephan Mission

Building a New State

As for the rest of the diocese, the coming of the railroad had transformed it. With their household goods, machinery, stock, seed and family too, loaded on an immigrant car, the newcomers were able to go easily wherever tracks had been laid. By 1890 all of the land in our diocese was settled, and there were 329,000 people in the new State of South Dakota.

The settlement of the land, the building of homesteads and the many little towns that came into being were reflected, too, in the growth of the Church. The rare log church, such as the one built in Bruyer Settlement in 1860, the makeshift meeting place for the celebration of the mass at the stations, gave way to the typical prairie church, usually frame, with its rather imposing spire. Out-of-the-way places were abandoned in favor of those on the railroad.

National parishes had been the rule of the first years, though there were exceptions. The French along the river, the Bohemians west of Yankton, the numerous German communities scattered throughout the territory, a Swiss and a Polish setttlement—these were the early arrivals. The latest of this kind were the German-Russians who followed the main line of the Milwaukee Railroad west of Aberdeen. They formed many parishes and by 1890 they numbered eight thousand people.

Now it was the iron fingers of the railroads that fed life onto the prairies. Townsites were created at about ten mile intervals along the rights of way. Sometimes the railroads gave land for the establishment of parishes. Their inducements to settlers helped to bring them to the land. These railroad towns were usually chance gatherings of unrelated people, lured by the promise of free land or by the opportunities in trade and service that a new community seemed to offer. A percentage was usually Catholic, and when they were sufficient in number they sought the regular ministrations of a priest.

Finding a priest for the growing communities was the great problem. Bishop Marty turned to his order, to Germany, to Ireland, to Bohemia, to France and to the older eastern states to find priests. With native vocations almost non-existent, these men who responded to his appeals built the churches and administered the sacraments in the first years. Thomas Flynn was the first priest ordained in our diocese. A native of Wisconsin, he spent a fruitful lifetime at Flandreau and at Madison where he died in his old age in 1926.

159

Something for dinner

Buffalo bones are plowed under

After the storm

The prairie is my garden

A few drops of rain

I am the Resurrection and the Life

Perhaps Father Robert Haire, who came to the diocese from Detroit in 1880, is the extreme example of a kind of priest common in this time. His parish assignment was from the Minnesota line to the Missouri; it covered the north half of our diocese and even a bit of North Dakota. He had no church in his parish. He built the first one with his own hands, a sod church at Columbia. Headquartering at Columbia, and later at Aberdeen, he traveled constantly to take care of his huge parish. As the people poured into the territory, he went, by every available conveyance, to baptize, to instruct, to marry and to bury the dead. His ports of call became parishes in time, and new priests came to share his work. A convert, and a man of intense political convictions, Father Haire found himself often at odds with authority, but his energy and accomplishment left their mark on the land.

Father Haire invited the Presentation Sisters to come to Aberdeen in 1886. The Benedictines had established a motherhouse at Zell in 1883 and later transferred it to Yankton. These were the establishments that would in time identify themselves with the diocese, and through the years their labors in schools and hospitals would be of increasing benefit to the Church in the Diocese of Sioux Falls. The Benedictines were of German-Swiss origin. Much of their early recruitment came from their homeland. The Presentation Sisters were from Ireland, and Irish girls came to help them in their work. But soon the girls of the Dakota parishes began to see this life as an inspiration and model for their own, and national characteristics were less in evidence. Other communities too served the diocese—the Mercy Sisters, the Sisters of Saint Agnes, the Ursulines—but the work of these two communities has been most significant in the development of the Church in the Diocese of Sioux Falls.

In 1889, the year in which South Dakota became a state, Bishop Marty moved from Yankton to Sioux Falls which became the see city of the newly created diocese. The decline of river traffic and the transfer of the territorial capital to Bismarck, North Dakota, had perhaps suggested the change. A small church had been built in Sioux Falls in 1879. At the time of Bishop Marty's coming, Sioux Falls had a small brick church, dedicated to Saint Michael, which now became the procathedral.

160

Bishop O'Gorman

In 1895 Bishop Marty left the diocese to go to Saint Cloud, Minnesota. His successor was Thomas O'Gorman, professor of history at the Catholic University of America, Washington, D. C. The appointment of Thomas O'Gorman to Sioux Falls came as a surprise to many—perhaps even to himself. He had attended "Latin School" in Saint Paul with John Ireland. When he was but ten and Ireland fifteen, they had gone to France to study for the priesthood. Father Augustin Ravoux made the trip with them. After his ordination Father O'Gorman was a pastor, then rector of Saint Thomas Aquinas' Seminary in Saint Paul, then a professor at the Catholic University. His erudition, his willingness to declare himself, his oratorical talent—all these had served to distinguish him. His *History of the Catholic Church in the United States* and his enduring friendship with Archbishop Ireland added further to his renown. The "unknown western diocese" of Sioux Falls did not seem an appropriate appointment for one already so distinguished. But Bishop O'Gorman put his varied talents to the assigned task, and the growth and development of the state offered him opportunity. The less than 400,000 people in the state grew to more than 637,000 in the twenty-five busy years he spent here as bishop.

The increase of Catholic population in the state now brought a further and final division of territory. The state was divided into two dioceses in 1902, Sioux Falls retaining the east and Lead being given the west, with the Missouri as the line of demarcation.

These were no longer pioneer days. Now the diocese was a land of family farms, with sound little trading towns to support them and to be supported by them. Good dry weather roads ran everywhere, though track was still being laid into areas not yet served by the railroads. New parishes and missions were established. To urge the establishment of parishes in the towns that did not have them, and to give instructions in those towns in which a church was not feasible, the bishop sent priests to Washington, D. C., to train in the Apostolic Mission House. In 1912 the mission band began its work. In rented halls, in stores, in their chapel car, these missionaries worked with a truly apostolic zeal.

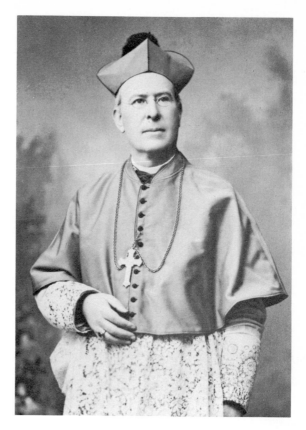

Bishop Thomas O'Gorman

Monsignor P. T. Monahan, Monsignor John Brady, Father J. R. O'Mahoney, these worked in this crusade and many small parishes owe their beginning to their apostolate. In 1917 the mission priests went with the soldiers to France. Father Coleman O'Flaherty of Mitchell, who also went as a chaplain to France, was killed there on the field of battle. When the war was over, the moment of value for the mission band had gone by, and it was not reorganized.

Meanwhile Bishop O'Gorman planned and built the imposing Saint Joseph's Cathedral. A church of majestic proportions, its beauty remains the pride of the diocese. It was dedicated in 1919.

Catholic Education

The Third Plenary Council of Baltimore had urged the establishment of parish schools in every parish. This was both unrealistic and impossible for the parishes of our diocese. A plan that had been used elsewhere without attracting much

161

attention was adopted by a few parishes in the Archdiocese of Saint Paul in the 1890's. By this plan the parish leased its buildings to the public school system for a nominal sum. The sisters were retained as teachers, paid by the public schools and subject to them. Religion was excluded from the curriculum, but the children were kept a half hour when the day's classes were done for religious instruction. This plan seemed to offer relief from the burden of separate schools and was inaugurated with the knowledge and blessing of the archbishop. However, Ireland met most severe criticism, not only from Protestants who saw in it an alienation of tax money, but, more surprisingly, from Catholics. Catholic oppostion came from the German parishes who wanted independent Catholic schools in which the German tongue could continue to be used. Opposition came, too, from the Jesuits, who saw in it an abandonment of the Catholic school system in which they were involved in the upper levels. Bishop O'Gorman knew of the trouble, and the furor it had caused reached even to the congregations in Rome and to Pope Leo XIII. He made no effort in his own diocese to find a place within the framework of the public school system. The child went either to public or to parochial school. It was only in the larger parishes that a parochial school was possible. Here the priest and the sisters had the best chance to influence the minds of the coming generation.

But who can praise too highly the priest in the smaller parish, who, at home and in his missions, carried the load alone. He taught his children, or directed and trained their teachers. Often he built the fires that heated his little churches. He baptized, witnessed marriages, sat at deathbeds. He collected money, planned and administered the affairs of his parish and from his pittance found some to send to the bishop, some for the far-off missions and some for the Holy Father. In his parish he was the embodiment of the Church. He formed the mind of Christ in his people. He declared the law, saying the difficult "no" when it had to be said. Only God can know the labor and sacrifice of these lonely men, whose lives were lives of devotion and obscurity. They were neither pioneers nor moderns, for they exist in every age. They work without worldly ambition, without preferment.

They, more than the notable figures, are the heart and soul of the apostolate on the prairies, and their name is legion. Names in the unsung apostolate spring to mind, but they are too many, and to name one is to do an injustice to the rest. To know them is to know the work of the Diocese of Sioux Falls.

In 1909 the Bishop purchased the buildings of a government Indian school at Chamberlain. With the Viatorian priests to staff it, he opened a college for men. Columbus College, never large, did a fine work in Catholic education, but the war brought a decline in enrollment, and an appeal was made to the bishop for advice and help. Concluding that the remote location of the college precluded any chance for its development, the bishop decided to move the college to Sioux Falls. An imposing building was constructed to house the school, and it opened its doors in 1921. But two days before the college opened, the bishop suffered a stroke and a few days later he was dead.

Bishop Mahoney

Bernard Mahoney, spiritual director of the North American College in Rome, became the third bishop of the diocese. He, like O'Gorman, came with a sense of being exiled, but it was providential that he came when he did. Throughout the administrations of his two predecessors the state had known constant progress. Setbacks were temporary and local, but the general trend was one of expansion and development.

Now the diocese was on the threshold of other times. Evidence of a declining economy was already at hand. Banks, having expanded credit in the prosperity of the war years, now began to call in their loans. The farmer and the businessman, themselves overextended, could not meet these obligations. Bankruptcies followed. The banks began to fail, and each failure invited others, until it spread over the land in a chain reaction. The bank that stood the shock was the exception, and the failures took a toll on the entire community. The climax came with the stock market crash in 1929.

These were days of discouragement for the Church. Life in the Catholic home and in the Catholic parish became a life of retrenchment. It was a time to accept losses or at best to hold

Bishop Bernard Mahoney

off defeat. Missions and schools closed, and curtailments threatened all parishes. New debts, where contracted, could not be paid. The debt on the cathedral and that on many parishes remained static. Turton, White Lake, Geddes, Woonsocket, De Smet and others could not meet their obligations.

This time, too, saw another development of far-reaching effect. In 1862 the government had adopted the 160 acre farm as the proper homestead. With much work, a man could support his family on such a farm. Horses, cattle, pigs, chickens, a garden and the inestimable blessing of health, and all would be well. But now tractors and complicated farm machinery skyrocketed the cost of farm operation. Since the tireless tractor could outwork the horse, more land became the solution. Three hundred and twenty acres became standard in the eastern part of the diocese, and the wheat farms to the north and west often were massive operations. In an almost exclusively agricultural diocese the effect of this change was tremendous. Farm and

town population declined. Good roads and the automobile had already hurt the small trading towns, and now many of these gasped and died.

Surprisingly, Monsignor John Brady expanded his parish school at Mitchell during these years, opening the only parochial Junior College in the nation in 1922. Staffed by the Presentation Sisters his college flourished during these most trying times.

Father Sylvester Eisenman, O.S.B., left Stephan in 1921 to begin a new mission in Charles Mix County. Throughout the period of drought and depression his mission, Saint Paul's at Marty, flourished. An entire mission plant, crowned by an imposing church, came into being. Perhaps his finest accomplishment was the formation of the Oblate Sisters of the Blessed Sacrament, who enrolled as their first members seven Indian girls.

In 1923 Bishop Mahoney invited the Oblates of Mary Immaculate to come to the diocese and gave them Roberts County with its considerable Indian population as their field of operation. A school, hospital and orphanage for Indians have been built there and most recently a home for the aged. In 1927 the Sacred Heart Fathers purchased the old Columbus College buildings at Chamberlain from the Viatorians and began a school for Indians there. Taken generally, the institutions of the religious did not feel the effects of the depression in the same degree as did the individual parishes and the diocese.

The debt on Columbus College was huge. In the declining economy the bishop could not call on his people to do the impossible. In 1929 the college closed its doors, but the debt remained. The inexhaustible patience of the bishop in these times was a blessing beyond price. It was a time to wait, and he waited.

Fast on the heels of the economic disasters came the great drought of the thirties and the accompanying depression. The heavens were shut up. High winds sucked up the black soil from the dry land. The rains would not come. The indomitable people looked always to tomorrow to bring what today would not give. But many people left the state, and those who stayed lived directly or indirectly on the government. Seed loans, feed loans, commodities, the W.P.A. — this was the jargon of the times.

Priests and sisters shared the poverty of their people in these days. Bills accumulated and properties were neglected. This was a time of repairs, not of new construction. This was a time when the people knew the value of the faith, for, like Job, they saw God as their only hope. Bishop Mahoney sang the chant of tomorrow with all the rest on his confirmation tours, but his ready sympathy, his kindliness and wisdom were a balm in these days of sore trial.

The economy was in decline when Bishop Mahoney came and it was in the ascendant when he died, but he knew only bad days. Still, in 1937, he initiated a program to retire the debt of the diocese, and it enjoyed astonishing success during his lifetime. His health had not been good for some time, and he died in 1939. The financial program had to be concluded by his successor. One can only recall the words of the Roman Ritual for the consecration of a bishop: "The bishop ought to make decisions, interpret, consecrate, offer [sacrifice], baptize, and confirm." These spiritual works occupied Bishop Mahoney, and they are the measure of episcopal greatness in every man who holds that high office.

Steady Economic Recovery

The late thirties and the forties were the days of recovery. Marred by the war, still this economic recovery, like a spring rain, renewed and quickened the land. Farmers regained the farms they had lost to the banks and insurance companies, and others, sensing the return of prosperity, bought farms. New buildings appeared and paint was applied to the old. Debts were liquidated; new ventures considered and attempted. In this moment of opportunity, Bishop William O. Brady, young and vigorous, came to take charge of the diocese. A native of Fall River, Massachusetts, rector of Saint Paul Seminary, Bishop Brady came when rain and recovery made the thought of action tolerable. The program of Bishop Mahoney for the liquidation of the debt was continued and eventually concluded by Bishop Brady. He urged priests and people to work and sacrifice. The response was immediate and whole-hearted.

The austerity of the Second World War was a moment of pause. In addition, the memory of the difficult times in the past two decades made caution excessive. Conservatism was the order of the day. This conservatism, not wise in re-

Bishop William O. Brady

view, was suited to the temper of priests and people at that time, and any other course would have been foolhardy.

But new projects came. A diocesan paper was published and a lecture series inaugurated. New parishes were established in Sioux Falls, Saint Mary's and Christ the King, and Watertown, Holy Name. The tiny pioneer churches throughout the diocese were being replaced by larger and finer structures. Rectories, schools, parish halls were built. Homes for the aged were constructed by the diocese at Pierre and Milbank. Hospitals were built at Huron, Watertown, Tyndall and Hoven.

The Benedictine Monks came from Saint Meinrad to establish a monastery on the eastern escarpment of the *couteau des prairies,* overlooking the Whetstone valley, to train priests and brothers for the Indian missions under their charge. They named this monastery Blue Cloud Abbey.

The Presentation Sisters opened a college for women, Presentation Heights, at Aberdeen in 1951 and built a beautiful new motherhouse there. Notre Dame Junior College at Mitchell was closed and its faculty staffed the new school.

Bishop Hoch

In March of 1952 an event took place that seemed to mark the coming of age of the Diocese of Sioux Falls. For the first time a native of the diocese was raised to the episcopacy. Lambert A. Hoch, born at Elkton, and for nineteen years chancellor of the diocese, was consecrated at Saint Joseph's Cathedral and became Bishop of Bismarck, North Dakota. When Bishop Brady left the diocese to become Archbishop of Saint Paul, Bishop Hoch came from Bismarck to serve his native diocese. His years in the chancery had supplied knowledge of the affairs of our diocese, and he was able to make plans and inaugurate policies immediately.

The postwar prosperity that had marked the years of Bishop Brady's administration was destined to continue. The small town did not recover, but larger towns grew greatly, and the population of state and diocese increased. The pitiful clusters of dilapidated houses that were all that remained of once promising small towns contrasted sharply with the modern development of the cities. The parishes throughout the diocese prospered, for the farmer and businessman were again in a stable and often prosperous condition. It was a time of building for most parishes, and new parishes were established in Sioux Falls and in Mitchell. High schools were built for the entire cities, at Sioux Falls and Aberdeen, and a public school acquired for this purpose at Mitchell. Extensive building was done by the religious communities, particularly at Yankton and Aberdeen.

The diocese itself entered a period of extensive development. Newman centers were built to care for the Catholic students at the State College at Brookings and the University at Vermillion, and others are projected to serve the three teachers colleges within the diocese. Additional homes for the aged have been constructed at Mitchell and Aberdeen.

No age is free from concern. Despite growth in numbers, religious vocations among women have not been able to keep pace with the need and demand of the Church. This has created problems, still unsolved. The advent of the lay teacher to the Catholic school is still too new to be appraised. Possible federal aid, given exclusively to the public schools, should this come, will aggravate the problem. Ideas, not unlike those that brought criticism on Archbishop Ireland, are being discussed. Meanwhile every effort is being made to continue the familiar way of the past. A hopeful sign has been the establishment of a new motherhouse of Benedictines at Pierre. The new house is a division of the parent establishment at Yankton.

Vocations to the priesthood, while not as critical a problem as the vocations of religious women, are in short supply. In an effort to meet this need Bishop Hoch called on his people to assist him to construct a minor seminary, and this newest venture will open its doors in the fall of 1964.

No one can observe the Sioux Falls diocese at this time and question its vitality. Its interests are varied—education, welfare, worship, the renewal of properties, all contribute to the primary spiritual purpose of the Church. The reappraisal of Catholic life that is taking place at the Second Vatican Council will find its reflection in our diocese in ways that we cannot now determine. But so much has the diocese been in harmony with the Holy Father, and with the bishops appointed by him, that his intentions rapidly become those of all the Catholics in the diocese.

The review of the years is the review of accomplishment. Not all is success. The Indian is often still out of adjustment with his time and with the faith, but generous men and women labor in his interest. Perhaps our greatest hope arises from the deep appreciation of the faith that is the mark of select people in most of the parishes of our diocese. This does not have a parallel in the past, and it promises well. God has been near and we must look to Him in gratitude. Others must write the appreciation of the chapter of diocesan history which this generation lives, for we are too close to see it in true perspective. There are indications that it is in accord with that which has gone before.

Architect's sketch of Blue Cloud Abbey, Marvin

Benedictine Convent of the Sacred Heart,
Yankton

Mother of God Priory, between St. Mary's
Hospital and a home for the aged, Pierre

Motherhouse and College of Presentation Sisters,
Aberdeen

RELIGIOUS IN THE DIOCESE OF SIOUX FALLS _____

Benedictine Fathers (Blue Cloud Abbey)
Benedictine Fathers (Conception, Mo.; Lisle, Ill.)
Dominican Fathers
Franciscan Fathers
Oblate Fathers
Polish Franciscan Fathers
Sacred Heart Fathers
Society of the Precious Blood
Viatorian Fathers

Benedictine Sisters of Pontifical Jurisdiction (Mother of God Priory)
Benedictine Sisters of Pontifical Jurisdiction (Convent of the Sacred Heart)
Bernardine Sisters of the Third Order of St. Francis
Daughters of St. Mary of Providence
Dominican Sisters of the Third Order of St. Dominic
Oblate Sisters (Indian) of the Blessed Sacrament
School Sisters of Notre Dame
School Sisters of St. Francis

Sisters of the Blessed Sacrament
Sisters of the Divine Saviour
Sisters of St. Francis of Blessed Kunegunda
Sisters of St. Francis of the Immaculate Heart of Mary
Sisters of the Third Order of St. Francis of Assisi
Sisters of the Third Order Regular of St. Francis of the Congregation of Our Lady of Lourdes
Sisters of the Presentation of the Blessed Virgin Mary of Pontifical Jurisdiction

BISHOP LEO F. DWORSCHAK — *St. Mary's Cathedral* ▶

Forts Daer and Pembina on the Red River, 1822

DIOCESE OF FARGO

by the Reverends A. A. A. Schmirler
and Gerald W. Weber

CHURCH ORGANIZATION in the area now comprising the Diocese of Fargo began almost 150 years ago. In 1818 a parish was established in Pembina in the northeast corner of the state. This was the first Catholic congregation with a resident priest within the entire area now covered by the Province of St. Paul. Another center of Catholic activity developed later in the Turtle Mountain territory where in 1850 Father George Anthony Belcourt erected a mission cross at St. Paul's Butte. This was the predecessor of the parishes now enclosed within Bottineau and Rolette counties. In addition to these general areas in which several parishes were organized, there was an isolated parish at Wild Rice, south of Fargo, by the middle of the century.

Much earlier than this Catholic explorers, fur traders and missionaries had crossed the northwest corner of the present Fargo diocese enroute to the village complex of the Mandan Indians on the Missouri River. Among these early travelers were members of the Vérendrye expedition who crossed this area in 1738. A fur trader known simply as "Old" Ménard who spent winters among the Mandans beginning in 1778 contributed more information about the geography of the area than any other man prior to 1803 when he was murdered by a band of Assiniboine brigands west of Willow City, North Dakota. There is no record, however, of missionary endeavor within the Fargo diocese at that time.

Before 1800 the fur traders Peter Grant and Charles Baptist Chaboillez had set up trading posts at Pembina and at St. Vincent, Minnesota. Subordinate posts were established farther upstream along the Minnesota-Dakota border. Pembina had developed as an offshoot of the Selkirk colony at Fort Douglas, now St. Boniface, Manitoba.

In 1818 two priests from Montreal came to Pembina to attend to the needs of a community composed largely of immigrants and Metis, later augmented by Chippewa and Assiniboine Indians, transient buffalo hunters, traders and surveyors. The priests were Father Joseph Norbert Provencher, later to become the first Vicar Apostolic of Western Canada, and Father Severe Joseph Nicholas Dumoulin. The first mass was offered here in September, 1818, by Father Dumoulin.

Father Dumoulin remained for five years, and for a time his parish was larger than St. Boniface where Father Provencher had established his headquarters. These words, written by the late Monsignor James M. Reardon in 1952, describe the parish at Pembina:

> Except for occasional visits from Father Provencher, Father Dumoulin was the only priest in a territory where now nine bishops and nearly sixteen hundred priests minister to the needs of a thriving church. When it was finally determined that Pembina was in the United States and not a British possession, it was abandoned by Father Dumoulin who returned to Montreal in July, 1823, leaving a record of 800 baptisms of children and adults, 120 marriages celebrated or validated, 48 burials and 150 first communions, with a large number preparing for baptism or communion.

For the next twenty-five years the parish had no resident pastor, but it was served sporadically by various priests. Records show priests named Thomas Destroismaisons, Harper and Boucher. Bishop Provencher, too, made frequent visits and in 1843 he passed through Pembina county with the first recorded Red River oxcart train. He was on his way to St. Paul with a caravan of thirty-five carts. This homespun vehicle of commerce, the oxcart, made Pembina a halfway house between St. Paul and Winnipeg.

The work of Father Dumoulin was taken up in 1848 by Father George Anthony Belcourt whom Bishop Shanley considered "North Dakota's greatest pioneer priest." Born and educated in Quebec Province, Father Belcourt was ordained a diocesan priest at Nicolet Seminary in 1827. Before coming to Pembina where he served as pastor for eleven years, Father Belcourt was formed as a missionary by work among the Chippewa for whom he compiled a tribal dictionary.

Red River oxcart train

Father George Anthony Belcourt

At Pembina the multitude of Father Belcourt's activities is described by Monsignor Reardon:

He built a chapel, dedicated to the Assumption of the Blessed Virgin, a school for the spiritual and educational training of the neophytes and founded a religious community of native, half-breed young women, known as the Sisters of the Propagation of the Faith, who, because they were familiar with the language and customs of the Indians, were well qualified to conduct a school in English, French, and Indian. The community was not very numerous, perhaps never more than seven, and ceased to exist when Father Belcourt left the mission in 1859. A few years after settling in Pembina, in 1853, Father Belcourt opened another mission at St. Joseph, later Walhalla, now Leroy, about thirty miles west and took up his residence there, ministering to a congregation of about fifteen hundred souls while retaining charge of Pembina under the direction of his assistant, Father Lacombe. There he built a log chapel under the patronage of St. Joseph, a presbytery, a school and a flour mill, the first in North Dakota, and from that center traveled throughout the state and in a special way evangelized the Turtle Mountain region and erected on Butte St. Paul, the highest point in the vicinity, the saving symbol of our holy faith....In his pastoral work he had such well known assistants as Father Lacombe, already mentioned, afterwards the famous Oblate "blackrobe" among the Indians of Western Canada; Reverend John Fayolle, second pastor of the original frame church of St. Anthony in Minneapolis; and Reverend Joseph Goiffon whose experience in a blizzard in November, 1860, is a thrilling episode in the annals of the Church in the Northwest.

The Father Goiffon mentioned above became known as "the frozen priest of Pembina"; his story was read with interest in America and Europe. In October of 1860, riding horseback from St. Paul, he crossed the Red River and became lost in a blizzard. Rescued only by chance when his lower body was already frozen and after he had kept alive by eating the meat of his frozen horse, he was eventually taken to Winnipeg because of constant hemorrhaging in his limbs. The cathedral rectory in which he was hospitalized caught fire, a fortunate fire for Father Goiffon. The attendants who carried him from his room dumped him, in their excitement, in a snowbank and left him there. His legs froze again and the bleeding was stopped! Father Goiffon lived to the hearty old age of eighty-six.

After Father Belcourt and his assistants ended their term in 1861, the Pembina area was assigned to Father Alex André and other Oblates. Thus in the sixties, a hundred years ago, the Oblates composed the priest corps in the Red River section of the Dakota Territory while the Jesuits evangelized on the Missouri.

This period cannot be closed without reference to a somewhat controversial figure, Father J. B. M. Genin, who came up the Red River in 1867. He celebrated mass, administered the sacraments and preached to soldiers, settlers, traders, Metis and Indians. He visited Pembina, Fort Abercrombie, Wild Rice, Fort Ransom and Butte de Coeur where, Father Genin writes, he erected a cross—this in addition to his activities on the Minnesota side of the Red River. Aside from historical controversies which were fought over him, he failed to achieve major importance. He easily formulated grandiose plans, but he quickly became petty in the execution of them. Concern for his personal financial security, a real problem for missionaries, seemed at times to dominate his thoughts to such an extent that it chilled the good will of his contacts.

In 1870 the Northern Pacific Railroad crossed the Red River at Fargo. It reached Bismarck on the Missouri before the panic of 1873. The railroad linked up steamboat traffic between the two rivers and a new era began.

In the seventies parishes with resident pastors were established at Leroy, Wahpeton and Grand Forks, and religious orders of women came to Dakota.

The First Sisters

The first of these were the Grey Nuns of Montreal. Two Grey Nuns stepped off the train in 1872 at the cluster of shacks that was Jamestown. They stood facing the ninety miles of empty prairie between them and Fort Totten which they had come to investigate as a possible location site. But finding no one to conduct them there, they reluctantly returned to Montreal.

However, the Grey Nuns again took up the project two years later; and that year is noteworthy for other reasons. A Sioux girl, Anapao or Josephine Nebraska, that year privately decided to give herself to Mary in charitable service. The Catholic Indian Bureau was founded in 1874. John Shanley, later to become the first bishop of Fargo, was ordained. Enactment of compulsory military service brought about the migration of German-Russians to the Americas —and Dakota Territory.

At this time the first public schools in Dakota Territory were being opened in the southeastern corner without maps and blackboards and with very few books. The first bank at Vermillion still hauled silver and currency on a weekly schedule from Iowa by horse carriage in order to make change for checks and script money. By contrast, the universities of Nebraska, Syracuse, Ohio State, Loyola of Chicago, California, Oregon and Nevada were opened that year. Sisters had come to Willamette Valley in Oregon thirty years earlier, and in 1864 the Sisters of Providence from Montreal began their residence in Montana. But none had come to a place so uninhabited as Dakota. When four Grey Nuns left Montreal for Fort Totten in 1874, they took the stride that brought Catholic culture to the geographic heart of the American continent.

The first group consisted of Mother Clapin, Sisters Lajemmerais, Drapeau and Allard with Father Louis Bonin, a diocesan priest, as chaplain. Thus the Sioux, who had displaced the Cheyennes in the area of our diocese by their cruel warfare, were themselves about to be conquered by a means more gentle.

At Fort Totten the nuns were greeted by James McLaughlin, an eventual successor to Major George Forbes in office, who, with his wife, would render great assistance to the nuns. The "Annals of the Grey Nuns" records their arrival:

Steamboat and railroad meet in Fargo, 1879

171

A few hours after their arrival [at the Agency House] an Indian chief came to see them; he... seemed happy; he was followed by a good number of Indians and many women in their dancing costumes, their faces and bodies painted, [and wrapped] in multicolor blankets, red decorations in their ears... and a mass of neckbeads of enormous size. They looked more like demons [to the sisters] than human beings; but after looking at them more attentively there was found something amiable in them; and each of them showed joy in shaking hands with the sisters.

The conquest begun, the "Annals" relate how on the second day they unpacked a library in a building provided by the government for the teachers. The medicine dance was still being used to cure illness when the sisters made their first visit to the sick. The first class was devoted to several hours on personal hygiene, and each subsequent day's curriculum placed an emphasis on the domestic arts. By extraordinary efforts the sisters managed to grow a garden for themselves after three years. But their work was largely undone in one night when buffalo trampled most of its produce.

That year, too, Father Genin came to Fort Totten and caused a great disturbance by organizing a hunting party to obtain hides by which he might meet church debts he had incurred. The tragedy lay in the fact that everyone else on the reservation had been trying to settle the Sioux, to eliminate the excitement of the doomed hunting economy and way of life. At this time, in northwestern Dakota Father Martin Marty was risking his life in order to make a treaty with Sitting Bull recognizing the realities of the Dakota situation. But Father Genin's hunt seemed to turn back the clock. The sisters' chaplain, Father Bonin, though deprived of priestly company, refused to see Father Genin.

The "Annals" continue to record a life of loneliness and mental anguish. "We are in complete isolation." For there was always trouble: with the Indians, with the agent, with the government, with living facilities, with the chaplain, with each other. Where could they go at such times? For recreation sister might climb to "the steeple which affords such a beautiful view out over the prairie." More often she might take refuge before the tabernacle. The focus of their lives is brought out by the way the day's

entry always notes how our Lord was moved from here to there, when, for example, they calcemined the chapel or the temperature was too low to heat the chapel or for various other reasons.

The roster of visitors recorded by the "Annals" at Fort Totten includes outstanding personalities of the region. Visitors today can tour the military compound, the most complete quadrangle of original buildings and parade grounds in existence in the United States. By driving the eight miles to St. Michael's they are also able to visit the site of an early victory of Christianity over paganism in the Diocese of Fargo.

Because a successor to Father Bonin, Father Jerome Hunt, O.S.B., did the work of chaplain on the reservation so early, so long and so successfully he is sometimes thought to have been there from the beginning. But Father Bonin made the initial sally. After four years he quietly determined to take up parish work. From Pembina he founded the parishes of Oakwood and Neche.

In the later years of his life at Riviere des Prairies, Canada, it was Father Bonin's proud boast that in 1876 he was the only priest in the present state of North Dakota. This was probably true for several months; for Benedictines Marty and Chrysostom Pfoffa resided near Kenel, South Dakota; Father Le Floch at Walhalla and Father Simonet at Pembina had been temporarily withdrawn; and Father Louis L'Hiver was still on the way to Grand Forks.

Decade of Settlement

The great wave of North Dakota settlement was due in great part to tales of bonanza farming in profitable wheat crops published all over the United States and Europe. It is a fascinating story in itself. The sudden change can be briefly illustrated. At Pembina in the 1770's Charles Bottineau farmed ten acres; Charles Grant, five to eight; Antoine Gingras, twenty to twenty-five; and John Dole, two to three, largely for home consumption. Now, in a span of ten years, the sale of wheat alone became a million-dollar item. Dakota Territory, which counted a population of 135,000 in 1880, totaled 350,000 in 1885. That the wave crested in North Dakota at over 600,000 then began to subside to a less than normal rate of growth in the 1940's is well known. Church organization flooded into the country districts simultaneously with population—and receded with it.

With the increase of population came new groups of sisters. The Presentation Sisters at Fargo became the second group to enter the diocese in territorial days, coming to Fargo on Father Joseph A. Stephan's invitation, July 26, 1882. Across the river from Fargo the Benedictine Sisters had located in Moorhead, Minnesota, three years earlier. A third group, the Ursulines, came to Grand Forks in 1883. And moving from the present state of South Dakota, as had the Presentation community, was a fourth sisterhood, the Mercy Sisters, now in Devils Lake and Valley City, although their original foundation was in Belcourt. Benedictine Sisters came to Wahpeton in 1886 and the Sisters of St. Joseph of Carondolet came to Jamestown after statehood, as did many others.

The story of the third group, the Ursulines, illustrates the changing times in the Vicariate of Dakota. On July 21, 1883, Sisters Stanislaus Rafferty and Augustine Enright, American-born members of an Irish foundation of Ursuline nuns in Illinois, arrived in Grand Forks. They founded what today is St. James High School. This school was advertised: "St. Bernard's Ursuline College. No eastern Academy maintains a higher grade of education. Nuns are devoted exclusively to teaching." In the main all this was true.

However, the Ursulines were to encounter some of the pioneer experiences of the Grey Nuns a decade earlier. On February 29, 1884, Sister Stanislaus, a novice named Sister Louise, Miss Marie Howard and Miss Margaret Sullivan set out in a sleigh, the train being snowbound, for a place sixty miles west of Grand Forks and nine miles south of the tracks. Their objective was to prove up on two 160-acre homesteads by a six-month residence. Time was running out on the claims. The group reached the destination in four days. Sister Louise may well be the only nun in history who made good her claim to 160 acres of real estate and made her novitiate at the same time!

The residence of the sisters and their companions was located on Stump Lake in Nelson County. It was popularly known as "The Shanty." The Ursulines christened it "St. Martin's on the Lake." Priests who took a turn at a monthly visit—Fathers Ahne, Hunt, Flanigan and Schirra

—as well as the Grey Nuns who exchanged one visit, called the residence the "Hermitage." It was a primitive place. Their cellar was a hole in the ground covered with a loose board. The nearest grazing for the milch cows was four miles away.

Despite the hours of work entailed in mere survival the sisters by June had prepared seventeen children of Catholic settlers scattered far from the church for confirmation. A duly respectful letter apprised the bishop at Yankton

MINNESOTA HISTORICAL SOCIETY

Typical shanty

that the sisters would bring the children to a rendezvous anywhere at the tracks if His Excellency could manage to stop the train. The bishop replied, "Tell her I will be at the Shanty on the fourth of July."

The Shanty, a cathedral-for-a day, stood in all its stark beauty, a 20x20-foot square shiplap construction, 8 feet at the eaves and 12 feet at the gable peak, sides and roof sealed with black tar paper. There were a few 20x18-inch windows and every door had a latch. For confirmation the interior was somehow divided into three compartments. One end, as far as the wall paper extended, became the bishop's room; it also contained the altar which was resplendent with bunches of wild flowers drenched by leaks in the roof. The middle room, containing the boys and their equipment, was also to be used for the examination in Christian learning of the entire class, a mandatory procedure in those days. The third section must have bulged at the seams or, more properly, strained the lathes holding the tar paper outside. This, the kitchenette, contained cooking utensils, an army drygoods box used as a table, a smaller box doubling for the pantry, an oven, the sisters and the girls. Pots and pans were scattered throughout all three divisions in this prairie ark to catch the rain dripping through the roof.

This was the setting which greeted Bishop Martin Marty. His soaking wet apparel replaced with something simpy draped over his shoulders, he armed himself with a pail, sat on a drygoods box, summoned the class, put his feet in the oven and began his instruction. In all the Dakota vicariate was there ever a class confirmed with a better shepherd-flock relationship than Minnie and Ida Hennessey, Marie Huard, George Lamb, Mary Lozo, James, Rita and

Hannah Cronin! Heavy rains had prevented the remaining nine members of the class from reaching the Shanty for the occasion.

It took till 1914 for the effort rooted at Stump Lake to fail, not too surprisingly, because of financial difficulties. Times and conditions had changed. Whereas, among the pioneers, a Father Dumoulin or a Father Belcourt had fabricated buildings, Father John Considine, the first priest ordained specifically for Dakota, had farmed, only to become somewhat embittered as a result — the days of the bumper crops were passing. Settlement had caught up with Dakota by 1884, and a decade later a priest farming at Oakwood was considered somewhat unusual. It was too late in the day for religious to homestead.

But it was not unusual that Catholic and Protestant college ventures failed during these years: Ripon (North Dakota), Tower City, Jamestown and St. Gall's south of Devils Lake. St. Gall's, however, through the determined efforts of Vincent Wehrle, O.S.B., eventually was crowned with success as Assumption Abbey at Richardton, North Dakota, in the present Bismarck diocese.

A sod church, 1895

Abandoned St. Gall's Priory

To the present day the Diocese of Fargo remains without a Catholic college or a full-fledged monastery for men.

Nonetheless, St. Gall's enriched the Fargo diocese because it centralized the type of circuit riding done by Bishop Wehrle and his Benedictine confreres. They followed the rails to the state line in the west and north, and maintained the buggy-swing around the seventy-mile lake to the south, exercising a formative influence upon at least forty-three hopeful congregations.

Diocesan priests pushed forward with equally optimistic zeal. Father Lorenz Spitzenberger, a Bavarian based at Perham, Minnesota, evangelized more than fifty places in Dakota on his Red River Valley circuit between 1878 and 1883, authorized only by Bishop Rupert Seidenbusch, then Vicar Apostolic of Northern Minnesota. In the southeastern counties of North Dakota Father M. M. Tierney carried out an extensive horse and buggy apostolate. Later on Carrington and Jamestown became the hub of missionary work.

The parish at Rugby was originally developed by Father Seraphim M. Roumie, a priest of the Melkite rite. When most of his Syrian railroaders had moved to larger cities, Father Roumie sold land taken up in Dakota for $400 to help establish a Melkite parish on Twelfth Place in Chicago.

The names of many ghost towns in North Dakota, unmarked on the latest maps, were once hallowed by church work — Ruby, Calmer, Tiffany and Ransom, to mention a few. His-torians cherish each for its story. Tarsus, for example, was a country church in the Turtle Mountains where the French-Canadian Catholic continuity maintained itself strongly. Here on Sunday mornings everyone attended mass. On Sunday afternoon all met again at the church for prayers. Social events included occasional horse racing, ball games and cock fights.

In 1906 Monsignor Theophile Campeau brought in the French Presentation Sisters whose academy at Willow City has given such a firm base to Catholicism in the old Mouse River loop. He himself had once been an Indian missionary in Canada. Among the Indians who came for miles to make their Easter duty with him annually was a "Granny" Bellegarde. Each year she came, sat on the rectory step and waited till visitors were dismissed with polite firmness. Then Monsignor Campeau and Granny went into the office. From a desk drawer the monsignor took a corn cob pipe which Granny smoked while they conversed in Cree.

Continuity of Indian missionary work at the Turtle Mountain Reservation must be credited mainly to Father Hildebrand Elliott, O.S.B., the sisters and Catholic people of Belcourt. This parish numbers more persons today than any other in the diocese. Each July, in observance of St. Anne's day, a spectacular procession with the Blessed Sacrament, comprised of 2,000 to 8,000 people, moves in reverent fashion down the slope to the village and back again to the red brick mission complex on the hill, with green "turtle-back" heights as a backdrop.

What is also remarkable is that this annual event continues a tradition inaugurated by Father J. F. Malo in the 1880's. Over the high altar in the Romanesque chapel stands a hand-carved, larger than life statue of St. Anne, ornamented in deep colors. It is proof of the document in which some of the oldest pioneers in the Turtle Mountains petitioned on July 6, 1890, that St. Anne be the patron of their church. As Father Malo recorded them they are:

Rahish Pah	Rapotince	Tootoosh
Bado	Riskimanacho	Napock
Piashish	Chichick	Chockokam
Nemakooshish	Paquagikan	Namkhaukhowenin
Pecpeeshesh	Achiwenin	Esselthuwa
Rayenee	Napochikonis	Atstamau
Rakanence	Achkaskonce	Ratigena
Pandawatoon	Rishenoo	

Episcopal residence and cathedral in Jamestown

Distinct groups of several nationalities came to North Dakota during the decade before the establishment of the Diocese of Fargo. Bohemian parishes sprang up at Wahpeton, Mooreton, Lidgerwood, Lankin, Pisek and Veselyville while the Polish started parishes at Cayuga, Geneseo, Courtney, Fried, Warsaw and Minto—all in the Fargo diocese. Hungarians were well represented at Fingal, Oriska and in the vicinity of Langdon. German-Russians began coming into North Dakota in Emmons County where the Benedictines from Standing Rock Reservation served their needs. Father Bernard Strassmeier, O.S.B., built a frame church with their help at Zeeland in 1889. The German-Russians constitute the most numerous element of Catholic population in the Diocese of Fargo today.

Jamestown only North Dakota Diocese

Jamestown was the see city of all North Dakota from November, 1889, to August, 1891, when John Shanley, its first bishop, moved to Fargo.

For some time prior to 1889 rumors predicted a division of the Vicariate of Dakota. Father Collins, the Fargo pastor, had a promotion scheme in mind when he boarded a train at St. Paul in October of 1887. On the same train, bound for the west coast, was James Cardinal Gibbons of Baltimore who had great influence in American ecclesiastical affairs. But Father Collins failed in his endeavor to persuade the cardinal to stop at Fargo to see for himself that it would be a suitable see city. What effect, if any, Collins had in influencing later events is not known. What is known is that Bishop Marty recommended both Jamestown and Fargo for consideration as the see city. A Jamestown delegation called on Archbishop Ireland of St. Paul to point out the good points of its own city.

Soldiers who came to "Jimtown" in 1872 said it had no claim to distinction except that it was at the crossing of the non-navigable James River, about halfway between the Red River and the Missouri. One Dakotan wrote many years later what she saw on her first trip to the town on July 13, 1872:

176

At that day and hour (10:30 P.M.) our overland journey from Fort Totten was completed, and from the bluff I first beheld Jamestown. On the bluffs west of the river the campfires of soldiers were burning brightly, while in the valley below the twinkling lights of the town gleamed merrily through the darkness.

An English immigrant in 1884 wrote that the aim of the citizens "appears to be to make their young city as much like the older established cities of St. Paul or Chicago as possible." Accordingly, he noted the red brick courthouse and jail, banks, a schoolhouse "somewhere," hotels, restaurants, two "huge" grain elevators, hall and opera house, grocery, hardware and dry-goods stores, flour mill, any number of liquor shops, beer and billiard rooms . . . "you can have anything and everything if you have the wherewithall to pay for it." That he was not favorably impressed by what he saw is also evident from the following:

> Jamestown consists mainly of one street running almost due north and south. Fifth Avenue, as it is named, contains the principal buildings. Branching off on either side from Fifth Avenue are numerous smaller thoroughfares . . . a few steps at right angles to Fifth Avenue, and lo! behold when we raise our eyes from the ground the city has vanished, and we have come to the end of the wooden sidewalk. All beyond us is prairie, dotted here and there, in a straggling fashion with tiny buildings; surrounding us are solitary houses or sheds, and stack upon stack of lumber. In the distance the muddy waters of the James River meander between low banks covered with a growth of bushes or stunted trees. The city of Jamestown is not all built yet . . . our mind is eased, for there is evidently something remaining to do or build after all.

To this untidy town on the James River came Bishop John Shanley to begin his administration of a diocese that was loosely organized, inadequately staffed and materially impoverished.

On arriving in Jamestown he inquired as to where the episcopal residence might be and after some difficulty succeeded in locating it. It was a bitter, cold evening, about twenty-five degrees below zero, and the bishop and his episcopal guests began to feel that they had not struck a very propitious spot. In the priest's house, now the bishop's house, there was neither heat nor food of any description.

In these words John Shanley described his arrival in Jamestown on the evening of January 23, 1890, as North Dakota's first resident Catholic bishop. The episcopal guests to whom he referred were James McGolrick and Joseph Cotter who had been consecrated with him on December 27, 1889, by Archbishop John Ireland as suffragan bishops of newly created dioceses in the Province of St. Paul. Their train had been delayed by an accident, and the elderly pastor of Jamestown, infirm in body and mind, had made no preparations for their arrival.

As we look back on the pioneer days of the new diocese in North Dakota, we understand only with difficulty the primitive conditions which the Church survived in North Dakota. Jamestown had only 1,500 inhabitants of whom some 350 were Catholics. Most of them—and this is true of the majority of the inhabitants of the new state—were recent immigrants from the East or from Europe, of rural background and with small material means. They had come to North Dakota because of sensational stories about its cheap land and bumper wheat crops. The Catholic church in Jamestown suddenly named the cathedral, was a simple frame building which had been built in 1882 at the cost of $6,000. The rectory was a small building which copied the local Presbyterian parsonage. Conditions were no better elsewhere in the state.

The Territory of Dakota had been divided by an act of Congress on February 22, 1889, and on November 2 of the same year the two states, North and South Dakota, were admitted to the Union. Shortly thereafter, on November 12, the Diocese of Jamestown was created by the apostolic constitution, "Quae Catholico Nomini," and on November 15, 1889, John Shanley, the thirty-seven-year-old pastor of the Cathedral of St. Paul, was appointed by Rome as its first bishop. The state and the diocese, established in the same year, existing in identical social and economic conditions and influenced by common geographical and political factors, developed and marked progress side by side.

When John Shanley took up residence in Jamestown, the state government, as yet only in the formative stage, was not able to exercise effectively its authority. One could see only dim outlines of organized society and the order based on law which we today take for granted. Living

Bishop John Shanley

conditions were very primitive. Sod houses and wooden shanties dotted the vast sweep of the prairie horizon. John Shanley immediately recognized the unfavorable circumstances in which he began his episcopal career. The impressions of his first days in North Dakota have been recorded for posterity in his diary (1897):

> In 1890, Jamestown was one of the most unpromising places in America for a bishop to begin work. As a matter of fact no place in North Dakota was ready to receive a bishop in 1890 .... After six years of suffering I begin to see some rays of hope for the future, and I can now write calmly my convictions on a subject about which, so strong were my feelings, I scarcely dared allow myself to think during the past six years. When I think back ... I wonder sometimes how it is that I did not go insane. There was nothing but trouble or disappointment whether I went away or came home from a trip. Thank God things have changed for the better.

The first order of business in Jamestown was to provide suitable living quarters for himself. He remodeled and enlarged the rectory, now his episcopal residence. He built a sacristy large enough for a winter chapel. He purchased the sanctuary furniture necessary for pontifical services.

But spiritual concerns also occupied him. He dismissed the awkward young fellow who served mass and selected a dozen little boys whom he himself trained. He organized a Sunday school and taught classes himself. He established an altar society. He preached every Sunday at both masses and in the evening he gave lectures on some aspect of Catholic life. Through these pastoral activities and the retreats and triduums he preached to the various classes of people, he suc-

ceeded by degrees in infusing some spiritual life into the members of the cathedral congregation.

However, even while he was organizing and building in Jamestown, he knew that the town was not destined to remain his see city. His first tour of the Red River Valley shortly after his arrival had convinced him of the impossibility of remaining in Jamestown. Its sole merit lay in the fact that it was on the main line of the Northern Pacific Railroad. Yet this was of little practical importance, since to visit many sections of the diocese, he first had to make a four-hour train journey to Fargo, often at unreasonable hours, then change trains to finish the trip. It was a waste of both time and energy.

Fargo, the railroad center of North Dakota, was the strategic point in the state. Years after he moved to Fargo he justified his transfer in these emphatic words:

> I lived in Jamestown from January, 1890, to August, 1891, when I moved to Fargo. The reasons for the change were:
>
> 1. The impossibility of governing the diocese from Jamestown.
>
> 2. The impossibility of making a living in Jamestown. Writing now as I do, six years after the occurrence, it may well be presumed that I do not exaggerate. I reaffirm ... it was impossible to govern the diocese and I could not get enough to keep body and soul together.

He soon discovered to his dismay that Fargo, although the largest town in the state with a population of 4,300, was little improvement over

Fargo at the turn of the century

Catholic Indian Congress, Fort Totten, 1909

Jamestown. Around one hundred families were registered in the Catholic community in Fargo. The building that now became his procathedral had originally been a Methodist church. Bishop Shanley in the *Bulletin* which he edited in 1909 has left us his impressions of it. "It was not a thing of beauty but a horrible shack. Passion Sunday is a joy for it begins the temporary concealment of our inartistic statuary."

As a river town on the frontier, Fargo had been the base of the fur trader, the voyageur, the missionary. It had seen the Red River cart and the Red River steamer. In the early days of Bishop Shanley, Fargo still had its share of colorful and troublesome characters, whiskey men, gamblers and adventurers. Reminiscing about this period of his life, the bishop later wrote: "In spite of the character of the people and the uninviting surroundings I determined to take steps for the future location of the see in Fargo, and with this end in view I looked the town over carefully for a good location for a cathedral." Find one he did. The present site of the cathedral was for sale at $7,500. At that time, as he remarked afterwards to a fellow priest, he did not even have enough money for a return ticket to Jamestown. Nevertheless, he went unaccompanied to the First National Bank, introduced himself and borrowed the money for the purchase of the property. Shortly after this transaction the citizens of Fargo, as an inducement for him to speed his transfer to their town, gave him a gift of $11,000, two-thirds of which was subscribed by non-Catholics.

With this money he built the basement of his church, the first step on a very long journey toward the erection of a new cathedral in Fargo. Immediately after the foundation was completed, lack of financial support forced an indefinite suspension of further work. The crops of 1891, 1892 and 1893 were either total or partial failures. Moreover, in 1893, a fire razed much of Fargo, causing financial losses to many families. Every fund-raising project failed. A plan to impose a $10 tax on every family in the diocese was rejected by the clergy. It was impossible to obtain a loan from any bank or financial agency in the country. North Dakota was considered a poor risk.

Shanley's personal record of these years of defeat and frustration is preserved for us in the *Bulletin*.

> The bishop has been obliged to support himself, to take steps towards the erection of a church in which episcopal functions may be performed with some degree of decorum, besides a multitude of other necessary works which require expenditure of money. We have succeeded in doing a great deal. But how? Not from the resources of this diocese, but by our own hard labors in the missionary fields outside of North Dakota. For three years we went about giving missions in various parts of the United States, earning money for our maintainance by the hardest of work; nor did we cease those labors until our health was seriously impaired. In the years 1891 and 1892 we received as cathedraticum or salary, the sum of five hundred and eighty-one dollars. For the year 1893 the amount for the support of the bishop was $797.32.

To supplement his meager income and to raise money for diocesan projects, such as completion of the cathedral and episcopal residence, during these years he preached more than thirty missions, gave five clergy retreats and a goodly number of triduums. In later years, referring to the labors of preaching by which he supported himself, he often said, "My house came out of my throat."

After eight years of exasperating delays work on the superstructure of the cathedral was finally resumed in 1898. At that time a loan of $50,000 was secured through the good graces of Father Joseph Lemieux, rector of St. Mary's Cathedral, from a Mr. Roberts of Montreal, Canada. On May 30 of the following year, the silver jubilee of the ordination of Bishop Shanley, St. Mary's Cathedral was dedicated. The jubilarian had the consoling privilege of pontificating in a building worthy of the title of cathedral. To add to his joy ground was broken also for a new episcopal residence.

The cathedral was completed, but with borrowed money. The struggle to pay off the mortgage is another story in itself, a few glimpses of which Bishop Shanley has left us in his diary.

> The people of Fargo gave $3,572.15 for the building of the cathedral—the superstructure.... The interest on our loan amounts to $5,106 payable semi-annually.... From May 30, 1899, to June, 1900, nothing was done by the Fargo congregation towards meeting the interest. In June, 1900, I told the people of Fargo that I had paid their interest for one year, and now they must bear their share of the burden; that henceforth on the first Sunday of each month a church debt collection would be made. I also levied a tax in the fall of 1900 on all the parishes, $50 a parish, thus placing half the debt on the diocese, the other half on Fargo. That is in theory, because the bishop has been forced to carry one-third of the debt. Last June (1903) I paid the tenth interest coupon, and still I live and can pay for my supper tonight.

With this story of staggering financial problems and tireless efforts to build a cathedral and episcopal residence, we have a fuller appreciation of the problems inherent in the bishop's labors as he organized and administered the affairs of the diocese, promoted the spiritual and temporal welfare of the Indian and worked for social reform.

When the diocese was formed in 1889, some forty Catholic churches were scattered throughout the state, all of them without exception frame shanties. There was one academy for girls, one Catholic hospital and three parochial schools. Of the 19,000 Catholics in the state, almost 8,000 were half-breeds. Active within the diocese were thirty-two priests, but twenty-one belonged to other jurisdictions, and they were free to leave when they wished.

More of Shanley's Problems

The reasons why these men had left their former dioceses or religious communities were many and varied. Some had come for most praiseworthy, noble motives: missionary work among the Indians or pastoral work with early settlers. Others had come for less noble reasons: maladjustment in their former assignments, open conflict with their respective superiors or expulsion for personal reasons. Most of them had labored for years in missionary territory, in an unorganized society, with the minimum of immediate ecclesiastical supervision. To mold these men into a coordinated body of clergy was no easy task. Some of these men resented not only episcopal authority, but even more the strong measures the bishop adopted to promote order and discipline among them and the laity.

During the first ten years of his administration Shanley saw the coming and going of dozens of priests for one reason or another. On a number of occasions it was necessary to suspend a priest or expel him from the diocese. There were times when a large number of clergy were in opposition to their superior, at times each for his own personal reasons, but at other times making common cause against him. The reasons for these strong feelings between clergy and their bishop are found in Shanley's diary, in pertinent correspondence in the archives of the Diocese of Fargo and in the *Bulletin* edited by Bishop Shanley.

The problem of securing and keeping a cooperative and stable clergy weighed heavily on the mind and conscience of the bishop. The organization of the diocese and the consolidation of spiritual gains was impossible with a constant clergy turnover. To administer effectively the far-flung areas of the diocese it was imperative to have a sufficient number of dedicated, able and cooperative priests. Bishop Shanley never lost sight of this vital fact.

The methods Bishop Shanley adopted to secure financial support for diocesan projects caused great dissatisfaction among the clerical malcontents in the diocese. In many instances they actually refused to cooperate with his program for reducing the debt on the cathedral and episcopal residence. To educate the people to the fact that North Dakota was a true diocese, a Laymen's Convention was convoked in Fargo in 1895. Bishop Shanley sent out 3,000 letters of invitation to representative laymen in every parish. He wanted the opportunity to talk directly to the laity because he had received reports that in some parishes laymen had been forbidden by their pastors to approach the bishop on episcopal visits. In a few instances the people had been told from the pulpit that the Irish bishop had no use for German and French people.

More than 600 laymen attended the convention. For three days, in forenoon and afternoon sessions, the bishop instructed them about their respective duties and privileges as Catholic laymen in the Diocese of Fargo. Moreover, the various parish delegations were received in private audience by the bishop. Not a small number of priests were critical of the convention and the attitude of the bishop which they felt gave the laymen too much latitude in church affairs. In reflection on the convention and the criticism of the clergy, Shanley made these comments in his diary on the effects the convention had on the growth of the diocese which he often compared to "the movement of an Alpine glacier":

> From the convention dates the growth of the diocese of Fargo. Priests and people knew from that date that order must be observed .... I realized the danger of the measure I adopted, but I adopted it as a last resort, and God blessed the undertaking.

The convoking of the Laymen's Convention also had its roots in the celebrated case of the Reverend Joseph Perrault. A word about this priest is necessary because the controversy in which he was involved affected the public image of the Church in North Dakota and in particular the good name of Bishop Shanley. Moreover, it is only in its telling that we can grasp the malicious nature of this particular problem and eval-

uate to some extent the atmosphere of distrust in the diocese, impeding both the work of the bishop and the progress of the Church.

Joseph Perrault was a French-Canadian priest whom Bishop Shanley transferred in 1892 from Mandan to Larimore after repeated complaints about him from the parishioners at Mandan. Offended by this disciplinary action Father Perrault circulated among his fellow priests a document containing more than fifty charges against the bishop. He sent this same list of charges to Archbishop Francis Satolli, a papal envoy on a special mission, who was visiting in St. Paul, and who a few months later became the first apostolic delegate to the United States. Principal among the accusations made against Shanley were these: autocratic and despotic government of the diocese, maladministration of diocesan affairs and favoritism toward the Irish clergy in the diocese. In his reply to Perrault Archbishop Satolli informed the priest that his charges against his superior were not substantiated, that no canonical investigation would be made and that he was to desist from making further charges. When Bishop Shanley was informed by Satolli about the charges of Perrault, he peremptorily demanded of the priest a public retraction. Perrault refused and was suspended.

Immediately thereafter Father Perrault gave all the documents and letters pertinent to the controversy to the *Grand Forks Herald* for publication. These were also reprinted later in the *Fargo Argus*. Father Perrault, at the same time, instituted thirteen lawsuits against Bishop Shanley, among them one for $50,000 in damages. The entire affair, by its public and sensational nature, caused considerable scandal. Moreover, one or another of the charges found a sympathetic ear among malcontents in the diocese. Even some loyal priests and laymen who denounced Father Perrault, at the same time became critical of the bishop for his adamant position, demanding as he did an unconditional retraction without first exhausting every means to effect a reconciliation.

Just how widespread this spirit of rebellious criticism grew the bishop discovered shortly after the Laymen's Convention in 1895 when he was about to depart for his *ad limina* visit. A long article echoing the spirit of the Perrault document appeared in the *Wahpeton Globe*. It

McIntosh County Catholics at their first church

stated that Bishop Shanley was being summoned to Rome because of maladministration of his diocese. Recognizing the author of the article by its style, Bishop Shanley forced the pastor of Wahpeton to retract over his signature every word of the article. In justification of this strong action he later commented: "It was the start of what was meant to be a very hot campaign against me, which would result, it was hoped, in my removal." Drastic as this action might seem today, it succeeded in preventing the movement from gaining momentum, compelled the discontented element in the diocese, lay as well as clerical, to recognize episcopal authority in the newly established diocese.

As can be surmised, Bishop Shanley was a man of action. If he saw an evil, he branded it as such in definite terms. In battle all his forces were marshalled for a frontal attack. Once his objective was clear in his mind, he never hesitated to adopt a course of direct and effective action. For him patient diplomacy was not a tool to solve the problems of a missionary diocese. The qualities which made him impatient with the slow progress of his diocese and intolerant of the imperfections of the clergy were also the same qualities which made him the decisive, strong-willed leader of a frontier church and the champion of every worthy cause. Not content with exercising his office among the faithful only or limiting his interest to their affairs, he threw the full weight of his influence into every good endeavor.

During his frequent travels throughout the state, whether to confirm, to dedicate a church or to lay a cornerstone, he would lecture if possible in the evening to an audience in which non-Catholics were well represented. He gave these talks in any convenient building—Catholic church, community hall or even Protestant church. He would speak with or without invitation. On one occasion in Fargo, in 1898, a number of Protestant ministers had been invited to address a rally to recruit men for service in the Spanish-American War. Bishop Shanley was pointedly ignored—the second time something of the sort had happened. Without invitation he attended the meeting, and when it was about to open he suddenly stepped forward and addressed the crowd. He talked freely on history and geography, foreign languages and science, until there was no time left for the other speakers. Then he left.

On another occasion he was in Devils Lake on a confirmation tour when he learned that on the previous evening a Chatauqua lecturer had attacked the Holy See. Although fatigued by his long journey from Fort Berthold he asked for and obtained permission to appear before the people who had assembled for another lecture. He delivered a two-hour address in which he answered the charges that had been leveled against the Church. He closed his talk with these forceful words: "Let this be a warning to lecturers on this Chatauqua platform to refrain from assailing God's Church, Peter's Church, Leo's Church, my Church." He gained an enviable reputation as a speaker through numerous public appearances such as this one.

He also attracted wide attention throughout

the state as a social reformer. It was largely through his persistent warfare against divorce that Fargo lost a growing reputation as the divorce center of the nation. At that time the state law in North Dakota permitted divorce action after a residence of only ninety days. Against this statute he wrote and spoke very often, urging that a residence of one year be required for divorce action. He even carried his fight against the statute to the doors of the legislature. In April, 1897, he rented the Atheneum, a public auditorium in Bismarck, and sent a general invitation to the public to attend a talk that he would deliver. For two hours he spoke in condemnation of the divorce law. As a result of his forceful discourse a bill to change the period of residence to one year was introduced into the legislature. It was approved by the house, but failed by one vote in the senate. Eventually, however, the bill was passed. The role of Bishop Shanley in this matter did not go unnoticed. The *Michigan City Independent* presented in an editorial the following commendation of him:

> The stern and unyielding opposition of the Catholic Church to our frightful divorce system is the only barrier left which safeguards the noblest instincts of our common humanity, broken down by the fierce tide of passion, overwhelming and submerging the homes of the land.

Such sentiments, however, were not shared by some people in Fargo who had profited by divorces. They openly showed their bitter hostility to him, but their opposition did not dissuade him from the strong position he had assumed. A record of his thoughts on this matter have been preserved in his diary:

> One great cause of my undeniable unpopularity is the fierce and successful warfare I waged against the divorce laws of this state. There were at one time over two hundred divorcees in Fargo . . . they spent money lavishly and were a bonanza to lawyers and tradespeople. I cleaned them out, and thus cut off a source of large revenue from many in Fargo. I have been made to feel it ever since.

In 1902 he again became involved in a public controversy. In that year a movement was begun by associations in Abercrombie, North Dakota, and Kent, Minnesota, to erect a forty-foot monument in memory of Father J. B. M. Genin

as North Dakota's greatest Indian missionary. Actually the priest, because of his eccentricities and misdemeanors, had been a disturbing element in Shanley's life. Among other things he had openly discouraged attendance at the Laymen's Convention; he attempted to unite the discontented national parties in the state against the bishop and forwarded to Rome for circulation there a number of unfavorable reports about Shanley (among them Perrault's document). His letters of complaint about the bishop to the apostolic delegate in Washington and to the Cardinal Prefect of Propaganda in Rome compelled those high church officials to threaten him with ecclesiastical censure.

For numerous reasons the bishop was determined to impede the erection of a memorial in his honor. To counter the laudatory and historically inaccurate articles being circulated about Father Genin in the press the bishop wrote three historical articles on the "Beginnings of Catholicity in the State" which were published in the *Grand Forks Herald* in the spring of 1902.

Although the misguided movement was temporarily halted, it was renewed in 1906 by Mrs. Linda Slaughter who submitted a ninety-two page historical sketch on early Catholic missions in North Dakota to the Historical Society of North Dakota for publication in the Society's *Collections*. The missionary labors of Father Genin were again exaggerated. When Bishop Shanley was informed about the article, he asked the Society not to publish it. At the same time he promised that he would submit for publication an article with accurate historical facts. The officers of the Society accepted his offer on condition that they would edit his article. When he rejected this condition, Mrs. Slaughter's article was published.

But the matter did not end there. When volume II of the *Collections* was ready for print, Bishop Shanley requested permission to address the members of the society. His request having been granted he appeared armed with a resolution signed by forty-four priests of North Dakota objecting to the errors in the article of Mrs. Slaughter and to the selection of Father Genin by the Historical Society for a place in the St. Louis Hall of fame. In his prepared address Shanley delivered a scathing rebuke to the Society. Concerning the controversial article he said:

Many pages of the above mentioned ninety-two are correct because copied literally, but without acknowledgement or quotation marks, from my articles in the *Herald*. The author would have done well to have copied my entire work. In any case, the committee on publication would have given us a more reliable volume had they taken the pains to compare the statements in the article in Volume I, as it stands, with the facts as related four years before their volume appeared by one who knew whereof he wrote.

I have, therefore, prepared this short address in the hope that it may appear in Volume II of our society's publications, and thus offset in a measure the harm done by the blundering article in Volume I.

To give all the historical facts, already mentioned in the *Herald* articles, would require more time than is now available. I shall, therefore, confine myself to pointing out a few of the more flagrant misstatements in the article for which our society by publishing it now stands sponsor. Twenty-one false statements will be enough for this address, though that number might be more than trebled.

The address was a definite answer to Mrs. Slaughter's article. After giving a short biographical sketch of Father Genin, he point by point corrected her inaccurate statements. The facts that he had marshalled admitted of no refutation. His address in its entirety was published as an appendix in Volume II of the State Historical Society's *Collections*.

John Shanley often took up the pen for the sake of truth. Throughout his life as a bishop, and even before that as a priest, he contributed numerous articles to the secular and Catholic press. All his writings, even his historical articles, were polemic in character. Invariably, he wrote as a participant in a debate or controversy. Written under these circumstances and for these purposes his writings cannot be classified as great literature or scientific history. Both training and experience had prepared John Shanley for his apostolate as founding bishop of a pioneer diocese in the Upper Midwest.

Bishop Shanley with Indians a few days before death

184

John Shanley was born in New York state on January 4, 1852. His parents, who had migrated from Ireland in 1832, moved to St. Paul when John was five. The future bishop felt a call to the priesthood at a very young age. By the time he was seventeen he had already attended minor seminaries in Minnesota and Missouri.

In 1869 he traveled with Father John Ireland, Bishop Grace's representative at the First Vatican Council, to Rome where he enrolled in the Propaganda College. After his ordination by Cardinal Patrizi on May 30, 1874, in the Basilica of St. John Lateran he returned to St. Paul where he was appointed assistant to Father Ireland. The lives of these two men remained closely interwoven throughout their priestly and episcopal careers. Until Shanley's departure for North Dakota they lived together in the cathedral rectory. John Ireland, who had been named the first metropolitan of the Province of St. Paul in 1888, recommended Shanley for the see of Jamestown in 1889. In his funeral oration at the bier of Shanley, Archbishop Ireland had this to say about his lifelong friend and protégé:

> He was the Christian youth before he was the priest; he was the irreproachable, devoted, zealous priest before he was the bishop, and when the head of the Church placed him among its rulers, he was the noble-minded and generous-hearted, the hard-working and the successful bishop. Under his administration there was intense life in the parish; every good work was accelerated; every duty was attentively and scrupulously performed. Father Shanley was the friend of everyone in the city, Catholic or non-Catholic; everyone admired his unstinted zeal, his courage in the presence of difficulties, his charity to the needy, his readiness day or night to hurry to the room of the sick and the dying; everyone understood the motives inspiring his every word and act, and loved in him even the occasional quickness of temper and apparent brusqueness of movement, which they knew were but tokens of his earnestness of purpose and his anxiety to take no time from pressing duties. The names of few priests in St. Paul will linger so long as that of Father Shanley upon the lips of present and coming generations.

In contrast to the bitter struggles of the early years of Shanley's episcopate, the last ten years of his administration were marked by great material improvements. The diocesan clergy, whose number had increased from 50 in 1899 to 106 in 1909, became a close-knit, dedicated body of men. The last five years of his life were the golden years of church building in the diocese. During the summer of 1906 alone thirty-six new edifices were erected. In 1907 and 1908 he dedicated fifty-eight churches, many of them substantial brick buildings still in use today. All-in-all, throughout the eighteen years of his administration, Bishop Shanley dedicated 205 churches.

The arduous schedule which Shanley kept throughout his life was not without deleterious effects upon his health. As a student in Rome his health was so delicate that some considered him a consumptive and feared that he might die before ordination. On the day of his consecration he was suffering from the flu which, as the bishop later wrote in his diary, "forced me to go to the hospital in Winona for treatment, where I remained over a week. The effects of that sickness remained and still remain in my system."

The rigors of the severe northern winters were a hardship for him. Father J. B. McDonald, a priest of the diocese, wrote in 1908:

> The Bishop, like his clergy, is perfectly familiar with the trail. During the eighteen years of his episcopate he has visited every nook and corner of his immense diocese. Unmindful of looks or personal comfort he has utilized every mode of transportation from a grain wagon to a broncho saddle.

In a notation in his diary the bishop described the conditions he experienced during his first five years in the diocese:

> Travel was not convenient, trains fewer, railroads not so numerous, and sleeping and other accommodations of the worst imaginable. Sod houses, buggy beds, no privies, long wagon rides of eighty and ninety miles. Day after day of that life, and weeks of it at a stretch. No wonder stomach, liver, kidney, nerves, brain and everything in the human machinery went to pieces. I marvel that I am alive this 20th day of July, 1903.

Through the years his health gradually declined. However, it was not until 1908 that his condition became serious. In October of that year, while traveling from Garrison to the Indian reservation at Fort Berthold, he was overtaken by a blizzard which forced him to remain for several days in a convenient farmhouse. Thereafter he complained of recurrent colds and high fevers. As the months passed, the symptoms of the fatal disease which afterwards struck him down became more and more pronounced. His physician, Dr. E. M. Darrow, urged him to give himself rest in a warmer climate. When this advice was not heeded, his condition grew so acute that he feared to leave his house. However, in March, 1909, he decided that an ocean trip might possibly bring some relief. On Easter Sunday he left Fargo for Lourdes. There he spent one week in spiritual retreat. Upon his return, after an absence of two months, he seemed somewhat refreshed, but his health had not improved.

After the annual priests' retreat in July he departed for Fort Totten where a Congress of Sioux Indians was in session from July 11 to July 14. He took an active part in the meetings and closed the convention by giving his blessing. Fatigued by these activities and the long trip back to Fargo, he arose late the next day and devoted himself to routine matters connected with the administration of the diocese. In the evening after he had composed a few letters and edi-

torials for the *Bulletin*, the diocesan publication which he had founded a few months earlier, he drew up the following resolution in behalf of his Indians for whom he had toiled during his episcopate:

> We, the Catholic Indians of the Diocese of Fargo in annual convention assembled, desire hereby to renew the expression of our belief in the Divinity of Jesus Christ, the Savior of the world, and in the Divine Mission of His Holy Church to whose every teaching we submit ourselves without reserve.
>
> In the chief Pastor of that Church, Pius X, the Bishop of Rome, we recognize the lawful successor of St. Peter to whom Christ said: "Thou art Peter (a rock), and on this rock I will build my Church. Feed my lambs, feed my sheep." To his infallible teaching and God-given authority we bow, as to the teaching authority of Jesus Christ Himself. In the Bishop of our Diocese we acknowledge another successor of the Apostles, whom the Holy Ghost had placed to rule the Church of God, and to him we promise loyal obedience. In his voice we hear the voice of the Divine Master, instructing us and leading us to our Heavenly home.
>
> In the Missionaries who have brought us to the knowledge of the true faith and who still labor among us, cheerfully enduring all hardships and looking for no reward, save an imperishable crown in eternity, we see the true shepherds of our souls, who are united through our Bishop to our Holy Father, the Pope, and through the Pope, to our Divine Master.

This was Bishop Shanley's last official act—an explicit declaration of faith which in the providence of God was written but a few hours before he surrendered his soul into the hands of his Creator. The next morning, July 16, 1909, the news spread throughout the state: the first resident Catholic bishop of North Dakota was dead.

When James O'Reilly (1910-1934) was consecrated as second Bishop of Fargo, the western part of North Dakota had just been established as the Diocese of Bismarck. Despite the years of drought and depression in the 1930's, Bishop O'Reilly consolidated the spiritual and material gains of his predecessor. Under his guidance the Diocese of Fargo continued to expand and grow: 34 new parishes were organized; 56 churches, 54 rectories, 24 schools, and 7 hospitals were built.

Aloisius J. Muench (1935-1960) was nominated third Bishop of Fargo at the height of the depression. He established the Catholic Church Expansion Fund to save mortgaged parishes and pro-

Bishop James O'Reilly

Aloisius Cardinal Muench

vide credit for future parish development. He founded a monthly diocesan newspaper, convened the first synod in the diocese, published a synodal book of diocesan legislation, established diocesan scholarships for needy seminarians and organized a mutual aid fund for disabled and retired priests. Bishop Muench was active in the Catholic Central Verein and the Catholic Rural Life Movement, serving two terms as president of the latter. With the cooperation of two priests of the diocese, Vincent J. Ryan and William T. Mulloy, both later elevated to the episcopacy, Bishop Muench edited the *Manifesto on Rural Life.*

In 1946 Bishop Muench was appointed Apostolic Visitator to Germany. In 1950 he was grant-

ed the personal title of archbishop and the following year was appointed Papal Nuncio to Germany. In December, 1959, he was created a cardinal priest and elevated to the Roman Curia.

Leo F. Dworschak, as auxiliary bishop (1947-1959) administered the affairs of the diocese during the absence of Archbishop Muench whom he succeeded as fourth Bishop of Fargo in 1960. During his administration, 54 new churches, 21 rectories, 7 schools and 2 Newman centers with accredited schools of religion were constructed. Bishop Dworschak inaugurated the Diocesan Development Program to assure capital expansion and better support of the needs of diocesan, national and international programs and institutions. In 1962 he founded a diocesan minor seminary.

Chapel in Motherhouse of Sisters of the Presentation of the
Blessed Virgin Mary, Fargo

Motherhouse of Sisters of St. Francis,
Hankinson

Queen of Peace Convent, Belcourt

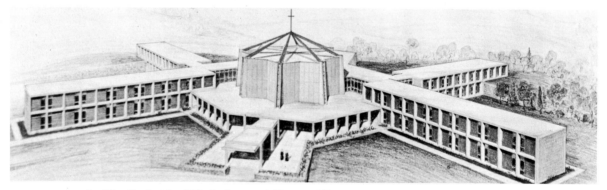

Architect's sketch of Motherhouse of Sisters of St. Mary of the Presentation, Valley City

RELIGIOUS IN THE DIOCESE OF FARGO

Benedictine Fathers (Blue Cloud Abbey, Assumption Abbey, St. John's Abbey)
Franciscan Fathers
Oblates of Mary Immaculate
Pallotine Fathers
Redemptorist Fathers

Benedictine Sisters (Queen of Peace Convent)
Calced Carmelites
Sisters of Charity (Grey Nuns)
Sisters of Mercy of the Union
Sisters of St. Francis of the Immaculate Heart of Mary
Sisters of St. Joseph (Crookston, Minn.)

Sisters of St. Joseph of Carondelet (St. Paul, Minn.)
Sisters of St. Mary of the Presentation (Valley City)
Sisters of the Presentation of the Blessed Virgin Mary (Fargo)
Sisters of the Resurrection
Sisters of Service
Sister Servants of Christ the King

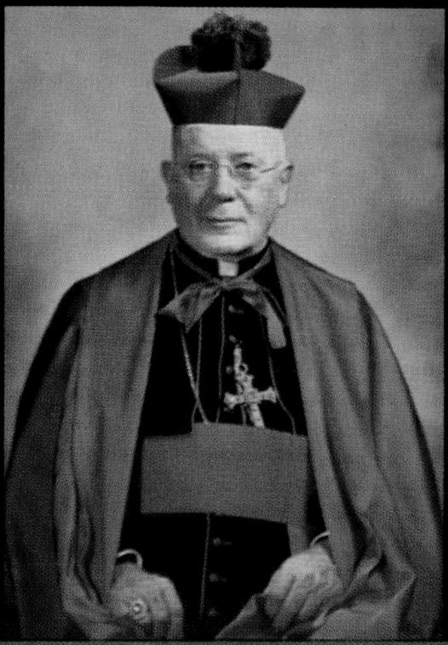

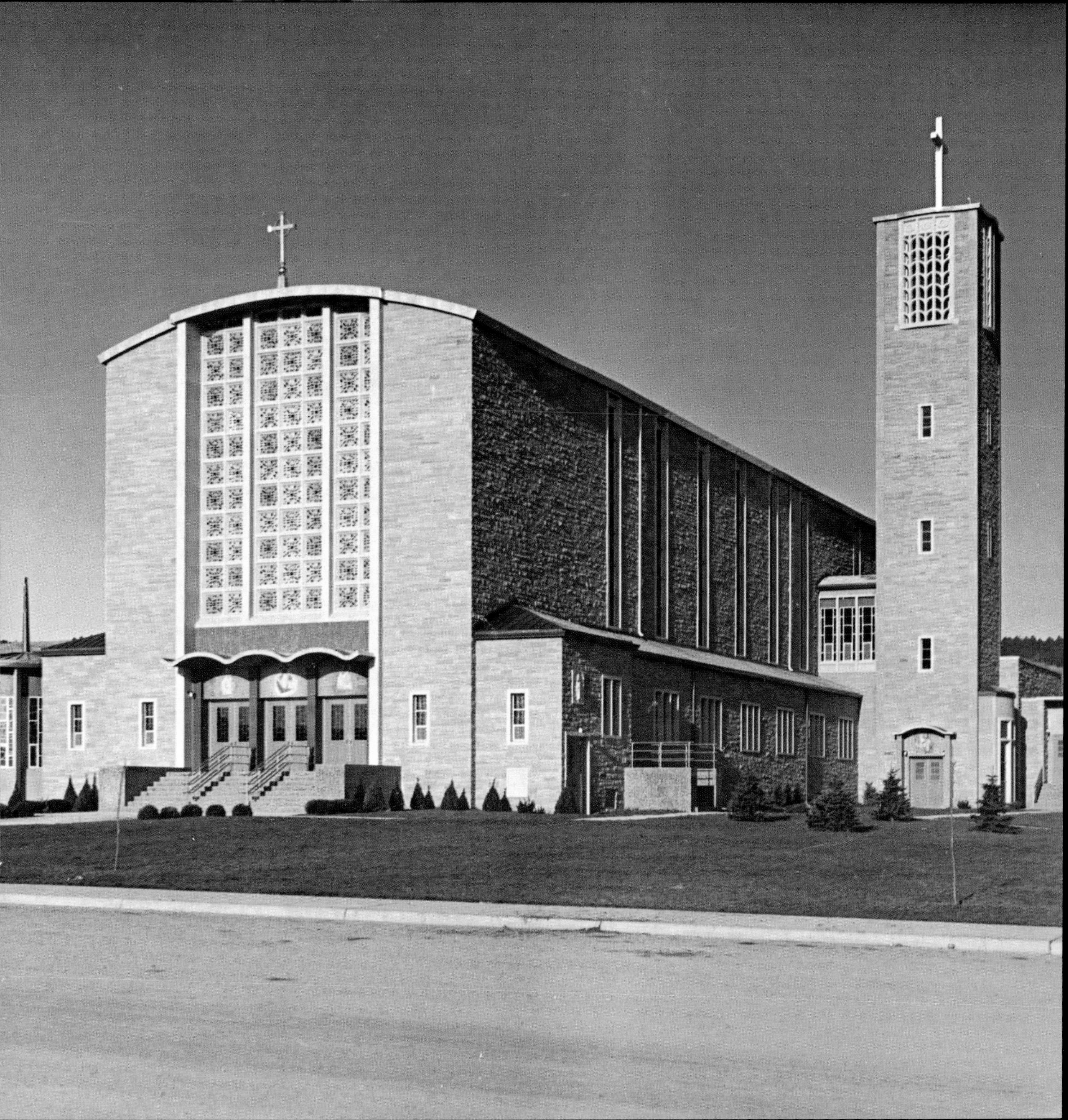

DIOCESE
OF RAPID CITY

by Right Reverend Monsignor Michael Costigan
and the Reverends Thomas Faulkner,
William O'Connell and Robert White, S.J.

THE HERITAGE of tomorrow, the knowledge of today, are understood only by looking back over the horizons of yesterday. Our history begins in the dreams of men stirred by tales of the beauty and bounty of our land. This is the story of those who came, of their visions and hopes, of their labors and hardships. It is the story of those who settled our land to make it the Diocese of Rapid City.

This is our land. It stretches from the west bank of the mighty Missouri River, across rolling prairies, encompassing both the stark, centuries-worn Bad Lands and the verdant summits of the sacred Black Hills. It is here that a great venture of the nineteenth century was sought and achieved. It was ripe for an adventure in human progress. It was more ripe for God's adventurers, the first missionaries.

Accounts differ as to when the first white man came to this land. Dates, places and names have been proposed, but they often contradict one another. It is certain, however, that the land was visited first by hunters, then by trappers and traders from the north. While these visits were important, they left no lasting impressions upon the mighty Sioux, the original inhabitants.

As word of bountiful game spread east and south, this Indian domain saw an influx of white men. With the hunters, trappers, traders and adventurers came zealous missionaries. It is said that priests from the south first offered mass at Fort Pierre on the Missouri River, while missionaries from the north, accompanying the

French traders, offered mass at Kenel and other places along the Missouri River.

As inexact and incomplete as is the prehistory of the area, this much is known. By 1870 a substantial number of settlers had moved into the southeastern corner of the present state. Both east and west river areas had been explored. Further increase of white settlers brought with it a full complement of priests. These early missionaries made the Black Hills and the prairies their new frontier. Their concern, their vocation was the salvation of Indian and white alike.

The bold vision which motivated the first settlers also moved these first priests. This is shown by the work of the early Indian missionaries. For centuries before Custer described the Black Hills area, the Sioux Indians called the area of the Rapid City diocese their homeland. In the summers they roamed the prairies surrounding the Black Hills, hunting the buffalo, and with the coming of winter they withdrew into the sheltered wooded valleys of the Hills. The Black Hills were sacred to the Sioux and in its secluded valleys they buried their dead.

Missionaries Among the Sioux

The Catholic Church first came to the Black Hills on a mission of peace between the Sioux and the whites who were gradually encircling them. In 1868 the Jesuit missionary, Father Pierre De Smet, set out from Fort Rice near

Bismarck, North Dakota, to seek out the hostile Sioux. He met them gathered in a huge encampment at the northern edge of the Black Hills near the towering Bear Butte. As he approached the Sioux tepees he unfurled his flag of peace, a banner bearing on one side the name of Jesus and on the other the image of the Virgin Mary surrounded by gilt stars. Thinking it was an American flag, bands of warriors galloped out of the camp with bows and arrows at the ready. But after seeing the banner of the Blessed Virgin they returned to the encampment reporting that it was not a war flag but an emblem of peace.

Father De Smet persuaded the Indians to send a delegation to meet the peace commissioner at Fort Rice. When he was ready to leave, the Sioux chiefs begged him to leave the "Banner of Peace" as a souvenir of his visit. Thus our Blessed Mother was introduced to the Sioux, and the mountains and rolling prairies of western South Dakota came under her protection.

The trip of 1868 was Father De Smet's first to the Black Hills area, but it was the climax of a long life of missionary work among the Indians of the upper Missouri Valley. In their many trips up the Missouri Father De Smet and his fellow missionaries had met the Sioux at the river trading posts and had instructed and baptized some. Father Christian Hoecken, S.J., at Fort Pierre on July 16, 1840, had baptized three children of Xavier Recontre and "a squaw." The record of these baptisms is the first written evidence of sacred rites performed by a Catholic priest in the present Diocese of Rapid City.

Father De Smet died in 1873 before he could realize his dream of establishing a mission among the Sioux. Meanwhile the encroaching circle of white men drew ever closer around them; the warriors under Chief Crazy Horse fought their last desperate battles. They were able to wipe out Custer's contingent in 1876, but the last of the buffalo had been killed, and the last recalcitrant Sioux, driven like sheep before the storm, came to the reservation agencies for food and shelter in the winter of 1877.

Five large Sioux reservations were established, stretching south from the North Dakota border along the west bank of the Missouri River to the Nebraska border and then along the Nebraska border west to the Black Hills. To the north, reaching into North Dakota, is the Standing Rock

Reservation; immediately to the south is the Cheyenne River Reservation. Still farther south, below the present capital, Pierre, is the Lower Brule Reservation. Then to the west along the Nebraska border are the Rosebud and Pine Ridge reservations.

In 1876 when the Sioux people were beginning to settle on the reservations, Chief Red Cloud asked for priests to come and teach them. But President Grant's peace policy determined that missionaries of only one religious denomination would be allowed on each reservation. Thus the Standing Rock Reservation, which held Sitting Bull's people, was allotted to the Catholic Church, and Red Cloud's people were assigned to Protestant groups.

In this same year, at the request of the American bishops, Abbot Martin Marty, O.S.B., of St. Meinrad Abbey, volunteered as a missionary to the Sioux. With two other Benedictines, Father Chrysostom Foffa (Pfoffa) and Brother Giles Langet, he went to Fort Yates on the Standing Rock Reservation and began the first permanent mission among the Sioux. So strong was this foundation that it still endures. Abbot Marty had the dream of a monastery foundation whose members would be recruited from the ranks of the native Sioux. This plan, inspired by St. Benedict's sixth century success in the conversion of the Goths, had been the great hope drawing Martin Marty to the American mission field. But it would be seventy years before this dream would be realized in the establishment of Blue

Kenel Indian Mission

191

Holy Rosary Indian Mission, Pine Ridge

Cloud Abbey at Marvin, South Dakota, in the present Sioux Falls diocese. In the ranks of the Benedictines at Blue Cloud there are several Indian men.

In 1878 four Benedictine Sisters from the Convent of the Immaculate Conception at Ferdinand, Indiana, came to teach at Abbot Marty's mission among the Sioux at Kenel. They were the first sisters in the present Diocese of Rapid City. Sister Gertrude McDermott was the first superior. In 1883 the school was placed under government auspices with the sisters and brothers continuing as teachers and supervisors. Monks from St. Meinrad Abbey withdrew from the Dakota missions when Father Martin Kenel, O.S.B., of Conception Abbey in Missouri took over the school. It thrived under his direction for almost twenty-five years.

After unsuccessful attempts by diocesan priests from Omaha to set up centers for Indians on the Pine Ridge and Rosebud reservations, Chief Red Cloud repeated his demands that Black Robes (Jesuits) be allowed to establish a mission and school among his people. Abbot Marty, who had become the first vicar apostolic of the Dakota Territory, also wanted missionaries for all the reservations. Divine Providence answered Bishop Marty and Chief Red Cloud in devious ways. Bismarck, the German chancellor at that time, had expelled all Jesuit priests and brothers. From these exiles missionaries were available for Bishop Marty. In 1886 Father Jutz, S.J., established St. Francis Mission among Chief Spotted Tail's people on the Rosebud Reservation,

then moved west to found the Holy Rosary Mission in 1888 for the people of Chief Red Cloud.

Katherine M. Drexel of Philadelphia, daughter and heiress of the financier, Francis A. Drexel, provided funds for the original buildings at both missions. Soon the Congregation of the Sisters of Christian Charity and Penance of the Third Order of St. Francis, from Buffalo, New York, began teaching in the new schools at the St. Francis and the Holy Rosary missions.

Many were the difficulties and dangers of these new missions on the isolated reservations. Finding a location with ample firewood and water was a problem on the Dakota prairies. Later, when coal was freighted in, the wagons were sometimes caught in the fierce blizzards of the northern plains. Once a barn had to be torn down and burned to keep the school children warm. Learning a strange language without the help of dictionary or grammar, calming the restless and bewildered Sioux who were forbidden to leave the reservations, battling the winter storms, summer droughts and traveling great distances on horseback or in crude wagons—this was the lot of the first missionaries. Their church buildings were the wide open spaces and lean-tos built of logs and branches. The missionary's bed was usually under blankets on the ground wherever night came upon him.

Sometimes real danger entered their lives. In the Ghost Dance trouble that came to a head in 1890 the young Sioux braves were anxious to prove their heroism. With ammunition strapped to their waists and carbines in their hands they

192

danced the Ghost Dance and waited for the mystical disappearance of the white man. Father Jutz, by then the superior of the Holy Rosary Mission, went out to the high butte where the recalcitrants held out. He induced forty men to come to the Pine Ridge Agency to confer with General John R. Brooke. But the next morning, before starting out, an Indian rushed in and shouted that the Sioux would be betrayed. Father Jutz then stepped forward and made the brief but courageous remark: "If what I said and promised is not true, then shoot me down." They followed Father Jutz to Pine Ridge and peace talks ensued.

However, not enough trust was established. Many of the Sioux left the reservations in spite of the government prohibition. Encircled by the military, they were forced to return to Pine Ridge. In disarming the men of the Big Foot band on Wounded Knee Creek, not far from Pine Ridge, a shot was fired and the surrounding American troops fired into the Indian camp with Hotchkiss guns. Before that cold December day was over, more than 300 Sioux men, women and children had died, and Holy Rosary Mission became a refuge and hospital for the frightened survivors. A Catholic Church was later built near the scene of the massacre.

But the missionaries brought to the Sioux people the peace of Christ, and their labors were soon fruitful. One of the Sioux who witnessed the early efforts of these missionaries said at a later date:

> I recall how we old-time Indians acted when we first attended Mass. It was our custom, while assembled in council, to sit on the floor in a circle and pass the pipe. To us, at that time, attendance at Mass was but another council where we came to hear a message for our benefit. So we came into the church and sat down on the floor, while one of the party filled a large redstone pipe, lit it, and sent it around the circle.
>
> As the priest delivered the sermon, we listened carefully, and at each pause in his speech we voiced our approval in our usual way, "How! How!" During the sermon the good Father said that after Mass we Indians should come over to his house and he would give us a box of crackers and other good things. Immediately one of the party arose and lifted his voice in a "Glad Song" which was strictly according to our customs, but not entirely proper within the sacred precincts of the church as we later learned.

The Cheyenne River Reservation was first served by the Benedictine Fathers from the mission on the Standing Rock Reservation to the north. But in 1886 Father Pius Boehm, O.S.B., of St. Meinrad Abbey established Immaculate Conception Mission at Stephan, South Dakota, on the Crow Creek Reservation. It was just across the Missouri River from the Cheyenne River and Lower Brule reservations. The Benedictine Fathers from Stephan, especially Father Fuldan, O.S.B., sowed the seeds of the faith on the Cheyenne River and Lower Brule reservations with great fruit. From July 5, 1891, to February 2, 1896, 308 baptisms were recorded.

As earlier hunters, traders and soldiers had brought back accounts of our land to the people of the east, so also the missionaries returned with their tales to the eastern cities and the European communities. Father De Smet, who had come originally from France to the St. Louis Province of the Jesuits, returned frequently to St. Louis to speak of the wonders of the missions, the beauty of the territory and the treasures of the Hills—gold.

The Church in Mining Towns

On April 8, 1876, Maurice Manual, miner, soldier of fortune and prospector, discovered a rich vein of gold in the northern Black Hills. As news of this strike spread, the fever of the forty-niners rose again. Here was an area rich in gold and easily accessible to the adventurous easterners. Wagons were purchased, supplies loaded, trains formed and the push westward was begun. Across the states of Missouri, Iowa, Minnesota and Nebraska and eastern Dakota Territory they moved: not hunters or trappers, farmers or ranchers, but a new breed, men and women with only one vision, gold.

Fording the Missouri and the Platte in their anxiety to establish claims, fearless of the warnings of the angry Sioux, on they pushed. Past Bad Lands and buffalo herds to the sacred hunting grounds of the Black Hills. The prospectors came for profit, anxious to strike it rich at any cost.

Small mining camps were established throughout the Hills, camps where might made right, where guns were the law, where only the strongest could survive. Many camps were settled, but a few took the spotlight of prominence and notoriety. One of these was the gold camp at Deadwood. Located in the heart of the northern Black Hills, it became the center of activities for all the camps. It was to this town that the stage coaches came; it was here that the soldiers of fortune set up shop.

Aware of the spiritual needs of these people Bishop James O'Connor, Vicar Apostolic of Nebraska, sent Father John Lonergan to Deadwood. It was his job to establish, despite hardships and opposition, the first Catholic church in the Black Hills. This he did in 1877.

Father Lonergan's impressions of the people and the place are better left unsaid. Singlehanded he had to combat the immorality of the area, the gold-centered minds of the men. He had to overcome the language difficulties of the various nationalities that made up his parish. Father Lonergan was succeeded by several diocesan priests, appointed by the Vicar Apostolic of Nebraska.

The Territory of Dakota became an ecclesiastical unit in 1879, and Abbot Martin Marty was consecrated Vicar Apostolic of Dakota the next year. Seeing the need for a resident priest in the gold-rich Black Hills, he brought the Holy Cross Fathers from Notre Dame, Indiana, into the area. Among the first priests was Father Peter Rosen, who had to contend with the same difficulties that faced Father Lonergan and his successors. Father Rosen wrote a *History of the Black Hills,* a rare book today, which is considered the only authentic history of the early times in the Black Hills country.

But if the frontier of saloons and gambling halls, of murder and vice was difficult for priests, imagine the dismay and shock of the first Sisters of the Holy Cross when they arrived in Deadwood and Lead City in 1878 to found hospitals and schools. The hardships and humiliations of these valiant women are not generally known, but it is history that after three years they returned to Indiana.

Wild Bill Hickok, Calamity Jane, Jack McCall and Poker Alice are names that live on from this era, but human activity was not confined to the rough and ready inhabitants of the gold towns of the Black Hills. Other little settlements were arising all over the Hills area, and by 1878 scattered communities also began to dot the plains. These people, too, had souls to be cared for. It is true that the priests were not as glamorous or as well

known as Wild Bill or Calamity Jane, but their lives were more adventurous than anyone can imagine. These early missionaries were circuit riders, priests whose parish was the whole prairie country. It was not uncommon for them to live on horseback for months at a time. Father Anthony O'Hora's records reveal his journeyings up and down the west river country, baptizing, preaching, teaching and administering the sacraments. Old-timers bless his memory and thank God for his untiring zeal.

These early missionaries carried only saddlebags with mass supplies and the minimum of personal items. They moved across this vast area offering mass, instructing and witnessing marriages, now in one place, now in another. Rarely did they stay in a place more than a day or two. These adventurers of God were sowers of the seed of faith. Proof of their success exists in today's well-established parishes and missions. Credit for these foundations must go to the early missionaries.

In 1889 the Dakota Territory was divided and admitted to the Union as twin states, North and South Dakota. Bishop Martin Marty, the Vicar Apostolic of Dakota, was appointed Bishop of Sioux Falls in the State of South Dakota. It was his task to see to the Catholic faith for the people of the entire state. Communications and transportation between east and west were slow. To serve better the people of the west river area, Bishop Marty appointed a second vicar-general in the Black Hills.

In 1890 Bishop Martin Marty established a community of sisters in the Hills when a group of five from the Benedictine Convent of St. Nicholas of the Flue in Melchthal, Switzerland, under the leadership of Mother Angela, came to Sturgis to found a convent and school. The children of the miners, traders and ranchers would now have instruction in their faith.

In 1894 Bishop Marty was transferred to St. Cloud, Minnesota, where he died in 1896. To his successor, Bishop Thomas O'Gorman, fell the task of the spiritual care of South Dakota. Bishop O'Gorman frequently wrote of his worries about the tremendous area of his diocese and his special concern for the western part of it, the present Diocese of Rapid City. He considered it impossible to serve the spiritual needs of the priests and people properly, since he lived so far from them in Sioux Falls. During his tours of the west river country in 1896 and 1898 he recorded many things which needed closer attention by the bishop. So in 1900 he placed before the Holy See his recommendation that the Diocese of Sioux Falls be divided.

The Diocese of Lead

Upon the recommendation of Archbishop Ireland of St. Paul and Bishop O'Gorman, and because of the development of the area west of the Missouri River, Pope Leo XIII established the Diocese of Lead on July 28, 1902. Its boundaries stretched from the Missouri River west to the Wyoming state line and from the North Dakota boundary south to the State of Nebraska, some 44,000 square miles.

The Very Reverend John Stariha, vicar-general of the Archdiocese of St. Paul, was appointed the first Bishop of Lead. Many problems faced the new bishop, but the most pressing was to end the era of the circuit rider and to establish permanent parishes throughout the diocese.

Under the hardships and privations he endured to carry out his duties, Bishop Stariha's health failed. In 1909 he returned to his native Austria where he died in 1915. In 1910 Pope St. Pius X named Father Joseph Busch, moderator of the diocesan mission band in St. Paul, as the second

Bishop Joseph F. Busch

bishop of Lead. He was consecrated by Archbishop Ireland on May 19, 1910, together with Bishop John J. Lawler who would one day be his successor. The dynamic Bishop Busch took up the arduous task of his predecessor with his accustomed vigor. He sought to establish parish life on the prairies and in the Hills. As a young priest, Bishop Busch had conducted missions in South Dakota. He was familiar with its needs and especially with the needs of the workingmen of the Hills area. He did all in his power for them. His letters to his priests and faithful show that he had much the same difficulties and hardships as his predecessors.

One must keep in mind the conditions and problems that existed in the prairie missions. The land which looked so promising to homesteaders was as poor as the majority of the people who came to till it. The climate was cruel and the earth was barren. With dreams built upon the calm and beautiful farm life of the east, these people came to plow, to plant, to sow and to reap. Little did they realize, as they trudged over dry grass and through thick gumbo, the battle that lay ahead with the arid soil and severe weather. Catholics found themselves a small minority in this western world away from the big cities. The one thing they shared with their

Bishop John Stariha

First cathedral of diocese, St. Patrick's Church, Lead

non-Catholic brothers was the poverty of the times.

In this environment the construction of simple churches was begun by the farmers and ranchers. Priests were assigned to care for a parish church and several small, usually distant, missions. All too often the pastor found himself far from human companionship, but the prairie priests bore this additional burden as one more personal sacrifice necessary for the spread of the faith.

Bishop Busch did much for the growth of the diocese in the six years that he was ordinary. But in 1915, when he was transferred to the Diocese of St. Cloud, Minnesota, an able successor was appointed by the Holy Father as third bishop of this missionary diocese. It was to be the lifework, spanning some thirty-three years, of Bishop John J. Lawler to spread and preserve the faith in the distant missions of his diocese.

Bishop Lawler was installed in St. Patrick's Cathedral, Lead, South Dakota, on May 4, 1916, by his good friend Archbishop James J. Keane of Dubuque. From the moment of his installation Bishop Lawler ruled the diocese with determination.

It was apparent to the new bishop that more priests were an absolute necessity if the people of the prairies and the Hills were to keep their faith. Settlers who saw a priest only once or

twice a month could not be expected to remain good Catholics. They had to come in contact with priests and teachers of religion more frequently. So Bishop Lawler set out to recruit helpers in this work of faith. He traveled in the east and in Europe, bringing back priests who were willing to assume the hardships and burdens of prairie life. This recruiting of priests, increasing the workers in the field of faith, could stand as perhaps his greatest work.

Yet Bishop Lawler did not stop there. Many small churches and mission chapels were founded during his episcopate. Built with the help of local residents, financed with money from eastern parishes and the Extension Society, these centers of worship and parish life were set up wherever several people could be gathered in the name of the Lord. Perhaps, in looking back, this policy of the third bishop could be criticized from a merely human point of view. But no criticism is valid when one considers that the "least of Christ's brethren," whether they lived in mud huts or frame lean-tos, were being nourished in the faith, their immortal souls looked after by the priest who shared their lonely existence. The establishment of this type of parish life, difficult as it was for the priests in those days, was the cohesive force that brought the Catholic families of these rugged times to the practice of their faith.

Bishop John J. Lawler

196

Mission church and rectory at Herrick

Bishop Lawler insisted upon a full Catholic life in every parish and mission and demanded that mass be celebrated as frequently as possible in every place. In his pastoral letters he placed great emphasis on catechism classes every week, on the Holy Hour and devotions, on parish missions and on visitation of the homes, especially in the case of weak Catholics. Wherever possible the bishop saw to it that a school was constructed, often at great sacrifice, so that the children would receive further training in their faith.

Indian Missions after 1900

The progress of work among the Indians kept pace with that of the Church among the white men. By the turn of the century missions were solidly established on each of the reservations. The pattern of missionary activity was quite similar everywhere. The mission began with the building of a large school emphasizing the industrial arts. Lay brothers and nuns taught the children and maintained the mission. Frequently the missions were close to the great central encampment on each reservation. But after 1900 the division of the reservations into allotments of 160 acres for each adult scattered the Sioux about the reservations. The camping grounds became little neighborhoods of log cabins along wooded creeks separated by grassy ridges.

A handful of missionaries covered each reservation by setting out on horseback or wagon from the central mission, going from neighborhood to neighborhood on trips that sometimes lasted for many weeks, just as the circuit riders did among the white population. The missionary ate and slept in the Indian cabins, instructed a handful of families for a few days or a week and then moved on to other families. In the meantime catechists taught the people their prayers and the most basic catechism, drew the families together for prayer each Sunday and prepared all for the next visit of the missionary.

One of the most significant factors in the spread and deepening of the faith among the Sioux was the establishment of the St. Mary and St. Joseph societies. Bishop Marty, a man of vision and deep insight into the culture of the Sioux, cited their natural love of meetings and oratory in advising that these societies be formed. Father Jerome Hunt, O.S.B., then at Devils Lake, North Dakota, organized the men and women into groups which, at first under the direction of the priest, but later on their own account, studied and discussed the truths of their religion and their application to practical life. These discussions were interspersed with hymns and prayers.

The requirements for membership in the societies were rigorous. At all public ceremonies these organizations held a prominent place. While the men proudly displayed their badges, the women were distinguished by their blue veils and medals. The list of officers indicated the variety of their duties. In addition to the usual offices of president, vice-president, secretary and treasurer, there were in the St. Joseph Society: singer, critic, standard-bearer, instructor, doorkeeper, visitors of the sick, waiters, herald, gravediggers, church marshall, haircutter, horse trader and church and rectory overseer; in the St. Mary Society: singer, standard-bearer, doorkeeper, seamstress, visitors of the sick, waiters, cooks and church servant.

Because of the extraordinary success of the organizations at Devil's Lake, the Benedictine Fathers at Standing Rock Reservation invited leaders of the societies to come to Fort Yates to organize similar units among their Indians. Gradually they spread to all the Sioux reservations. Their frequent meetings and activities became part of the life of each reservation neighborhood.

The annual Indian congresses were another of Bishop Marty's efforts to use the native institutions of the people. The Sioux were accustomed to an annual summer meeting when all the sub-tribes of the nation gathered in one great encampment. Old friends and relatives saw each other

again, great feasts were held, and the affair was climaxed with the central religious ritual of the Sioux, the Sun Dance. Selected men pierced their breasts with leather thongs leading down from a sacred pole. Then, leaning back till their weight pulled at the thongs, they gazed at the sun and made a sacrifice of the excruciating pain. The whole tribe participated in this ritual of bravery and heroism in some way and sought to obtain blessings upon the people.

The new Sioux converts missed sorely the festivity of the annual encampment; but the new annual congresses transformed the pagan ritual into the central event of Catholic lives. The first congress was held at the Standing Rock Reservation in 1891. The Sioux gathered from all over the reservation and from surrounding territories. Each St. Mary and St. Joseph society elected and sent delegates.

The meeting opened with the handshake in which all present took their turn walking about the circle of visitors greeting friends and relatives unseen perhaps for years. During the days of the congress, conferences were held to take up specific religious problems of the people. Catechists and priests exhorted the slothful and negligent to approach the sacraments. From early dawn the missionaries were occupied in the confessionals. At sunrise criers called the Indians to prepare for the holy sacrifice of the mass. Catechumens were baptized daily, and the climax came with the visit of the bishop and confirmation of the converts of the past year. The congress closed with a great solemn procession of the Blessed Sacrament led by a mounted Indian chief carrying the processional cross.

The annual Indian congress has been held since 1891 and has attracted as many as 3,000 people. In 1963 the seventy-first annual congress was held at Holy Rosary Mission to celebrate the seventy-fifth anniversary of that mission.

As the Sioux became settled on the reservations they learned from the missionary how to run cattle in common herds on the open range. They planted large gardens and were taught how to store great quantities of dried beef, potatoes, squash and many other garden vegetables for the long Dakota winters. As a more settled life developed in the little neighborhoods, the missionaries built small frame chapels in each community.

These churches became the center of the sim-

Catholic Indian celebration

ple but rich rhythm of life. On the Pine Ridge Reservation alone thirty churches were built between 1900 and 1938. More than twenty churches were located on the Rosebud Reservation. At Standing Rock Reservation there were ten. On the Cheyenne River Reservation there were seventeen and on the lower Brule Reservation there were four, all of the latter being cared for by Benedictine Fathers from Stephan Mission and diocesan clergy until the early 1920's. Outstanding among these early priests were the Reverend John Vogel, now deceased, and the Right Reverend Monsignor Joseph N. Golden, now chaplain of St. Joseph's Hospital in Deadwood, South Dakota. The Indians remember both these priests with great love.

In 1923 the Sacred Heart Fathers took charge of the Cheyenne River and Lower Brule reservations. In 1927 the old Columbus College near Chamberlain, South Dakota, formerly operated by the Viatorians, was purchased by the Sacred Heart Fathers and opened as St. Joseph's Indian School. Eventually the Benedictine Sisters from Yankton, South Dakota, came to teach in the school, where they have remained to the pres-

ent day. Although the school is located across the Missouri River, in the Sioux Falls diocese, it serves the Catholic Indian children from the Cheyenne River and Lower Brule reservations.

Mention should be made of the establishment of the St. Paul Indian Mission at Marty, South Dakota, also located in the Sioux Falls diocese on the old Yankton Sioux Reservation. Although not in the Diocese of Rapid City, it too has served to educate many children from the adjacent west river reservations.

Life went on and the Church developed despite the Roaring Twenties and the Black Friday of 1929. A new impetus to this development was given in 1930 when the Holy See transferred the diocesan see from the gold mining town of Lead to the new center of life and growth, Rapid City. This significant action took the activities of the diocesan government from the sometimes inaccessible Hills to a fast-growing trading town. The Church had been in Rapid City before the turn of the century. Its native stone church, St. Mary's, was made the cathedral of the Diocese of Rapid City. Under the title of Our Lady's Immaculate Conception, it served in that capacity until 1962.

199

**Church of the Immaculate Conception,
Second Cathedral**

Depression and Drought

While the population of Rapid City increased and its importance as a trading center turned it from a small town to a city, all was not well on the prairies to the east. As financial crises gripped the nation and bread lines became a common sight in large eastern cities, a more terrifying crisis grew on the plains. Across the western skies came horde after horde of grasshoppers. These insect enemies of grain and grass feasted not only on the hard-won crops, but they consumed even the fence posts and parts of frame buildings. To add to the catastrophe, while the semi-arid land of western South Dakota was being stripped bare by the invaders, rainfall stopped completely. This brought another plague. The dread drought produced parched river beds, caked water holes and dry wells.

Many who had braved hard winters and fought the summer elements were crushed under these new burdens. Small farms and ranches were abandoned as their broken and disconsolate owners fled east and west in search of a more benign way of life. Yet some remained, and through it all, despite the aridity of the soil and the cruelty of the elements, the faith was maintained and nurtured by supernatural elements. The priest and his mission church stood fast with the help of the bishop, the Catholic Church Extension Society and other friends of the home missions.

Many settlers stayed on. Grasshoppers could not live forever. Rain must come someday. But before the grasshoppers would die, and before the parched earth would again yield its fruit, a third plague descended on these prairie towns. Out of the southwest it came, and by its power it turned day into night. For weeks on end the wind blew and the dry land became flying dust, as topsoil from Oklahoma, Kansas, Nebraska and South Dakota turned the western plains into the great midwestern Dustbowl. A man without faith would have seen these three terrible plagues, coupled with the economic depression afflicting the entire nation, as a sign of divine wrath. Fortunately Bishop Lawler, his priests and people were men of faith. They believed in God and they hoped in His divine providence which would one day take them and their diocese out of these dreadful conditions. Hard-pressed, frequently without adequate food or clothing, the people and their priests stuck to this land. By the grace of God and the talent of men they conquered it.

After grasshoppers, drought and dust had passed, the land had indeed changed. Entire communities had ceased to exist. Population was down, and photographers could record the wreckage of the three plagues in the abandoned farms, empty homes and boarded churches. But pictures could not show the despair of families or the depression of the priests.

But the shepherd knew. He had lived it out with his flock. Together they had weathered the storms. The needs of the flock were more urgent than ever. Their faith had to be bolstered and increased, and so with determined dedication Bishop Lawler set about to re-establish parishes, to reopen churches and to cause the faith to flourish once again.

The years following their hardships of the thirties were painful ones for the citizens of South Dakota. But the poverty of the people was slowly overcome and self-sufficiency restored to them. The federal government played an important part in the process. The CCC and the WPA of the New Deal government brought opportunities for work to men who had been jobless for years. Construction of new roads, repair of the older ones, building bridges and dams, establishing forest conservation projects and reclamation efforts, all helped bring economic recovery to the stricken area. During this period many of the scenic lakes and picturesque roads of the Black Hills were constructed. Reclamation and conservation services started then have continued to this day to develop and protect the natural beauty of the area.

In 1936 and the years following, Bishop Lawler established the religious vacation schools for children throughout the diocese. For many of the mission communities, the sisters who came to teach their children were the first they had ever seen. The religious vacation schools brought about a new awareness of the faith. Through the efforts of the devoted sisters, priests and seminarians, the children received a deeper understanding and appreciation of their faith that they would later impart to their own children. Parents too became aware of the fond care the Church seeks to exercise over her members and they thus benefited by the visits of the sisters.

A New Era Begins

The forties saw the spread of war throughout Europe and Asia. This Second World War affected lasting changes on the face of South Dakota, as it did on the whole of the nation. Spiritually, materially and economically the state and its people prospered and developed. The seed of the faith, planted by the earliest missionaries, began to bear fruit under the stress of war. Most of the able-bodied young men of the area were called to service in the armed forces; for those who remained behind life was not the same. As the reality of war, with its separation of families, its heartbreak and sadness, began to affect the lives of those living on the remote prairies and in the small Hills communities of the diocese, the mettle of their strength was in their faith. For many it was a first experience in human contacts outside their home environment.

As the war affected the people, so it also brought about changes in the economy of the area. The developments of that era can be seen in their effects today. They are traced directly to wartime effort and production. The present Ellsworth Air Force Base, then called Wheeler Air Base, was established in 1940. Its importance to the area, especially the Black Hills, was and is significant in the material growth of the city and the diocese. With personnel numbering more than 10,000 men and their families, the air base has brought new stimulus to the merchants and work force of the district. Government contracts were awarded for work on the base and later for work on the many missile sites in western South Dakota, giving rise to a demand for labor. Employment was available to local residents, as well as to many others who moved into the area in search of jobs. All of this brought material prosperity and new opportunity to the west river country.

Correlative to this new growth, the mines and lumber industry, the cattle, grain and produce markets kept pace with the demands of the time. Farms and ranches prospered. The cattle industry especially influenced a healthy economy. Land, once thought useless because of lack of moisture, was found most suitable for grazing cattle. Vast tracts were fenced in and watered by means of dams and other water conservation methods. The federal administration of the time brought the farmers and ranchers the highest degree of material prosperity they had ever experienced.

In June of 1946, the Right Reverend Monsignor Leo Dworschak, vicar-general of the Diocese of Fargo, North Dakota, was appointed coadjutor bishop for the Diocese of Rapid City. But in 1947, when Fargo's Bishop Aloisius Muench was retained in an important diplomatic post in Germany by the Holy See, Bishop Dworschak returned to Fargo. In April of 1947, Pope Pius XII appointed the Most Reverend William T. McCarty, C.SS.R., as coadjutor bishop with the right of succession. He had been the provincial of the Eastern Province of the Redemptorist Fathers when he was appointed a bishop. He was consecrated on January 25, 1943, by Archbishop Francis Spellman for the Military Ordinariate, where he served until his transfer to Rapid City.

Bishop John J. Lawler, after thirty-three years as shepherd of the diocese, died on March 11, 1948. Bishop McCarty became the fourth and present bishop of the Diocese of Rapid City.

Mt. Rushmore National Memorial

During the fifteen years since his installation, the diocese has grown both spiritually and materially. It has finally reached the maturity envisioned by the pioneer bishops and priests who prepared the way.

Bishop McCarty's Administration

After the war, family vacations and the desire to see the country brought tourists and vacationers to the Black Hills. They now came to "explore" the places of past history, to enjoy the beautiful scenery of the state and national parks in the Badlands and the Black Hills and to gaze at the monumental sculpture of the four presidents on Mount Rushmore, carved from solid granite by Gutzon Borglum. The area is ideal for those who wish to get away from the busy life of the city or those who seek a change from the rather routine life of the small midwestern town or farm. The tourist industry continues to grow and flourish, bringing in nearly half the income of the area. Motels, tourist attractions and services add to the growing economy.

The Church, too, benefited from the new influx of tourists. Churches must now be planned not only for the stable community which they serve for the major portion of the year, but also for the Catholic tourists who flock in during the four months of the tourist season.

Another significant factor in the economic and religious development of the area has been the urbanization of the population of western South Dakota. Communities with opportunities for employment, housing, schools and churches expanded and prospered. As farming and ranching became more complex and competitive, many moved from the farms and ranches to seek employment in larger population centers. For example, in 1948 the population of Rapid City numbered some 25,000 inhabitants. Since that time the population has more than doubled.

Bishop McCarty realized that the face of the diocese was changing, and he adapted the apostolate of the Church to meet its needs. Missions, no longer necessary in the age of the paved highway and automobile, were closed; parish life and activity were centralized so that more could be offered the people of the area by the priests who served them. This centralization quite naturally lifted some of the financial burden of church support from the people of the far-flung communities. Rather than maintain a series of smaller missions, the people of a given area could more easily support one larger central church. Gradually, the older frame churches which had served the early inhabitants were replaced by solid structures of stone and steel.

On the prairies the people enjoyed the new ease of transportation. The full day's drive to mass of an earlier day was now a matter of a few miles and a few minutes. County seats, with their larger schools and county payroll, became the centers of commerce, shopping and parish life. The sacrifices of today's Catholics in building the Church to its present stature in South Dakota have accomplished great things because they stand upon the labors and hardships of our forefathers in the faith.

Since the Second World War the Sioux reservations have entered upon a new era, one in which the rhythm of life in the isolated little neighborhoods has begun to slow down. During the war all able-bodied men left the reservations for the armed services—many leaving the reservation for the first time—and hundreds of families moved off to nearby towns and cities to work in defense plants. The Sioux got a taste of a life they had never known before. The men in the armed services sent home money and the people still on reservations could buy cars and travel to nearby towns.

To meet this new era in the life of the Sioux the Church has adjusted its missionary efforts.

Thousands of Sioux settled in Rapid City and by the late forties Bishop McCarty decided that special provision would have to be made for the Catholic Indians in Rapid City. At the same time the alumnae of Marymount College, Tarrytown, New York, were anxious to erect a memorial to the late Mother Joseph Butler, R.S.J.M., the founder and first president of the college. They provided the financial support to build the original recreation center which provided a temporary church for the Catholic Sioux in Rapid City. The complex became known as the Mother Butler Center. Thanks to the efforts of a great Sioux missionary, the late Father Joseph Zimmerman, S.J., and others, between three hundred and four hundred Catholic Indian families became associated with the center. In 1957 a large frame chapel was dedicated and placed under the patronage of St. Isaac Jogues, S.J., for their use.

Today the Mother Butler Center is headed by two Jesuit priests. Five Sisters of the Society of the Daughters of the Sacred Heart have charge of the home for working girls, give catechetical instruction to the Indian children, staff a medical clinic and maintain a used clothing store for poor Indians of Rapid City and the surrounding area. Most of the Catholic Indians still call the Mother Butler Center their church, but many are gradually becoming part of the general parishes in Rapid City and of the diocese. Slowly the Sioux are moving from a mission status toward full diocesan participation.

The development of tourism and possibly industry on the reservations also portends a new era for Catholicism there. The Catholicism of the reservations had been built upon such unique institutions as the catechist, the St. Mary and St. Joseph societies and the annual congress. With the isolation of the reservations broken down and the Indians themselves being urbanized, reservation Catholicism is being brought closer to the mainstream of American Catholic life.

In an earlier time the missionaries best served

Church of St. Mary, Lemmon

the people by locating a little chapel in each neighborhood and offering mass there every two or three weeks. To accustom families to attend mass every Sunday, the mission districts have been consolidated so that mass can be offered for everyone on the reservation each Sunday. Enrollments in the mission schools have grown as the need for education and trade skills is realized. Young Sioux are being given intensive schooling to prepare them for college and vocational training after high school.

The surest sign of the maturity of the missionary efforts to establish the Church is the number of priestly and religious vocations. To date there are more than twenty Sioux nuns in various congregations and orders, one brother and several candidates for the priesthood.

After his coming, Bishop McCarty had indeed used his energies and those of his priests and faithful to satisfy the spiritual needs of his people, Indian and white. But one pressing need still remained. When he was installed as ordinary in the small Cathedral of the Immaculate Conception, he saw at once that the diocese needed a fitting cathedral. His hope and dream ever since his arrival had been that one day a beautiful new cathedral would stand in Rapid City as testimony of the faith, love and generosity of the people of the diocese. Since 1930 the small, inadequate sanctuary of the old cathedral had served as the setting for the bishop's official functions. With the tremendous growth of the Cathedral parish and the city, the church was soon too small to accommodate the large number of parishioners. The founding of two other parishes in the city did not help relieve the crowded situation. A new cathedral was indeed a necessity.

But even before such a pressing need could be realized, it was essential that better facilities be built for the school children of the Cathedral parish. To accommodate the grade and high school children, the Cathedral Auditorium was built in 1952. It also served as a temporary church for the Cathedral parish on Sundays and holydays until the completion of the new cathedral.

The new Perpetual Help Grade School was completed in 1961 and opened for the school year of 1961-1962. Built to meet the growing needs of the parish, the school will accommodate over 1,000 children and operates at present

Bishop McCarty meets a member of his flock

with a student enrollment of 800. The school is a modern functional building with all the space and equipment necessary to meet the highest standards demanded by our present educational system.

But the pressing need for a cathedral itself remained. Yet apparent as it was, there was an obvious lack of funds necessary for such a bold undertaking. The construction of a new cathedral would surely test the generosity and the spirit of sacrifice of the Catholic people of the west river country. Inquiries were made throughout the diocese as to the possibilities of raising the money. The response indicated that the clergy and faithful were willing to make the necessary sacrifices. With the solid assurance of his flock, Bishop McCarty went ahead. Plans that had existed only as hopes and dreams now began to take on reality as architects began their sketches. It was the bishop's hope that the cathedral would express in stone, steel and glass the simplicity and strength of the faith of his

204

Catholic people. Enshrined in the cathedral would be a large, faithful reproduction of the original painting of Our Lady of Perpetual Help, to whom he, as a Redemptorist, had deep devotion, a devotion he has caused to be spread diocese-wide even as it is world-wide.

A commanding hilltop on the southern edge of the city was selected as the site. Construction of the new cathedral was begun in the winter of 1960 as Bishop McCarty broke ground. The building progressed rapidly, and soon towering steel girders rose high above the city, revealing the majestic proportions of the modern structure.

On Easter Sunday, April 2, 1961, the bishop laid the cornerstone for the new cathedral, surrounded by a group of clergy, religious and faithful. On the Feast of the Assumption of the Blessed Virgin Mary the following year, the first solemn

Interior of Cathedral of Our Lady of Perpetual Help

Pontifical Mass was offered by Bishop McCarty in the newly completed structure. Dedication ceremonies took place on May 6, 1963. Bishop McCarty, assisted by the cathedral clergy, performed the ceremony of dedication, and Archbishop Egidio Vagnozzi, Apostolic Delegate to the United States, offered the Solemn Mass. The Most Reverend Leo Binz, Archbishop of St. Paul and Metropolitan of the Province, preached the sermon. Many bishops, priests and people assisted on that great occasion.

Bishop McCarty had indeed accomplished the great task of building a cathedral worthy of the title—worthy, too, of the people who built it and would look to it as their mother church. With the willing assistance of his own priests and people, Bishop McCarty had realized a dream which his predecessors could not attempt to bring to reality.

With the dedication of the new cathedral, the history of the Diocese of Rapid City enters a new era. Evidence of the new religious growth is witnessed not only by the new cathedral church, but also by the new St. Martin's motherhouse for the Benedictine Sisters. After seventy-five years of service and life in the Sturgis community founded by Bishop Marty, the Benedictine Sisters of St. Martin's transferred their motherhouse from Sturgis to Rapid City. Since 1889 the Sisters had worked zealously for the growth of the faith in the diocese. Conducting religious vacation schools in the mission parishes during the summer, instructing those who attended their four grade schools during the winter months, maintaining an academy high school for the girls of the diocese and caring for the sick in their hospitals, the sisters live out their vocation to God and to the people of our diocese. Their seventy-five years of work and prayer are surely bearing fruit.

In order to meet the needs of the diocese and of their own growing community as well, the sisters decided to build a motherhouse and academy for girls in the see city. These simple but beautiful buildings are situated on the western outskirts of Rapid City. Future plans call for the construction of a junior college for women, which will be the first Catholic college in the diocese.

That was the past. This is the present. As to the future, let us go "over the horizons of yesterday, into the heritage of tomorrow."

Architect's sketch of **St. Martin's Priory**

RELIGIOUS IN THE DIOCESE OF RAPID CITY _____

Benedictine Fathers (Conception, Mo.)
Third Order Regular of St. Francis
Jesuit Fathers
Redemtorist Fathers
Society of the Sacred Heart of Jesus

_____

Benedictine Sisters of Pontifical Juris-
   diction (St. Martin's Priory)
Daughters of the Heart of Mary
Franciscan Sisters of Blessed Kune-
   gunda
Handmaids of the Precious Blood

School Sisters of Notre Dame
Sisters of Charity of the Blessed Virgin
   Mary
Sisters of St. Francis of Penance and
   Christian Charity
Sisters of the Presentation of the Blessed
   Virgin Mary

BISHOP HILARY B. HACKER — *Cathedral of the Holy Spirit* ▶

DIOCESE OF BISMARCK

by Reverend Louis Pfaller, O.S.B.

WHEN THE PROVINCE of St. Paul was established in 1888, the area now known as the Diocese of Bismarck was included, but only in 1910 did it enter the province as a distinct diocese. Actually, though, the lands on the upper Missouri had belonged to many ecclesiastical jurisdictions before 1888.

When France claimed the Mississippi and Missouri Valleys, the Bishop of Quebec ruled these remote regions. This lasted from 1658 until 1777, when religious authority over the whole Louisiana Territory passed to the Bishop of Santiago de Cuba, and then to the Bishop of St. Christopher de Havanna. Between 1793 and 1826 the Bishop of New Orleans ruled the trans-Mississippi region. In 1826 the Diocese of St. Louis was formed, embracing the northern portion of the original Louisiana Purchase.

Up to this date (1826) the entire Missouri Valley belonged to the successive bishoprics; now the dividing line was formed by the Missouri and White Earth rivers. From 1851 until 1859 the land west of these rivers belonged to the Vicariate Apostolic of Indian Territory, and from 1859 until 1879 it formed part of the Vicariate Apostolic of Nebraska. In the meantime, the land east of these rivers lay in the Diocese of Dubuque from 1837 until 1850, in the Diocese of St. Paul from 1850

until 1875 and in the Vicariate Apostolic of Northern Minnesota from 1875 until 1879. Dakota Territory was made a separate vicariate in 1879, and in 1889 the new states of North and South Dakota gained their own dioceses. Twenty years later the Diocese of Bismarck was established.

Though this area was part of some diocese or vicariate for three centuries it has only been in the last hundred years that any effective missionary work has been carried on within its limits. Before 1872 there was not a single town in the area, not one chapel or mission nor any resident priest. Yet the presettlement period has a romantic and colorful history of Catholic explorers, fur traders and roving missionaries.

Vérendrye and Fur Traders

As far as we know, the first white men to enter North Dakota were members of the La Vérendrye expedition which reached the Missouri River in 1738. For seven trouble-filled years La Vérendrye had labored to build a chain of forts from the Great Lakes to Lake Manitoba. They were to be steppingstones to the fur-producing plains and a possible passage to the Pacific. La Vérendrye was primarily a commerical adventurer, but he was spurred on to a great extent also by the desire to convert the natives of the prairies.

The missionaries of Canada longed to meet Indians who were farmers and living in somewhat permanent villages, so that they could carry on mission work with a stable people. When the nomadic tribes told La Vérendrye that such a tribe lived on the river to the west (the Mandans or Gros Ventres), chaplains were immediately assigned to accompany the explorers and to establish a mission among the "Mound Dwellers."

Father Jean Pierre Aulneau, S.J., therefore belongs in spirit to the Diocese of Bismarck. He did not intend to tarry at Fort St. Charles on the Lake of the Woods but was so anxious to get to the "Mantannes" that he planned to go ahead of the expedition in the fall of 1736. Had it not been for his unfortunate death at the hands of the Sioux on June 8, 1736, he would have been the first missionary to enter what is now the Diocese of Bismarck. As it was, more than a century elapsed before the first missionary arrived on the upper Missouri.

Statue of La Vérendrye

In the meantime, French and Spanish traders trickled into the region to secure furs from the Mandan, Hidatsa, Arikara, Sioux, Assiniboine and Chippewa tribes. Their chief fur posts were Forts Union, Berthold, Clark and Manuel Lisa. Many of the traders became "squaw men" and had great influence over the Indians.

The majority of the trappers and traders were Catholics, and though they were not always model Christians they awaited with eagerness the visits of missionaries and somehow they aroused in their Indian spouses and friends a desire for the Christian faith and the saving waters of baptism. It was not uncommon for them to teach prayers to the Indians and to baptize the infants and the dying. Sacajawea, the "Bird Woman" whom Lewis and Clark met among the Mandans in 1804, was married to the trapper Toussaint Charbonneau and was presumably baptized by one of the French traders.

Father De Smet's Indian Apostolate

The fur traders had a long wait for the first priests to come up the Missouri, but in 1840 they finally arrived. In June and July Father Christian Hoecken, S.J., came up from Council Bluffs on the annual steamer. At Fort Clark, some fifty miles upstream from modern Bismarck, and at Fort Union, west of modern Williston, he found nearly a hundred fur traders and their families. He baptized seventeen half-breed children and two Indian wives of the traders.

Father Hoecken has the distinction of being the first priest to visit what is now the Diocese of Bismarck, but the second missioner was the one who for the next two decades was practically the only priest to visit western Dakota. He was the most famous and beloved of all Indian missionaries, the rotund, jolly Belgian Jesuit, Father Pierre J. De Smet. He is popularly known as the "Apostle of the Rockies," but actually he did more apostolic work along the Missouri in Dakota than he did in the Rocky Mountains.

In the fall of 1840, returning from his visit to the Flatheads in western Montana, Father De Smet purposely traveled along the Yellowstone and Missouri rivers so he could minister to Catholic traders at the fur posts. In all, he visited the area eleven times; 1840, 1842, 1846, 1851, 1859, 1862, 1863, 1864, 1866, 1867 and 1868. At first his visits were only incidental, occasioned by his return from the missions in the Rockies, and aimed principally at helping the men in the fur posts; but gradually the Indians became his chief interest.

In 1851 he ascended the Missouri as a peace-

Father De Smet

maker for the government. When he neared Fort Clark he procured a horse and galloped on ahead of the slow-moving steamer so he could have time to instruct the half-breeds and Canadians and baptize all their children. Hearing of this, the Indians in the villages nearby came to beg the missionary to baptize their children, for an epidemic of cholera was abroad. He realized that the majority of the infants would die before reaching the age of reason, so he consented to baptize 186 Arikara children. Later he learned that the cholera had taken most of them. "What a consolation," he wrote, "that by the sacrament I unlocked the gates of heaven to them!"

Though Father De Smet was stationed in St. Louis most of his life, his heart was with the Indians, and he sought every pretext for visiting them. In 1859, on his return to St. Louis from a peace mission in Oregon, he stopped briefly with each tribe or village of the Crows, Assiniboines, Hidatsas, Mandans, Rees and Sioux. On that trip he baptized about 900 children, many of whom were in ill health, "and seemed only to wait for this happiness to fly to God, to praise Him for all eternity." On his visits of 1862 and 1863 he baptized 1,400 more along the upper Missouri.

That the missionary had a keen sense of humor we know from his description of a ceremony in which he baptized 292 Mandan and Hidatsa children at Fort Berthold in 1864:

Everything passed off in the best order, though not altogether without noise. During the ceremonies, we were honored from time to time with a deafening chorus. All that was needed was for a young savage, seized with terror at the approach of the Black Robe, to exhibit the strength of his young lungs in piercing yells, to set all his comrades going in the same key. It was really enough to split one's ears. The dogs on the outside added to the uproar by reinforcing the cries of the children with their frightful howls and roars. But all in all, the 10th was for me a beautiful and consoling day. The religious ceremonies occupied it all. Through the constant bending of my somewhat obese body, to give the baptism, I was scarcely able to move for several days afterward, *met het geschet in den rug:* with a "crick" in my back.

Such was the Black Robe's reputation for fairness and honesty that he could travel unmolested almost anywhere in the Indian country. Five times the United States government employed "the man who did not speak with forked tongue" to conciliate the aroused redskins. His greatest triumph as a peacemaker came in 1868 when he journeyed overland some 300 miles from Fort Rice (south of Mandan) to the mouth of the Powder River in Montana to visit the hostile Sioux camp under Sitting Bull. He induced the Indians to send representatives to Fort Rice for a peace conference.

BODMER ATLAS

Interior of Mandan Earth Lodge

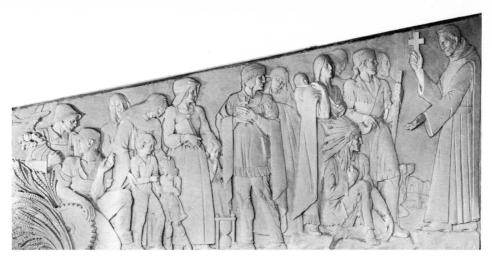

Bishop Marty Teaching
Bas-relief, Cathedral of the Holy Spirit

Responding to the repeated pleas of Indians, traders and government officials, Father De Smet spent the last years of his life in trying to secure enough money and missionaries to establish missions among the Sioux and the Fort Berthold Indians. Though he did not, or could not, realize his long cherished dream, his years of contact with the natives were not in vain, because he laid a firm foundation for future missionaries by winning the love and admiration of everybody he met in the entire upper Missouri region.

Early Settlements Under Bishop Marty

On one of his tours to Europe to recruit missionaries and solicit offerings for the missions, Father De Smet addressed the students of the Jesuit college in Fribourg, Switzerland. The master of ceremonies for the convocation was young Aloysius Marty, who idolized the great Jesuit and dreamt of the day when he could join his hero as an Indian missionary.

Soon after this the college was closed by a hostile government and young Marty joined instead the Benedictine Abbey of Einsiedeln and came to St. Meinrad Abbey in Indiana in 1860. When he became abbot of the monastery in 1870 it seemed that his dreams of mission work among the Indians would never come true. But in 1876 when the newly established Bureau of Catholic Indian Missions asked him for volunteers to carry out the founding of missions in Dakota as planned by Father De Smet, Marty startled all by leaving his abbatial office and setting out for Standing Rock Reservation as a precursor for others who followed.

When he arrived by boat at Fort Yates on July 30, 1876, Abott Martin Marty became the first resident priest in western Dakota. He was soon followed by Father Chrysostom Foffa (Pfoffa), O.S.B., and Brother Giles Laugel, O.S.B. They found a proud race of people, resentful of losing their hunting grounds to the whites. Some years later Bishop Shanley described the tense situation facing the abbot:

> Shortly after his arrival, bands of hostile Indians, under the leadership of Chief Kill-Eagle, who had just come from the bloody battlefield of Little Big Horn, made their appearance and tried to induce the Standing Rock Indians to duplicate the slaughter of Montana. They were all assembled on the plain west of the military post, mounted and heavily armed, in battle array. The inhabitants of the garrison were much alarmed, knowing the overwhelming strength and daring bravery of the Sioux warriors. At that moment of impending danger one could see a solitary horseman, attired in the garb of a Benedictine monk, galloping toward the sullen, hostile warriors, who received him with great respect. It was Abbot Marty. In him they recognized the black gown, and their former love and esteem for the great missionary, Father De Smet, whom they had known, roused their savage hearts to better sentiments. They listened to Abbot Marty attentively, and, submitting to his fatherly advice and pleadings for peace, dismounted and gave up their arms, which the soldiers gathered up in wagon loads. Thus was peace restored through the gentleness, courage, and apostolic zeal of that humble and holy monk.

211

Old St. Mary's Church, Bismarck

In time other monks came from Indiana and Missouri to build up the missions on Standing Rock Reservation. The Benedictine Sisters, too, the first nuns in the Diocese of Bismarck, came to Fort Yates to teach the Indian boys and girls. Sitting Bull encouraged the children to learn all they could at the schools "so that the white man cannot cheat us."

The Benedictine missionaries came to convert the Indians, but since there were no other priests in the area they found themselves in charge also of the whites. The missionaries often made a 700-mile round trip to visit the several hundred Catholic soldiers stationed at Forts Yates, Rice, Lincoln, Stevenson, Buford and Seward.

Bismarck, too, claimed their attention. After 1873 several priests from Minnesota had visited the few Catholics there. Father J. B. M. Genin had even built a small frame church there which he dedicated to the Immaculate Conception in June, 1875. But he had duties elsewhere, and so Father Chrysostom left Fort Yates to take up residence in Bismarck in 1877, with the neighboring army posts as his missions.

The next year he succeeded in getting four Benedictine Sisters from St. Joseph, Minnesota,

to open Bismarck's first parochial school. Eventually the Sisters established also St. Alexius Hospital (1885) and in 1947 they founded a separate Bismarck motherhouse, the Priory of the Annunciation.

In 1879 Pope Leo XIII erected in Dakota Territory a separate vicariate to be ruled by Abbot Marty. He was consecrated bishop on February 1, 1880, and he made Yankton his headquarters. Dakota was truly a mission territory. The railroads had come to the eastern part, but settlements were few and far between. Bishop Marty had only thirteen priests in the whole vicariate and four of these were stationed in the northwest quarter: at Bismarck was Father Chrysostom Foffa, O.S.B., and at Fort Yates were Fathers Jerome Hunt, O.S.B., J. H. Stephan and L. Hendrick.

Beyond Bismarck lay a howling wilderness. For six years (1873-1879) Bismarck was the end of the line for the Northern Pacific. Financial difficulties and the vigorous opposition of the Sioux were the causes. But powerful armies beat the Indians into subjection, and finally in 1879 construction west of the Missouri commenced. Before long towns mushroomed along the tracks, and the missionaries had to seek out their scattered flocks. The Yankees who established the town sites were rapidly outnumbered by German immigrants who came in great numbers to Morton and Stark counties west of the river and to Emmons, Burleigh and McLean counties east of the Big Muddy. Toward the end of the 1880's and continuing until the First World War, the German-Russians came in great numbers and settled what has been called "The German-Russian Triangle," with its base running from Aberdeen, South Dakota, to Hettinger, North Dakota, and its vertex at Rugby, North Dakota.

Many of the German-speaking settlers were Catholic and they formed the bulk of the future Diocese of Bismarck. Of the other nationalities represented, the Ukrainians and Czechs were most numerous.

It was no easy task for Bishop Marty to secure priests for the thousands of Catholic settlers. In 1881 he was fortunate to get the Benedictine Fathers from St. John's Abbey to take over the parish in Bismarck and all of the stations along the new railroad as it extended into Montana. Father Martin Schmitt, O.S.B., once had forty-four places between Mandan and Medora where he offered mass. At Medora he was fortunate to have a fine chapel. It was the gift of the dashing adventurer, the Marquis De Mores, to his wife, Medora von Hoffman. The brick chapel is still used by the Catholics of Medora; it is the oldest original church in the Diocese of Bismarck.

At first the northern part of the diocese developed much more slowly than the southern. It was not until 1886 that the Great Northern reached the site of Minot, and the nearly 5,000 boomers who flocked to the site set up as wild a town as was ever portrayed in a TV Western. Many pioneer residents of Minot recalled a certain railway conductor who would call out the name of the station: "MINOT, this is M-I-N-O-T, the end of the line. Prepare to meet your God!"

The first priest to visit the wild town soon witnessed the truth of the warning. Father Claude Ebner, O.S.B., came to Minot from Devils Lake in the summer of 1886. He walked around the town ringing a little bell to call together the Catholics for mass to be offered in a tent. One Sunday, ten minutes after the "devout" worshippers filed out of the tent, two gamblers got into a fight and one shot the other to death.

In time the lawless element left the town and a fine parish developed in Minot. Today the city has four parishes and Sacred Heart Convent, the motherhouse of the Benedictine Sisters who came from Pennsylvania in 1910 to teach the Indians on the Fort Berthold Reservation.

Bishop Shanley's Traveling Salesman

For more than a decade (1886-1898) the Benedictine Fathers at Devils Lake periodically visited some twenty-four mission stations along 275 miles of the Great Northern, from east of Devils Lake to Fort Buford, and even into Montana. The outstanding missionary of this period was Father Vincent Wehrle, the Swiss-born Benedictine who came to Devils Lake in 1888. With untiring zeal he traveled "as a salesman for the Lord" by rail, by buggy and by sled, to keep alive the faith of Catholics on his far-flung missions. At first there were no churches so he offered mass in farm homes, depots, halls and schoolhouses.

In the fall of 1893 he built St. Gall's Monastery on the shores of Devils Lake so that through it he might recruit fellow laborers for the Lord's harvest in North Dakota. Bishop Shanley of Fargo was deeply grateful to Father Vincent for his recruiting of German-speaking priests.

In the summer of 1893 Bishop Shanley sent Father Vincent to visit the neglected German settlements in Stark, Morton, Emmons and McIntosh counties. After his two-month tour he

Young Father Wehrle

213

returned to Fargo and reported to Shanley: "It is too bad these Catholic People cannot have a priest residing permanently among them. If taken care of, they will become a pillar of your diocese." During his long career, Wehrle worked so devotedly for these people that he was justly called "The Apostle of the German-Russians," a title of which he was proud.

Wehrle was Shanley's best trouble shooter when Germans were involved. In 1898 an altercation arose between the pastor and many people at Richardton. It grew to such proportions that Shanley found it necessary to send Prior Vincent there to restore order and peace. He patched up the "schism" but felt that it would be only a temporary solution unless more sympathetic priests were sent to Richardton and the surrounding German settlements.

In desperation Shanley wrote, "For God's sake and that of our own Faith, my dear Father Vincent, move your monastery to Richardton, where you will be in the midst of these people."

Move to Richardton he did, in June, 1899. Within a few years the parish at Richardton, once considered the worst in the whole state, became a spectacle of fervor and edification. The monastery became firmly established, and so successful were the labors of the priests under Prior Vincent that on November 25, 1903, the Priory of St. Mary was raised to an abbey with Father Vincent as first abbot. In May, 1904, he was installed in his new position.

The monks of Devils Lake and Richardton did a mammoth task of preserving the faith of the German people in North Dakota. Under their

zealous care, 55 churches were erected. No less than 115 places were served by them, about 60 of which are flourishing today with resident pastors.

Both Shanley and Wehrle agree that the 1890's were the most difficult in the development of the Church in North Dakota. Shanley later wrote:

> When I think back to the first ten years as bishop, I wonder sometimes how it was that I did not go insane. There was nothing but trouble and disappointment, whether I went away or came home from a trip. Oh, to think of those years of agony. God be praised, the work has been done, the Church has been founded, and is today one of the most flourishing dioceses in the United States of America.

Wehrle spells out more in detail just what these troubles were:

> For several years there seemed to be no progress for the Catholic Church in the whole state. Too many Catholic homesteaders left the state as soon as they had the homestead secured and found it impossible to sell it. During the first six years he [Bishop Shanley] said it was a mistake to erect a diocese. A vicariate apostolic would have been the proper arrangement. But during the last ten years he was confident of success.

Brighter days dawned after the turn of the century when the state experienced a tremendous growth, both economically and spiritually. As the railroad companies built branch lines to the remotest regions, homesteaders poured in. Along the tracks arose those twin skyline features of North Dakota—grain elevators and church spires. During Shanley's administration the western half of the state grew from only 5 churches with resident pastors in 1889 to 30 in 1910. In 1889 western North Dakota had in addition only 3 mission chapels and 14 mission stations, but in 1910 these had increased to 47 mission churches and 42 stations.

Some idea of the increase of the Catholic population and of their fervor for religion can be gauged from the fact that in the summer of 1906 alone the people erected 36 new edifices and enlarged or repaired a similar number. In 1907 and 1908 Bishop Shanley had the joy of dedicating 58 churches and many schools throughout the state. Most of these churches were beautiful structures which even today are ornaments to their communities. Some of the outstanding churches were St. Mary in Bismarck,

Assumption Abbey in 1908

Catholic Indians at Elbowoods

St. Patrick and St. Joseph in Dickinson, and St. Leo in Minot. When Bishop Shanley blessed St. Leo on Thanksgiving, 1908, he referred to it as "by far the best" of the 29 churches which he had dedicated in North Dakota during 1908. Even so, many people of Minot criticized the pastor, Father J. L. Raith, for thinking "just too big," and for having over-enthusiastic illusions about the growth of the Catholic population of Minot.

An even more grandiose piece of architecture was the new abbey church at Richardton, which the newspapers called "the gem of the prairies, the most beautiful building in the state."

Bishop Shanley was highly pleased with the growth of the Church in North Dakota. He recalled that when he took charge of the diocese in 1889, "I found in North Dakota thirty priests, forty churches and no ecclesiastical students. . . . In January, 1908, I was able to report for the [Catholic] Directory one hundred two priests, among them one abbot, two hundred ten churches and a Catholic population of 65,571. Twenty-three students belonging to the diocese are now in various seminaries."

The zealous builder did all he could to provide priests and churches for the burgeoning Catholic population. He literally wore himself out for his people. Towards the end of October, 1908, he undertook yet another tour of church dedications and confirmations. As he journeyed by team from Garrison toward Elbowoods he was overtaken by a North Dakota blizzard which rendered travel impossible. He sought shelter in a farmer's house, where he remained snowbound for several days. On his return to Fargo he complained of having a heavy cold and high fever, which greatly weakened his once robust system. He died quite suddenly at Fargo, July 16, 1909, just one day after participating in the Indian Congress at Fort Totten.

A New Diocese in North Dakota

As early as the spring of 1909 there were rumors afloat that North Dakota would be divided into two dioceses. Bishop Shanley was not a little displeased by the speculation, as can be seen from his comments in the *Bulletin* published just a month before his death:

The present Bishop of Fargo has not asked the Holy See to create a new diocese in this Diocese, but he is quite willing to transfer his heavy cross to any worthy priest at any time . . . .

When the time comes for a division of the Diocese of Fargo, the Bishop of Fargo, whoever he may be, will ask the Holy See to make the division, and he will divide the Diocese so that the Bishop of the new Diocese may be able to live without preaching missions, retreats, etc. in the east as was the lot of the first Bishop of Fargo.

Nevertheless, the rumors were based on reliable speculation. Less than two months after Bishop Shanley's death, the bishops of the Province of St. Paul met on September 8, 1909, at the residence of Archbishop Ireland and drew up a petition addressed to the Holy See, asking for a second diocese in North Dakota. The reasons given were these:

1. The State of North Dakota is far too large for one bishop. The state embraces 70,195 miles, and it requires a journey of 350 miles to reach some of the missions, and then often in wintery storms. It would be better, therefore, if the people had a bishop closer at hand.

2. Recently the immigrants have asked that railroad branch lines be constructed, so if another diocese were established soon a great number of Catholics would be willing to settle there, and the new diocese would have a firm and secure foundation.

3. Bishop Shanley has just died, and before a new bishop takes charge, it would seem to be an opportune moment to divide the state into two dioceses.

4. It should be noted that the immigrants in the western half of the state are predominantly of German or Slavonic origin, and it is therefore fitting that they should have a bishop whose mother tongue is German; and that since the settlers in eastern North Dakota are English speaking, they should have a bishop whose mother tongue is English.

The bishops therefore asked that the new diocese comprise all of the territory west of the eastern boundary of the counties of Emmons, Burleigh, McLean and Ward. They concluded the petition with the statement: "This division of the region seems most fitting both by reason of the railroads that run there and by reason of the language which the settlers there use."

When Archbishop Ireland and his suffragans discussed the possible candidates for the proposed "German" bishopric, they agreed that the outstanding German was Abbot Vincent Wehrle, the tireless champion of the German-speaking immigrants. Wehrle's name was very fresh in Ireland's mind, for at the end of July the abbot had written to him complaining that the Germans in North Dakota had not been treated with sufficient tact and that their interests should be considered in the choice of a new bishop. "We need a Bishop," wrote the abbot, "who has a warm heart for these German Russians and Hungarians. It may not be necessary for him to know their language, but he must be able to love and understand them. If we get such a Bishop, these people will soon be the joy of their Bishop and of their priests and the strength of Catholicity in North Dakota."

In the same letter he avowed that he had no episcopal aspirations and that he considered the spiritual and material building up of his abbey as his lifework. Before long, however, he seems to have changed his mind, for when he received advance and secret news that the new diocese would be erected and that he would be its bishop, he wrote to a close friend in Switzerland: ". . . under present circumstances it would be a mortal sin if I would not accept the appointment. We need a bishop who can understand the poor Russians and one who knows the poor condition of the diocese, so that he can act quickly. For this reason I yield to the will of God."

On January 8, 1910, Archbishop Ireland released the news of the creation of the new Diocese of Bismarck, and stated that a new bishop would be appointed without any great delay. Pope Pius X erected the Diocese of Bismarck on December 31, 1909. News of Wehrle's appointment as bishop did not reach the United States until April 9, 1910. When Archbishop Ireland's telegram arrived in Richardton, Abbot Vincent was away visiting the missions in southwestern Morton County.

The news spread like lightning throughout the new diocese. The laity all over western North Dakota knew and loved the veteran missionary and rejoiced in his appointment. The clergy were not so enthusiastic, it seems, for on December 5, 1909, Wehrle had written to a friend in Switzerland: "All the people wish, many of the priests fear, that I will be bishop."

Abbot Vincent was consecrated bishop in the St. Paul Seminary Chapel on May 19, 1910, in one of the most magnificent ceremonies in American church history. On that memorable day Archbishop Ireland consecrated six bishops destined for dioceses in North Dakota, South Dakota and Minnesota.

A festive parade led by prancing horses welcomed the new bishop to Bismarck on June 13. Three days later he was formally installed at St. Mary's Church by Archbishop Ireland. Many dignitaries, including Catholic Governor Burke, graced the civic and church celebrations that day.

At first the bishop lived in St. Mary's rectory, but in 1911 he purchased the Thompson house, once known as the "most elegant residence in the State of North Dakota." Palatial as it was for those times, it now became the residence and chancery of a man who continued to live the mortified life of a monk. He insisted on pecking out his letters on a typewriter, because "a secretary would just be in the way." He had a grand total of one servant to clean and cook for him—Brother Peter Werlen, O.S.B. The episcopal diet was simple and frugal. He lived like a poor man.

Soon after his installation, Bishop Wehrle performed an act very dear to his heart. On July 6, 1910, he dedicated the beautiful Richardton Abbey Church. A picturesque feature of the gala event was the part played by the Hungarians from Lefor and St. Stephen. They organized a procession of some 300 people who walked and rode the twenty-five miles to Richardton. With cross and banners in the lead and accompanied by a band and military societies from both parishes, they prayed several rosaries as they marched along.

The bishop rode out to meet the Corpus Christi-like procession and led them to the new church. There he welcomed them most cordially and told them that the faith he had in them had not been in vain. At one time he had considered the people of these parishes almost hopeless because of their liberal principles and lack of faith. Many a time the missionary sent out to them for Sunday did not receive enough remuneration to pay for his horse's fodder. But things had changed for the better and the wonderful demonstration of the parishioners did much to assure the bishop that his trials and worries on their behalf were bearing fruit at last.

Thirty Years of Growth

There were in the diocese in 1910 about 25,000 Catholics. Their number doubled in the next two decades. The deepening of the spiritual life of these children of God was a challenge to the bishop and his clergy to mutiply churches, schools and hospitals. In June, 1910, there were parochial schools in only five places—Bismarck, Fort Yates, Glen Ullin, Richardton and Dickinson. Wehrle lost no time in begging sisters to come to the diocese. To the Ursuline Sisters in Calvareinberg, Ahrweiler, Germany, he wrote:

> Dakota is a rich field of labor of great promise; it does not offer natural scenery, but if one seeks souls, one finds in our German-Russian and German Hungarian people a race of men that has a capacity for the good and the best. Under the severest tests these people have been true to their Catholicism and their German character. Should education, which has been lacking, come their way, then certainly will appear before long vocations to the priesthood and the religious life.

Moved by the appeal, the Ursulines opened schools at St. Anthony and Strasburg in the fall of 1910. Two years later they opened St. Agnes School in Kenmare. The Benedictine Sisters began teaching at Mandan in 1913, at Garrison and Fallon in 1916, and at Lefor and St. Patrick at Dickinson in 1929.

The Notre Dame Sisters came to New Hradec in 1917, to St. Pius of Scheffield in 1918, and to New England in 1924. The Sisters of Mercy of the Holy Cross staffed the school at Haymarsh, while the Franciscans came to St. Leo at Minot in 1926.

Mention should be made also of the role of the laity in religious education. In many country schools where all of the pupils were Catholic, it was common for zealous lay teachers to teach catechism under the supervision of the pastor. Without their valuable assistance, the priests with many missions and a huge territory to traverse would never have been able to instruct the children in the country districts.

For the adult German Catholics a means had to be found to combat the creeping materialism and socialism of the times. German newspapers were a necessity, so in 1904 Father Rabsteineck of Dickinson founded the weekly *Der Volksfreund.* Upon Bishop Shanley's advice, the Benedictine Fathers of Richardton took over the paper in 1907 and continued to publish it until 1924.

Another German Catholic weekly was the *Nord Dakota Herald,* established in Dickinson 1907 and continued to publish it until 1924. the two papers merged and they were published under the name of the latter until the summer of 1960, when publication ceased.

Through the press and by means of pastoral letters Wehrle kept in close contact with the German Catholics. He was especially vigilant in warning them not to be taken in by certain radical leaders in North Dakota poilitics who were "real Socialists, men who are infidels in the fullest sense and want to overthrow the present social order, instead of reforming the present conditions according to Christian principles."

Early in his episcopate, Wehrle was goaded into refuting "some childish gossip" to the effect that he intended to move the chancery to Richardton. "No one," he wrote in an open letter to the *Mandan Pioneer,* "would protest as much as I would if attempts were made to make Richardton the episcopal see. The only question that can ever come up is whether it will be necessary that I should remain the superior of the monastery at Richardton for some time longer; but this question will be settled between the Pope and the monastery and not by the newspapers."

By special permission from the Holy See he continued to rule as both abbot and bishop for five years until July 6, 1915. His successor, Abbot Placidus Hoenerbach, O.S.B., inherited a fine community of priests and brothers but also a sizeable debt on the abbey buildings. A series of bad crops and unwise investments brought Wehrle's foundation to the verge of ruin, and in 1924 the creditors forced the abbey into involuntary bankruptcy.

Wehrle's sorrow at seeing his community at Richardton disband was turned to joy when a group of the original monks in 1928 reopened the monastery under the aegis of the administrator, Abbot Alcuin Deutsch of St. John's Abbey in Minnesota. He sent one of his ablest priests, Father Cuthbert Goeb, O.S.B., to rule the revived foundation, first as prior until 1932, then as abbot until 1954. Bishop Wehrle had the happiness of seeing the abbey flourishing once more and continuing the missionary and educational work for which he had established it.

During most of Wehrle's administration the diocese was missionary in character. Most of the priests had several missions connected to their parishes. The age of the Model T had arrived; yet, since few could afford to buy a "gas buggy," most of the priests before 1920 had to rely on the "two-horse-power" vehicles of tried and proven reliability. It is not easy for young people today to visualize such a mission trek with its hardships and exciting moments. The experiences of these old-timers were typical of what the others endured.

Once when Father Benedict Peter, O.S.B., was driving his buggy from Richardton to SS. Peter and Paul's south of Hebron, he dropped the reins as he neared the church. The frightened horses circled around the church while he clung to the seat, and while the would-be mass-goers watched, the steeds galloped back to Richardton with the priest hanging on for dear life. On another occasion he was driving along very comfortably in his sled enjoying the warmth of his buffalo robe and his footwarmer, when the charcoal set the sled on fire. Tossing off the robe, he jumped from the flaming vehicle, and the horses ran wildly to escape the flames, strewing charred pieces for miles. On still another occasion Father Benedict (or was it Bishop Wehrle, as some claim?), while crossing the Missouri River on the Fort Berthold Reservation, broke through the ice. The horses, wagon and all of his effects were swept underneath the ice, while he barely managed to crawl and roll out of the icy water and get on solid ice. Years later an Indian found his valise containing his chalice and water-soaked missal on a sandbar.

Veteran missionary that he was, Bishop Wehrle did not shrink from hardships. Often he left Bismarck on weekends to take care of some parish whose pastor was ill. This was especially true in the fall of 1918 when the influenza swept six priests to their graves. After the funeral of Father Otto Wolpers in Dickinson, the bishop stayed on for some time to care for St. Joseph's

The age of the model T, Sunday mass at Hague

parish until Father George Aberle had recuperated enough to take charge.

Though the number of diocesan priests was steadily increasing, there were not enough priests for all of the churches and missions. So in 1920 Bishop Wehrle appealed to the Fathers of the Precious Blood from Ohio to take over several parishes. They gladly responded and in time took charge of Killdeer, St. Martin, Golden Valley, Dodge, Werner, Grassy Butte, Beulah, Hazen, Hazelton, Braddock, Linton and St. Aloysius near Hague.

One can gauge the poverty of the diocese during Wehrle's episcopate from his futile struggle to collect funds for the construction of a cathedral church. As early as 1921 he had an architect draw up plans for a beautiful shrine to the Holy Spirit, to whom he had a special devotion. But contributions from the impoverished farmers were so meager that construction was postponed from year to year. As late as 1935 the bishop planned to go ahead with construction, but did not have the heart to ask his poor people for the money. The depression had forced many a farmer into bankruptcy and many, therefore, left the state. Conditions became even more bleak in 1936 when for four months hardly a

drop of rain fell in some places, while scorching winds and choking sandstorms devastated the countryside. In view of these adverse conditions, Wehrle decided to leave the construction of the cathedral to his successor.

Though the cathedral was not built, there was extensive building throughout the diocese. In the period between 1910 and 1932 no fewer than 92 churches and chapels were built in places where there had been no churches before. Records reveal also that in that period 41 new or enlarged churches replaced smaller buildings.

Between 1911 and 1940 the personnel and facilities of the diocese practically doubled. The number of churches with resident pastors jumped from 30 to 74, mission churches from 44 to 82, while stations decreased from 44 to 6. There were 22 diocesan and 25 religious priests in 1911, while there were 60 diocesan and 45 religious priests in 1940. Hospitals increased from 1 to 4, and parochial schools climbed from 8 to 18.

Such progress was indeed remarkable when one considers that most of these years were times of economic depression. It demonstrates convincingly the spirit of faith and sacrifice on the part of the people. Proper credit should be given, too, to the Catholic Church Extension

Society for its generous help to the infant diocese. During Wehrle's administration the society contributed a total of $166,539.15 for the building of churches, schools and rectories.

The year 1935 marked the silver jubilee of the diocese; but Wehrle, asserting that "times are entirely too hard for a secular celebration," asked the Catholics of the diocese to forego civic festivities and confine their observances to religious exercises in the parishes. The pastoral letter read in all churches of the diocese, May 12, 1935, was in the nature of a parting message to his flock. "Being now nearly 80 years old," he wrote, "I shall certainly within a short time render to God . . . an account for all the souls belonging to my diocese as well as for my own soul."

For four more years the octogenerian continued to rule the diocese. More and more his health declined, so incapacitating him for his episcopal work that he finally agreed to resign from his office on October 17, 1939, to St. Alexius Hospital in Bismarck. As a resigned bishop, he received the honorary title of Bishop of Teos. He died on November 2, 1941, and was buried in a vault beneath the twin towers of the abbey church in Richardton.

Shortly after his resignation, the *Wanderer* of St. Paul epitomized his life with this tribute:

> Bishop Wehrle, as priest, abbot and Bishop, was a man of God. Ever conscious of his high calling as an ambassador of Christ, he labored unceasingly for the salvation of souls and the spread of the Faith.
>
> His whole life was dominated by this single purpose. He had no other interest in life. In his concern for the spiritual welfare of the people he was not unmindful of their material well being. He loved Western North Dakota and believed in its future.
>
> Bishop Wehrle has left a deep and lasting mark on the western part of North Dakota in the area which comprises the Diocese of Bismarck. The many churches, schools and hospitals built under his direction and inspiration are only the tangible evidences of his work.
>
> These material things do not represent the most important achievement of his long life. Of even greater significance was his achievement as priest, abbot and Bishop in fostering the Christian way of life among thousands of people. People of all faiths revered and loved the kind Bishop, the first Bishop of Bismarck.

Bishop Vincent Wehrle, O.S.B., and Bishop Vincent J. Ryan, in 1940

Bishops Ryan, Hoch and Hacker

Since Wehrle's resignation, three bishops have ruled the Diocese of Bismarck. Pope Pius XII appointed Monsignor Vincent J. Ryan of Fargo as second bishop on March 23, 1940. He died on November 10, 1951. A native of South Dakota became third bishop of our diocese when Monsignor Lambert A. Hoch, chancellor of the Diocese of Sioux Falls, was selected by the Holy Father on January 29, 1952.

In 1956 Bishop William O. Brady of Sioux Falls was transferred to the metropolitan see of St. Paul, and at the beginning of December it was announced by the apostolic delegate that Bishop Hoch would succeed Bishop Brady at Sioux Falls. Then, on December 29, 1956, the Pope chose as the fourth Bishop of Bismarck the Very Rev. Hilary B. Hacker, vicar-general of the Archdiocese of St. Paul.

The last quarter of a century has been a period of steady spiritual and material growth in the Diocese of Bismarck. Though the population of the western half of the state has increased very little, the Catholic segment has grown to more than 73,000, which is twenty-eight per cent of the total population of the area.

The prosperity of this period is reflected in the extensive building program carried on throughout the diocese. At least 150 buildings have been erected, and about one third of them are churches. In most cases the new churches replaced older structures dating back to homesteading days, but new parishes have also been added in fast-growing Bismarck, Mandan and Minot.

The outstanding church built in this period is the Cathedral of the Holy Spirit. Bishop Wehrle had bought the site back in 1917, but it was only in 1941 that actual construction got under way. The Second World War began (for the United States) soon after the foundation was poured, and construction was delayed by shortage of building materials. Finally on August 30, 1945, the beautiful shrine to the Holy Spirit was dedicated. It was the crowning achievement of Bishop Ryan's administration.

Institutions

In the field of education, the diocese has increased the number of elementary schools to 28, enrolling nearly 8,000 pupils. There are 11 Catholic high schools for 2,366 students. On the college level two fledgling institutions give promise of becoming great centers of learning. In the fall of 1960 the Bismarck Sisters of St. Benedict opened Mary College to the public as a four-year college for women. It is an outgrowth of the pre-existing St. Alexius School of Nursing and the junior college for the Sisters. A similar development took place at Richardton, where the two-year Assumption college for seminarians was expanded to include lay students in the fall of 1962. Assumption College is North Dakota's only Catholic men's college.

An educational institution that has captured the interest of the public on a national scale is the now famous Home on the Range for Boys. It is the realization of the dream of Father Elwood Cassedy who pitied boys from broken homes and wished to provide a ranch home for them *before* they could get into trouble. In June of 1949, the quiet, diminutive, perpetually smiling priest spoke in Deadwood at a convention of the Fraternal Order of Eagles of North and South Dakota. During his talk he mentioned his dream, and the idea caught on immediately. A small collection was taken up right after the speech.

A few days later Mr. and Mrs. E. B. Lievens of Sentinel Butte read in the *Bismarck Tribune* of the priest's desire to build a home for boys and began negotiations to deed 960 acres of their ranch near Sentinel Butte for that purpose. Ranchers of the area donated some fifty head of Herefords for a foundation herd for the support of the ranch. Others liked the idea of the home and sent in donations. Father Cassedy set to work remodeling a granary and moved into it with his first three boys in July of 1950. By the spring of 1951 he had a building for 28 boys, and in time another building was constructed by the Eagles to house 50 boys.

Though 9,900 young people attend Catholic schools in the diocese, about 11,000 more are not so privileged. Fortunately, the latter are not neglected, for a zealous army of priests, sisters, seminarians and lay people teach them religion in released time classes and in special summer vacation schools. A significant development is the growing participation of lay teachers in this apostolate. They have helped greatly to develop

Home on the Range

**Bishop Lambert A. Hoch
standing before portrait of Bishop Ryan**

poise and self-confidence in their teaching by the special courses offered to teachers by the Confraternity of Christian Doctrine.

Adults, too, have become better informed in spiritual matters and shown the depth of their Christian living by their sacramental sharing in the life of Christ and their promotion of parochial and diocesan projects and organizations. In recent years the men and women of the diocese have shown great interest in the retreat movement, the Christian Family Movement and such organizations as the Knights of Columbus, the Holy Name Society, the Christian Mothers and the Catholic Daughters of America.

Bishop Wehrle sought to maintain contact with his people mostly through his numerous pastoral letters. In 1941, Bishop Ryan established a diocesan newspaper, *Dakota Catholic Action*, with a circulation of 20,000—enough copies to reach every family in the diocese. In their writing for *DCA* and in their preaching on confirmation tours and at parish celebrations, the bishops have made their people conscious of their vital part in the life of the mystical body of Christ. They have exhorted parents and children to pray unceasingly for the increase of religious and priestly vocations, and apparently their prayers have been answered. In 1962 there were resident in the diocese 148 priests, 19 brothers and 440 sisters.

When Archbishop Brady preached the sermon at the golden jubilee celebration of the Diocese of Bismarck (June 19, 1960) he summarized very well the growth of Christ's mystical body in western North Dakota in these words:

Exploration, trade and missionary activity pressed into the New World simultaneously, or almost so. The Church accompanied Columbus on his voyages. The missions on the Florida and California coasts are essential to an understanding of those early American foundations. From the north, the same pattern developed. Priests pushed from Canada into what is now United States territory to save the faith which the explorers and traders had learned at home and to bring Catholic doctrine to the Indians who had never heard of either.

Now, 225 years following the first penetrations of these northern plains, great names and great ambitions are recorded in geographical locations, in shrines erected on holy spots, in the rediscovery of forts, burial grounds, chapels and trading places that once were isolated settlements in a wilderness.

Vérendrye and Garreau and Lewis and Clark, as explorers, are names to be honorably recalled. As we do, we match them with others: Aulneau, Dumoulin, Belcourt, De Smet and Hoecken who pioneered in the Name of God.

None of these explorers or missionaries could possibly have guessed that between their days and ours, the wilderness would be so fully cleared, the harsh Indians would be wards of the government and not masters of the forests, the white settlers would so rashly break the soil as well as the hearts of the Indians from whom they took it.

Not even Abbot Martin Marty could have foreseen as he left Einsiedeln and then St. Meinrad's to come to Fort Yates in 1876, that within four years he would be a bishop in the Dakotas, while within another thirty years, there would be four bishops in the same territory, or, that within another two generations, the Church yet to be established at Bismarck would have buried two bishops, seen a third ordinary come and leave again and that a fourth bishop of Bismarck would lead his priests and people in a golden anniversary by 1960.

What a change in such a short time! It would have been fantastic then to dream of more than 150 priests serving more than 65,000 Catholic people here. Yet, in the mercy of God it is true. Indian missions remain to be served and the Red Man has not come to his full possible stature as a citizen or as a Catholic. Whites from many origins followed the footsteps of the pioneers into the sometimes harsh acres of North Dakota, but not as temporary traders. They came, they stayed and they have become permanent people of a hardy civil state and a strong Catholic Church.

222

Assumption Abbey and Assumption College, Richardton

Annunciation Priory, Bismarck

Sacred Heart Priory, Minot

RELIGIOUS IN THE DIOCESE OF BISMARCK ————————————————

Benedictine Fathers (Assumption Abbey)
Benedictine Fathers (Conception Abbey)
Society of the Precious Blood

————————————

Benedictine Sisters of Pontifical Jurisdiction (Annunciation Priory)

Benedictine Sisters of Pontifical Juris-
diction (Sacred Heart Priory)
Benedictine Sisters of Pontifical Juris-
diction (Crookston; Pierre)
Dominican Sisters of the Third Order
of St. Dominic
Felician Sisters
School Sisters of Notre Dame

Sisters of the Holy Family of Nazareth
Sisters of Mercy of the Holy Cross
Sisters of Mercy of the Union
Sisters of the Precious Blood
Sisters of St. Francis of Penance and
Christian Charity
Ursuline Sisters of Mount Calvary

ACKNOWLEDGMENTS

The editor gratefully acknowledges the kindness of individuals, societies and publishers in furnishing their photographs and in permitting the reproduction of copyright and other material in this volume as follows:

C. J. Larson Studios, St. Paul; North Central Publishing Co., St. Paul; Photomatic, Inc., Minneapolis; Rev. Vincent A. Yzermans and Carl Fritz, St. Cloud; Power's House of Photography, Duluth; Edstrom Studio, Inc., Winona; Gene's Studio, Sioux Falls; Mabon Studio, Rapid City; Oswald Studio, New Ulm, and Mrs. Helene Thompson, assistant curator of pictures, Minnesota Historical Society, for photographs.

North Central Publishing Company: for quotations from *The Catholic Church in the Diocese of St. Paul,* by James M. Reardon; University of Minnesota Press: for quotations from *Minnesota: A History of the State,* by Theodore C. Blegen; Yale University Press: for quotations from *Catholic Colonization on the Western Frontier,* by James P. Shannon; Charles Scribner's Sons: for quotations from *Frontier America,* by Thomas D. Clark; Prentice Hall, Inc.: for quotations from *Western America,* by LeRoy R. Hafen and Carl C. Rister; and The Macmillan Company: for quotations from *Westward Expansion,* by Ray A. Billington.

COLOR SEPARATIONS — Photomatic, Inc., Minneapolis, Minnesota

BINDING — A. J. Dahl Company, Minneapolis, Minnesota

TYPE — Set photographically on Photon in Times New Roman and Univers

PAPER — Wedgewood Offset Enamel

COVER — Arrestox White Linen, Offset Finish

224

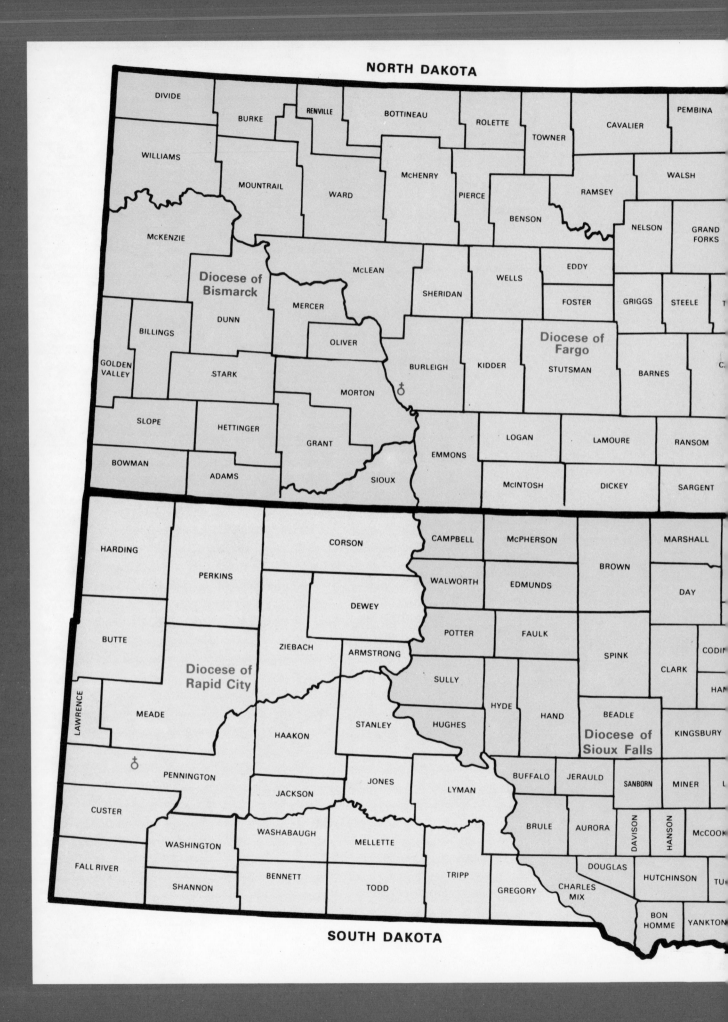